CONTENTS

SERIES EDITOR'S FOREWORD

This series of programmed texts has been written specifically for students meeting a subject for the first time on their engineering degree courses. Each book covers one of the core subjects required by electrical, mechanical, civil or general engineering students, and the contents have been designed to match either the first, or in the case of this volume, the first and second year requirements of most universities, both old and new.

The layout of the texts is based on that of the well-known text *Engineering Mathematics* by K. Stroud (first published by Macmillan in 1970, and now in its third edition). The remarkable success of this book owes much to the skill of its author, but it also shows that students greatly appreciate a book which aims primarily to help them to learn their chosen subjects at their own pace. The authors of this present series acknowledge their debt to Mr Stroud, and hope that by adapting his style and methods to their own subjects they have produced equally helpful and popular texts.

Before publication of each text the comments of a class of students, of some recent engineering graduates, and of some lecturers in the field have been obtained. Those helped to identify any points which were particularly difficult or obscure to the average reader or which were technically inaccurate or misleading. Subsequent revisions have eliminated the difficulties which were highlighted at this stage, but it is likely that, despite these efforts, a few may have passed unnoticed. For this the authors and publishers apologise, and would welcome criticisms and suggestions from readers.

Readers should bear in mind that mastering any engineering subject requires considerable effort. The aim of these texts is to present the material as simply as possible and in a way which enables students to learn at their own pace, to gain confidence and to check their understanding. The responsibility for learning is, however, still very much their own.

G.E. DRABBLE

PREFACE

This book offers an alternative approach to learning in fluid mechanics for those students for whom conventional textbooks and indeed taught courses do not always seem adequate.

The content is structured so as to help students reach a good level of understanding as rapidly as possible, and the programmed approach is designed to ensure that every step can readily be followed and understood.

In my experience, most students like to see practical applications of what they are learning as early on as possible. I have therefore included in the book many examples of the use of fluid mechanics in real engineering situations – examples such as calculating the force on a dam, investigating the stability of a car ferry, or estimating the thrust of a jet engine.

The subject matter is divided into nine areas, each of which is the topic of a separate chapter, or programme. The programmes are intended to be worked through in sequence, but those students who have the appropriate background knowledge can of course start at an intermediate point in the book: the index will suggest where to start.

Two of the programmes, 7 and 8, are about dimensions, similarity and the testing of models. Model tests are used more often in fluid mechanics than in other fields of engineering and science, which is why these topics are usually included in fluid mechanics text books; but exactly the same ideas apply to tests on models in any other field, whether it be a load test on a model structure or an investigation of heat flows in a model building. These two programmes are applicable in many areas besides fluid mechanics, and they should be useful reading for students in many disciplines.

As in any area of engineering, we generally need to measure fluid mechanics quantities in numerical terms, and a certain amount of mathematics is unavoidable. Familiarity with straightforward algebra and trigonometry is sufficient for almost all the work covered in the book. In one or two places there is a proof that goes beyond this fundamental material, but the reader can pass over this and pick up again from the result of the proof without disadvantage.

Early drafts of the book have been read and used by a number of students of Lancaster University, and I am most grateful to them for their helpful comments and corrections. Parts of it have also been read by colleagues in the Engineering Department at Lancaster, and the whole book has received the careful attention of Eddie Drabble, the Series Editor. To all of these my sincere thanks for their constructive suggestions.

MARTIN WIDDEN

HOW TO USE THIS BOOK

This book has nine chapters, or programmes, dealing with nine separate topics in fluid mechanics. Each programme is written as a carefully planned sequence of short sections, called frames, each of which contains a limited quantity of information. Most of the frames end with a short question or problem for you to tackle – this enables you to test your understanding of the material that you have just studied. The correct answer to each problem is given in the following frame.

This structure, which is common to all the books in the *Foundations of Engineering* series, is designed so that you can readily study on your own, and at your own pace. If you find a section easy and straightforward, you can work fast; any parts you find harder you can take more steadily.

When studying independently in this way, you are advised to work systematically through the book from the beginning, attempting all the questions at the ends of the frames. You should make every effort not to look at the next frame until you have answered the given question. A good technique is to have a piece of paper or card to conceal the next frame – you can use it for rough work if necessary.

At intervals throughout the book short sets of problems have been provided. Those placed at intermediate stages in the programmes should encourage you to revise what you have covered so far; at the end of each programme there is a test exercise, so that you can ensure you have mastered the knowledge and techniques you have learned before going on to the next programme.

It is of course possible to start at an intermediate point in the book, if you have the appropriate background knowledge; in this case the index will help you to find the right page to start. The index will also be useful if at a later stage you want to look something up in the book – to brush up on a particular topic, for instance.

Whatever pattern of study you choose, try to make a habit of mastering the content of each small section of the book before you go on to the next, and use the sets of problems to reinforce your new knowledge. If you work in this way, you should learn both efficiently and effectively.

Programme 1

FLUID MECHANICS FUNDAMENTALS

1

Introduction

This book is about fluids: that is, liquids and gases.

Unlike solids, a liquid or a gas does not have any shape of its own, but adopts the shape of its container. For example, water in a jug takes up the shape of the bottom part of the jug. If poured from the jug into a glass, the water quickly takes up the shape of the bottom part of the glass.

Water is of course a *liquid*. A *gas* also takes up the shape of its container, but with the difference that if we take a closed jar and allow a little of a gas into it, air for example, the air occupies the jar completely, however little we put in. With a liquid, a definite amount is required to fill the jar. A smaller amount of liquid will fill only part of the jar; it forms a free surface, with gas or vapour above.

So fluids have no shape. Which of the following substances are fluids (at usual temperatures)?

Air? Mercury? Oil? Ice? Rubber? Hydrogen?

2

Air, mercury, oil and hydrogen

Ice is the solid phase of water. Rubber is also a solid: it is quite easy to deform, but when released it returns to its original shape.

Air, mercury, oil and hydrogen all take up the shape of any container; they are all fluids.

Of these four fluids, which are liquids and which are gases at room temperature?

3

> Mercury and oil are liquids: air and hydrogen are gases.

Mercury and oil both settle to the bottom of any containing vessel and form a free surface; they are liquids. Air and hydrogen, on the other hand, will completely fill any container; they are both gases.

4

Putting the difference between liquids and gases another way, the volume of a given mass of liquid can hardly be varied at all by changes of pressure, whereas a gas is quite easy to compress. You can easily experience the compressibility of air if you block the exit of a bicycle pump with your thumb and work the handle. It will move half the way along without too much effort, and possibly two thirds or even further if you are strong enough. If the pump were to be filled with water instead, you would hardly be able to move the handle at all.

Because gases are easily compressible, and so their density can vary significantly, the fluid mechanics of gases is more complex than that of liquids. However, there are very many practical instances where the density of gases does not vary much, and in these cases it is reasonably accurate, and much simpler, to treat them as *incompressible* – in other words, as if their density were constant. The special behaviour associated with compressibility arises only when there is high velocity (approaching the speed of sound), or large changes of pressure, such as may be brought about by large changes of altitude.

In this book we shall only be dealing with incompressible behaviour.

Turn over now to frame 5

5

Viscosity

Another difference between solids and fluids is shown up when we compare their behaviour under the action of an applied force.

A force applied to a solid produces a definite deformation, for example as shown in the diagram below. Here the block of material, fixed at its base, is subjected to a shearing force F which acts over an area A; the force per unit area is called the *shear stress*, usually denoted by the symbol τ.

Writing this as an equation:

$$\text{shear stress} \quad \tau = \frac{F}{A}$$

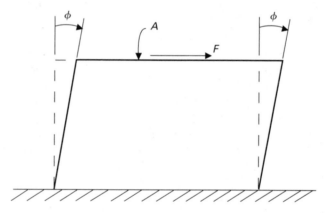

In response to the shear stress the block deforms through an angle ϕ. The angle ϕ is called the *shear strain*, and in a solid material such as this the deformation (that is, the shear strain) will not change as long as the shear stress τ remains constant.

On the other hand, a fluid subjected to a shearing force responds by *flowing*, that is, it undergoes a continuously-increasing deformation. The flow carries on for as long as the force is applied.

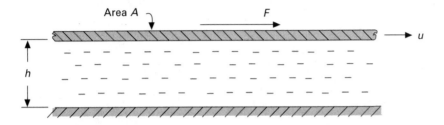

In this diagram we see two parallel solid surfaces separated by fluid. In response to a shearing force F applied as shown, one of the surfaces moves continuously relative to the other with speed u.

If the area of the surface to which the force is applied is A, the shear stress τ is given by the ratio F/A, as before. It seems reasonable to expect that the shear stress required will increase as the velocity u increases. We may also suspect that it will be more difficult to slide one of the surfaces over the other if the layer of fluid between them is made thinner, that is if the distance h is reduced. Experiments show that, for many fluids, the shear stress is proportional to the ratio of these two quantities:

$$\tau = \mu\left(\frac{u}{h}\right)$$

in which μ is a constant called the *coefficient of viscosity*, or simply the *viscosity*, of the fluid. The greater the viscosity of the fluid, the greater is the shear stress needed to produce a given velocity gradient. Treacle has larger viscosity than water, which in turn has larger viscosity than air.

This equation was first proposed by Newton, so fluids that obey the equation, such as water, treacle, petrol, mercury and all the common gases, are called *Newtonian fluids*. Fluids which do not behave in this simple way are called non-Newtonian; they include milk, blood, clay and gelatine. We shall not be attempting to treat non-Newtonian fluids in this book.

7

Example

To give some idea of the magnitude of the forces we are talking about, we will calculate the viscous force that resists the motion of part of the table of a small machine tool on its guide. The arrangement is shown diagrammatically below.

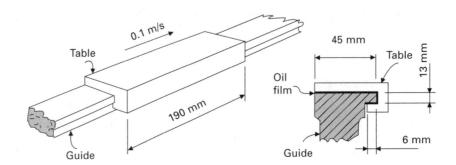

The table is able to slide along the guide, in a direction perpendicular to the paper in the end view above, at a maximum speed of 0.1 m/s. The gap between the table and the guide is 0.2 mm all round, and is filled with oil of viscosity $\mu = 0.04$ N s/m^2.

(In the SI system, the units of shear stress are N/m^2. The ratio (u/h) is a velocity divided by a length, so its units are [(m/s) ÷ m], i.e. s^{-1}. Thus the units of viscosity are [(N/m^2) ÷ s^{-1}], i.e. N s/m^2.)

If u and h have the same meanings as in the previous frame, what is the value of the ratio (u/h)?

8

$$\boxed{u/h = 500 \text{ s}^{-1}}$$

Using metre units for lengths, the gap is

$$h = 0.2 \times 10^{-3} \text{ m}$$

and so the ratio (u/h) is given by

$$(u/h) = 0.1/(0.2 \times 10^{-3}) = 500 \text{ s}^{-1}$$

So, what is the value of the shear stress resisting the motion of the table due to shearing of the oil?

> Shear stress $\tau = 20$ N/m^2

This comes straight from the equation

$$\tau = \mu(u/h)$$
$$= 0.04 \times 500$$
$$= 20 \text{ N/m}^2$$

The area over which this shear stress acts is a total of $(45 + 13 + 6)$ mm wide, that is, 64 mm wide and 190 mm long.

So now we can find the magnitude of the viscous force on the machine table. The force is ...?

> 0.24 N

Here is the working: the viscous force is the product of the shear stress τ and the area A on which it acts.

The area is 190 mm long and 64 mm wide, that is

$$A = 0.190 \times 0.064 = 0.012 \text{ m}^2$$

so the viscous force is

$$F = \tau \times A = 20 \times 0.012 = 0.24 \text{ N}$$

This is quite a small force: the viscous force in the oil does not offer very much resistance to motion of the table along the guide. This is the reason why sliding surfaces are lubricated.

The oil film always separates the two sliding surfaces. Often the film will be much thinner than in the example we have just done, and the shear stress will be correspondingly larger, but still much less than if the surfaces were in dry contact. In the next frame we tackle a case where the film is indeed much thinner.

11

Here is a different situation, where instead of being flat the oil film is in the shape of a cylinder. The left side of the diagram below represents a bearing in which the rotating shaft is supported in a fixed cylindrical housing from which it is separated by a thin film of oil (in virtually all engines the connecting-rod bearings and the main bearings for the crankshaft are just like this).

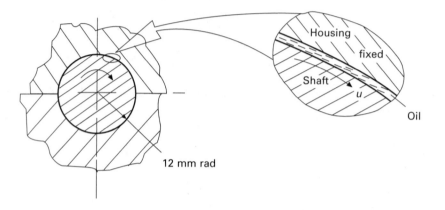

12 mm rad

In this example, the radius of the shaft is 12 mm and the thickness of the oil film is 0.0015 mm. The film is so thin compared with the radius of the bearing that if magnified the surfaces look virtually flat (see the right-hand side of the diagram), so it is reasonable to use our equation $\tau = \mu(u/h)$ in this case.

We shall take the following values: the shaft turns at 250 rad/s, the length of the bearing (perpendicular to the paper in our drawing above) is 30 mm, and the viscosity of the oil is 0.04 N s/m^2.

Remembering that the surface speed u of the shaft is the product of its radius r and the angular speed ω in rad/s, find the ratio u/h for the oil.

12

$$\boxed{2 \times 10^6 \text{ s}^{-1}}$$

Here is the working: the surface speed of the shaft is

$$u = r\omega = 12 \times 250$$
$$= 3000 \text{ mm/s}$$

so

$$u/h = 3000/0.0015$$
$$= 2 \times 10^6 \text{ s}^{-1}$$

(There is no need to convert u to m/s units and h to metre units here: since we are taking the ratio of them, we can leave them both in their millimetre units, as above.)

Now find the shear stress τ in the oil.

13

$$\boxed{80 \times 10^3 \text{ N/m}^2}$$

This comes directly from our equation $\tau = \mu(u/h)$.

The area of the surface of the shaft over which the oil is being sheared is the circumference times the length, i.e.

$$A = (2\pi \times 12) \times 30$$
$$= 2262 \text{ mm}^2$$

Now, the moment exerted on the shaft by the viscous force is the product of the force and the radius. The radius of the shaft is 12 mm, or 0.012 m, and the force is shear stress times area, so the moment is

$$2262 \times 10^{-6} \times (80 \times 10^3) \times 0.012 = 2.17 \text{ N m}$$

In a real case, the shaft may carry a load in a radial direction which will cause it to be offset from the centre of the bearing: the thickness of the oil film will then not be uniform. Nevertheless, the calculation we have done here gives a good estimate of the frictional torque imposed by the oil.

14

Particles of fluid that find themselves up against a solid boundary do not slide along the surface – it must appear to a molecule of fluid to be such rough terrain as to be virtually impassable – and so they must always stay with the solid surface. In the example of Frame 7 the particles of oil that are against the fixed guide of the machine do not move at all, and the particles that are against the moving table move along with it.

The fluid between these two extremes moves in layers that slide one over another. The velocity of motion of a layer is found to be proportional to its distance from the fixed surface, so we can draw a diagram to show how the velocity varies, called a velocity profile. It looks like this:

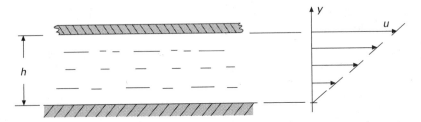

In the case shown, the lower of the two surfaces is regarded as fixed and the upper one moves with speed u. In terms of u, what is the velocity of the fluid layer that lies a distance $y = 2h/3$ from the lower, fixed plate?

15

The velocity is $2u/3$

Working: since the velocity of motion of a layer of fluid is proportional to its distance from the fixed surface, and the layer a distance h away is moving with velocity u, the layer that lies at $y = 2h/3$ from the fixed surface has $2/3$ the velocity of the moving surface, i.e. $2u/3$.

The slope of the velocity profile is called the velocity gradient. In this case the profile is a straight line, so its gradient is constant. In the next frame we examine a case where the profile is not straight and the velocity gradient is not constant.

When a fluid flows over a single surface (the bottom of an open-topped channel in which water is flowing, for example), a graph of fluid velocity against distance from the surface will *not* be a straight line. It will look more like this:

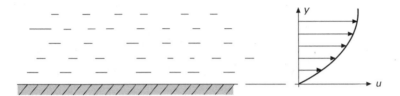

The arrows show the speed of the fluid relative to the surface, as before. Even if the fluid is stationary and the surface is the moving part, it is often more convenient to view the fluid from a vantage point on the surface, as if the surface were actually stationary and the fluid moving. A good example of this is the motion of a ship through water; if we look over the side of the ship, the water appears to be rushing past and the ship's side appears stationary. The water close to the side of the ship is visibly dragged along with it – its velocity relative to the ship is quite small – while at a distance from the side the water is virtually stationary, and so it appears to be rushing towards the stern of the ship. There is a sharp velocity gradient close to the ship's side.

Exactly the same happens as an aircraft moves through the air. Particles of air that are very close to the surface move along with the aircraft, and to an observer on the aircraft they appear virtually stationary (or would, if they could be seen).

In these cases, the shear stress τ at any particular layer in the fluid is still proportional to the gradient of the velocity profile at that layer, provided the fluid is Newtonian. Because the profile is no longer a straight line, we now have to write

$$\tau = \mu \left(\frac{du}{dy} \right)$$

In words, the shear stress is proportional to the velocity gradient (du/dy). The constant of proportionality is μ, the viscosity of the fluid.

Example: For a test in a ship tank, a long thin plank is submerged in the water and is pulled along at a constant speed. The viscosity of the water is 1.10×10^{-3} N s/m². In a layer of water close to the plank the velocity gradient is found to be 710 s^{-1}. Find the shear stress at this layer.

17

$$\boxed{0.78 \text{ N/m}^2}$$

The shear stress is the viscosity times the velocity gradient, i.e.

$$\tau = (1.10 \times 10^{-3}) \times 710 = 0.78 \text{ N/m}^2$$

Now, if the plank is 160 mm wide × 4.5 m long and so thin that its thickness can be ignored, calculate the total viscous force resisting motion of the plank through the water. Assume that the shear stress is constant over the whole area. Don't forget that a plank has two sides!

18

$$\boxed{1.12 \text{ N}}$$

Here is the working: the surface area of the plank is

$$A = (0.16 \times 4.5) \times 2 = 1.44 \text{ m}^2$$

The viscous force is the product of the shear stress and the area upon which it acts:

$$\text{Viscous force} = \tau \times A = 0.78 \times 1.44 = 1.12 \text{ N}$$

As in the first example we did on viscosity, this is not a very large force. Do not imagine that viscous forces are insignificant, though. Viscosity sometimes has the effect of completely altering the character of the flow of moving fluid, and it is certainly not always negligible.

Now here is a revision example. Work through it to make quite sure you have followed our work on viscosity, and then check your working with the solution set out in the next frame. Don't look at the answer before you have finished!

A mechanical damper consists of a single leaf of steel sandwiched between fixed steel walls, as shown below.

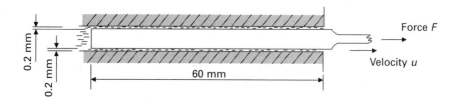

The viscosity of the liquid in the gaps is 4.7 N s/m². The width of the damper (in the direction into the paper in our diagram) is 40 mm.

If a force $F = 5.0$ N is applied, find the velocity u. (Don't forget there is liquid on *both* sides of the steel leaf.)

20

Solution

The shear stress is

$$\tau = \mu\left(\frac{\mathrm{d}u}{\mathrm{d}y}\right) = 4.7 \times \frac{u}{0.2 \times 10^{-3}}$$
$$= 23500\,u$$

The force is

$$F = 2 \times \tau \times A$$

(The factor 2 is included because the leaf has two sides.) So:

$$F = 2 \times (23500\,u) \times (60 \times 40 \times 10^{-6})$$

Thus if $F = 5.0$ N,

$$u = \frac{5.0}{2 \times 23500 \times 60 \times 40 \times 10^{-6}}$$
$$= 0.044 \text{ m/s}$$
$$= 44 \text{ mm/s}$$

All clear? If not, go back and look over the last few frames to check any gaps in your understanding before you continue. Then turn on to frame 21, where we come to a new topic.

21

Pressure

As we have seen, a gas in an enclosed space always occupies the whole space. It pushes continuously on the inner wall of the enclosure, as if trying to find its way out (owing to the repeated collision of the gas molecules with the wall). If an opening is made in the wall, the gas immediately begins to escape through it.

A liquid also exerts an outward force on its containing vessel, and for a similar reason.

If we think of the stationary fluid in a given space as divided into two parts, A and B, by an imaginary boundary, and then think what happens if one part of the fluid, say part B, is taken away, we know that the remaining fluid (part A) will flow into the space created. It was only the force exerted on A by B that prevented A from flowing out beforehand. Likewise, it was the force exerted on B by A that prevented B from flowing out. These two mutual forces are equal and opposite, in accordance with Newton's third law.

In all these cases, the force exerted per unit area is called the *pressure*.

Since the pressure will generally vary from place to place, a proper definition has to be based on a very small area over which the pressure varies hardly at all. We say that the pressure of a fluid is approximately the force acting on a small element of surface divided by the area of the element; if we allow the area to become smaller and smaller until it is no more than a point, the ratio is exactly the pressure at the point.

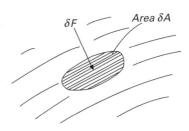

In mathematical terms, the pressure p is defined as

$$p = \lim_{\delta A \to 0} \left(\frac{\delta F}{\delta A} \right)$$

So the force acting on a small area δA is ($p\,\delta A$), and this is virtually exact provided the area δA is small. Is the direction of this force

Parallel to the surface?

Normal to the surface?

In some other direction?

Normal to the surface

The pressure force is caused by very large numbers of collisions of molecules of the fluid with the surface. Considering the direction parallel to the surface, some molecules will have a velocity component to the left, and some to the right. Overall, the forces they exert parallel to the surface will balance out to zero, and so the direction of the pressure force can only be normal to, i.e. perpendicular to, the surface.

Because the movements of the molecules are random, the magnitude of the force experienced by a small area around a given point is the same whatever its orientation. It could be a small horizontal surface (and so experience a vertical force), or a vertical one (with a horizontal force), or at any other orientation, and the force magnitude would be the same. In other words, *the pressure is the same in all directions at a point in a stationary fluid.*

In the next frame we are going to work out how the pressure in a fluid varies with the depth: turn over now.

23

Below we see a cylindrical element of liquid, which forms part of a large quantity of stationary liquid. The element is in equilibrium under the forces that act on it.

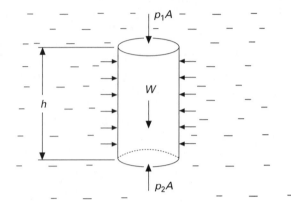

These forces are its weight, the pressure forces on the top and bottom of the cylinder, and the pressure forces on the sides. The volume V of the element is (Ah), and so its weight W is equal to $\rho(Ah)g$, where we have used the symbol ρ for the density of the fluid. (The density is assumed constant.)

For equilibrium in the vertical direction

$$p_2 A = p_1 A + \rho(Ah)g$$
$$p_2 - p_1 = \rho gh$$

Now here is an opportunity for you to try out this expression for pressure difference:

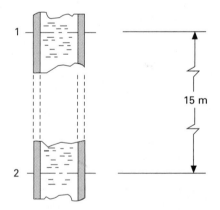

The pressure at level *1* in a pipe filled with acetone is 2.20×10^5 N/m^2. The density of acetone is 800 kg/m^3. Find the pressure at level *2*, which is 15 m lower.

$$338 \text{ kN/m}^2$$

Here is the working:

$$p_2 - p_1 = \rho g h$$
$$p_2 - 2.20 \times 10^5 = 800 \times 9.81 \times 15$$
$$= 118 \times 10^3 \text{ N/m}^2$$
$$p_2 = 338 \times 10^3 \text{ N/m}^2$$

This can be written as 338 kN/m^2, or alternatively as 3.38 bar. 1 bar = 10^5 N/m^2, and is roughly the value of atmospheric pressure at sea level. (Atmospheric pressure is always varying, and is only very occasionally exactly 1 bar.)

The vessel shown in diagram (a) below contains liquid at rest. The surface of the liquid is open to the atmosphere, and so the pressure at the surface is atmospheric pressure, which we shall denote by the symbol p_0.

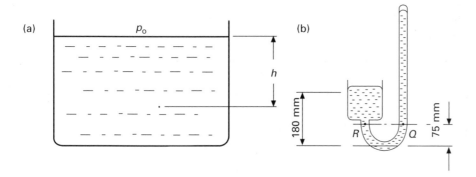

At any point at a depth h below the surface, the pressure is p, where

$$p = p_0 + \rho g h$$

This pressure p is the same everywhere on a horizontal plane a depth h below the surface. In fact, *the pressure is always the same everywhere on a horizontal plane in a body of fluid at rest.*

Bearing this in mind, find the pressure at point Q in the mercury in the vertical tube shown in diagram (b), if atmospheric pressure is $p_0 = 95$ kN/m^2. The density of mercury is 13.6×10^3 kg/m^3. (Remember that the pressure at Q must be the same as that at R, a point at the same level.)

25

$$\boxed{109 \text{ kN/m}^2}$$

Working: the distance of point R below the surface of the mercury is

$$h = 180 - 75$$
$$= 105 \text{ mm}$$

So

$$p = p_0 + \rho g h$$
$$= 95 \times 10^3 + (13.6 \times 10^3) \times 9.81 \times 0.105$$
$$= 95 \times 10^3 + 14.01 \times 10^3$$
$$= 109 \times 10^3 \text{ N/m}^2$$
$$= 109 \text{ kN/m}^2$$

There is probably no pressure gauge in existence that can measure pressure absolutely. In fact they all measure the *difference* between the pressure under investigation and a reference pressure, which more often than not is atmospheric pressure. For this reason the excess of the measured pressure over atmospheric pressure is called the *gauge pressure*.

In the example above, what is the gauge pressure?

26

$$\boxed{14 \text{ kN/m}^2}$$

The gauge pressure is the difference between the pressure p and the atmospheric pressure p_0, i.e.

$$p - p_0 = \rho g h$$
$$= 14.01 \times 10^3 \text{ N/m}^2$$
$$= 14 \text{ kN/m}^2 \text{ (to three significant figures)}$$

27

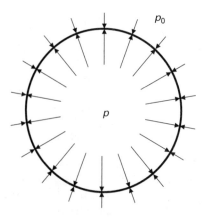

The diagram here shows a sectional view of a pressure vessel such as a steam boiler. The absolute pressures are p inside and p_0 (atmospheric pressure) outside.

The effect of the pressure inside is to place the wall of the vessel in tension: it tries to stretch it, like the wall of a balloon. On the other hand, atmospheric pressure outside, acting alone, would place the walls in compression and attempt to crush the vessel.

These two effects cancel each other if the two pressures are equal; the walls are only stressed if p differs from p_0. In all cases like this, it is the gauge pressure $(p - p_0)$ that is important, and not the absolute value of the pressure.

28

The examples we have done so far have all been related to pressures in liquids. The results apply equally well to a gas, provided the density of the gas is uniform.

The pressure difference between points at different heights in the atmosphere becomes apparent when our ears 'pop' in aircraft, on a ski-lift, or even in a car on a mountain pass.

What is the pressure difference involved in climbing a height of 500 m if the density of the air (assumed constant over the height in question) is 1.18 kg/m^3?

29

$$\boxed{5.79 \text{ kN/m}^2}$$

Here is the working: the pressure difference is given, just as before, by

$$p_2 - p_1 = \rho g h$$
$$= 1.18 \times 9.81 \times 500$$
$$= 5788 \text{ N/m}^2$$
$$= 5.79 \text{ kN/m}^2$$

This could also be written as 0.058 bar, and so represents a change of about 5.8% in atmospheric pressure. The smallness of this change suggests that, since the density of a gas depends on the pressure, our assumption of approximately constant density was justified, but 5.8% is by no means insignificant – certainly enough to make ears pop!

Of course, being a pressure *difference*, the result is the same whether p_1 and p_2 are absolute pressures or gauge pressures.

30

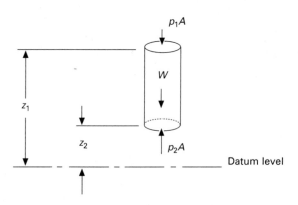

Sometimes, instead of the height difference being measured directly, the heights are measured from a horizontal datum level, as shown above. In this case the equation of vertical equilibrium for a cylinder of fluid is

$$p_2 A = p_1 A + \rho A(z_1 - z_2)g$$
$$p_2 + \rho g z_2 = p_1 + \rho g z_1$$

Notice that the two sides of the equation have the same form. It can be written as

$$p + \rho g z = \text{constant}$$

or, dividing through by ρg,

$$(p/\rho g) + z = \text{constant}$$

The equation applies to all points in a continuous body of stationary fluid whose density is the same everywhere.

31

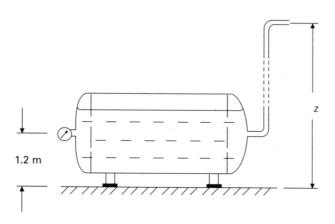

A vessel as shown is used to supply fresh water (density $\rho = 1000$ kg/m³) to the upper floors of a tall building. The air in the upper part of the vessel is at a pressure well above atmospheric.

A pressure gauge at height 1.2 m above the ground indicates a gauge pressure of 450 kN/m². To what height z can the water be raised? (Use the equation $(p/\rho g) + z =$ constant.)

32

$$\boxed{47.1 \text{ m}}$$

Working: remember that atmospheric pressure, when measured as a gauge pressure, is zero. So, using the equation $(p/\rho g) + z =$ constant between the level of the pressure gauge and the level of the outlet, where the pressure will be atmospheric:

$$(p/\rho g) + 1.2 = (0/\rho g) + z$$
$$z = (p/\rho g) + 1.2$$
$$= 450 \times 10^3/(1000 \times 9.81) + 1.2$$
$$= 45.9 + 1.2$$
$$= 47.1 \text{ m}$$

In the equation $(p/\rho g) + z =$ constant, z is clearly a length, and so the other two quantities, the constant term and the ratio $(p/\rho g)$, must be lengths also.

The ratio $(p/\rho g)$ is called the *pressure head*, or simply the *head*.

As we have just seen, the head of liquid is equal to the height the liquid could be raised above the point in question by the action of the pressure alone.

33

Pressure measurement

One way to measure the pressure in a pipe or vessel containing liquid is by means of an open-ended vertical tube in which the liquid can rise. A tube like this is sometimes called a *piezometer*.

The height h to which the liquid rises is equal to the pressure head in the pipe or vessel. This is related directly to the pressure, as we have just seen.

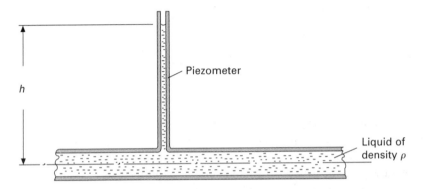

In the example shown here, the liquid in the pipe, and in the piezometer tube, is ethyl alcohol, whose density is 790 kg/m³. The alcohol rises to a height $h = 0.850$ m in the piezometer tube. What is the gauge pressure in the pipe?

34

$$6.59 \text{ kN/m}^2$$

The pressure head in the pipe is 0.850 m, and this is equal to $(p/\rho g)$, where p is the gauge pressure.

So

$$p = \rho g h$$
$$= 790 \times 9.81 \times 0.850$$
$$= 6587 \text{ N/m}^2$$
$$= 6.59 \text{ kN/m}^2$$

to three significant figures.

A piezometer is a very simple device, but it is not very often used in industry, for two reasons: it is only practical for rather low pressures, otherwise the tube needs to be inconveniently long; and it is no use for pressures below atmospheric – *negative gauge pressures* – because it simply allows air to enter the tube.

A device which can help us with one of these difficulties is the U-tube manometer. This consists of a U-shaped tube made of a transparent material, usually glass, in which the levels of liquid within the tube can be observed.

When the liquid in the U-tube has settled to its position and is at rest, the pressure at any two points at the same level within the liquid will be the same.

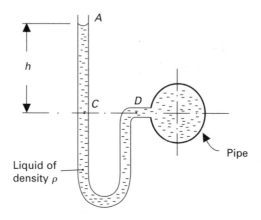

A U-tube manometer is shown connected to a pipe. The liquid, of density ρ, fills both the pipe and the lower part of the U-tube.

One leg of the U-tube is open to the atmosphere, so the pressure at the surface of the liquid (point A) is atmospheric; if measured as a gauge pressure, its value is zero.

At point C, which is a distance h lower than A, the gauge pressure is p_C, which is equal to ...?

$$\boxed{p_C = \rho g h}$$

Point D is on the level of the centre-line of the pipe, and is also at the same level as point C. All three locations lie within the same body of stationary fluid, so the pressure is the same at all three.

Thus the gauge pressure p in the pipe is given by

$$p = \rho g h$$

In the situation shown above, if the liquid is water (whose density is 1000 kg/m³) and the height is $h = 0.420$ m, what is the gauge pressure p in the pipe at a point on the centre-line?

37

$$\boxed{4.12 \text{ kN/m}^2}$$

The working is quite straightforward:

$$p = 1000 \times 9.81 \times 0.420$$
$$= 4120 \text{ N/m}^2$$
$$= 4.12 \text{ kN/m}^2$$

to three significant figures.
  Now here is another example:

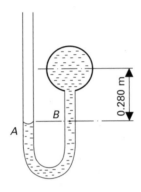

Again the pressure at point A is atmospheric. Point B is at the same level, and lies within the same body of stationary liquid, so the pressure at point B is ...?

38

$$\boxed{\text{Atmospheric}}$$

Referring again to the diagram above, if the liquid is kerosine, whose density is 790 kg/m^3, what is the pressure difference between point B and the centre of the tube?

39

$$\boxed{2.17 \text{ kN/m}^2}$$

Working: the pressure difference is

$$\rho g h = 790 \times 9.81 \times 0.280$$
$$= 2170 \text{ N/m}^2$$
$$= 2.17 \text{ kN/m}^2$$

to three significant figures.
  The centre-line of the pipe is *above* point B, so the pressure there is *less* than the pressure at B, in other words the pressure in the pipe is 2.17 kN/m^2 *below* atmospheric. As a gauge pressure, it is negative: -2.17 kN/m^2.

40

It is often convenient to use a liquid in the U-tube which is different from the fluid in the pipe or vessel.

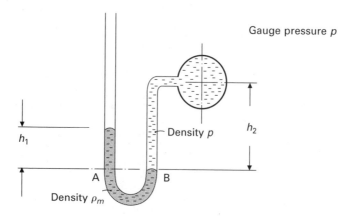

In the arrangement shown, the density of the liquid in the U-tube is ρ_m, and that of the fluid in the pipe (which may be either a gas or a liquid) is ρ. The two fluids must not mix with each other – oil and water, or water and mercury, are examples of suitable pairs of liquids – and ρ_m must be greater than ρ, so that the manometer liquid stays beneath the other fluid and has a clearly-defined boundary with it.

Points A and B are at the same level in the same body of stationary fluid, and so the pressures at A and B are ...?

41

$$\boxed{\text{Equal}}$$

Looking at the right-hand limb of the U-tube, we see that the gauge pressure at point B is

$$p_B = p + \rho g h_2$$

Similarly, in the left-hand limb the gauge pressure at A is

$$p_A = \rho_m g h_1$$

But these two pressures are equal:

$$p + \rho g h_2 = \rho_m g h_1$$

So

$$p = \rho_m g h_1 - \rho g h_2$$

Now try the example in the next frame.

42

Example 1

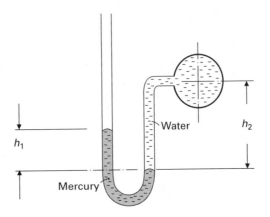

The liquid in the manometer U-tube is mercury, whose density is 13.6×10^3 kg/m^3. In the pipe, and above the mercury in one limb of the manometer, is water (density 1.0×10^3 kg/m^3).

If the heights are $h_1 = 360$ mm and $h_2 = 520$ mm, what is the gauge pressure in the pipe?

43

$$\boxed{42.9 \text{ kN/m}^2}$$

Here is the working: the gauge pressure is

$$p = (13.6 \times 10^3 \times 9.81 \times 0.360) - (1.0 \times 10^3 \times 9.81 \times 0.520)$$
$$= (48.0 - 5.1) \times 10^3$$
$$= 42.9 \times 10^3 \text{ N/m}^2$$
$$= 42.9 \text{ kN/m}^2$$

We shall see later on (in Programme 5) that we often need to find the pressure difference between two points in a pipe along which fluid is flowing, for example when the fluid is flowing through a restricting orifice as shown here. The gauge pressures are p_1 upstream of the orifice and p_2 downstream.

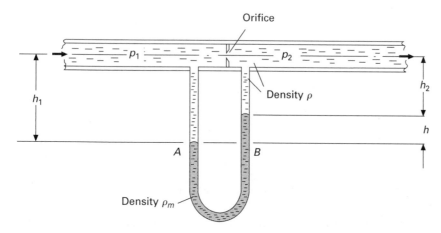

The fluid in the U-tube is stationary, and so the pressures are the same at points A and B, which are at the same level in the same body of stationary fluid.

At A the gauge pressure is $p_A = p_1 + \rho g h_1$
At B the gauge pressure is $p_B = p_2 + \rho g h_2 + \rho_m g h$

Equating these pressures, we get

$$p_1 - p_2 = \rho g h_2 + \rho_m g h - \rho g h_1$$

and, since $h_1 = h + h_2$

$$p_1 - p_2 = (\rho_m - \rho)g h$$

The pressure registered by the manometer is in the usual form, '$\rho g h$', but in this case the density to use is the *difference* between the densities of the manometer liquid and the fluid in the pipe.

In the next frame you can try out this expression on an example.

45

Example 2

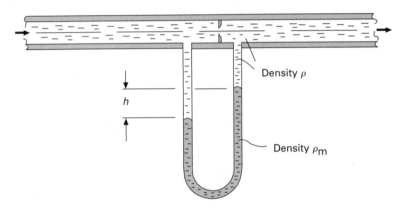

Density ρ

Density ρ_m

The fluid flowing along the pipe shown is sea-water, whose density is $\rho = 1025$ kg/m^3, and the liquid in the manometer U-tube is mercury (density $\rho_m = 13.6 \times 10^3$ kg/m^3).

If the level difference in the manometer is $h = 248$ mm, find the pressure difference across the orifice.

46

$$\boxed{30.6 \text{ kN/m}^2}$$

To find this value, all we need to do is to substitute the quantities given into the equation we found in Frame 44:

Pressure difference $= p_1 - p_2 = (13.6 - 1.025) \times 10^3 \times 9.81 \times 0.248$

$$= 30.6 \times 10^3 \text{ N/m}^2$$

Because mercury is a very dense liquid – the most dense known – a small difference in levels in the U-tube represents a relatively large pressure difference. A manometer using mercury as the manometer liquid is said to be of *low sensitivity*.

The sensitivity of an instrument may be defined as the ratio of a change in the reading on the instrument to the change in the quantity being measured. In the case of the U-tube manometer, the sensitivity s is given by

$$s = \frac{\text{difference in levels}}{\text{difference in pressures}} = \frac{h}{p_1 - p_2} = \frac{1}{(\rho_m - \rho)g}$$

We see from this expression that the greater the difference is between the density of the manometer liquid and the density of the fluid whose pressure is to be measured, the less will be the sensitivity of the manometer.

If we wish to measure rather small pressures, a manometer with high sensitivity will be necessary. An obvious way of achieving this is to use a manometer fluid whose density ρ_m is only a little greater than that of the fluid whose pressure is being measured.

In the next frame, there is an example where this is done.

48

Example 3

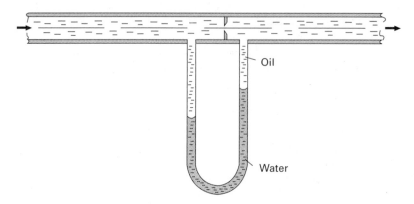

Oil

Water

In the system shown above, a thin oil of density 900 kg/m^3 is flowing along the pipe, and pressure differences in the region of 300 N/m^2 are expected to have to be measured. It would be impossible to do this accurately using mercury as the manometer fluid, because the level differences would be too small. However, the density of water, being 1000 kg/m^3, is close to that of the oil, and water and oil do not mix, so this combination will provide a satisfactory manometer.

Find the difference in the levels of the water in the U-tube when the pressure difference ($p_1 - p_2$) is exactly 300 N/m^2.

49

$$\boxed{306 \text{ mm}}$$

Here is the working:

$$p_1 - p_2 = (\rho_m - \rho)gh$$
$$300 = (1000 - 900) \times 9.81 \times h$$
$$h = \frac{300}{100 \times 9.81} = 0.306 \text{ m}$$
$$= 306 \text{ mm}$$

50

If the fluid in the pipe is itself water, we can achieve a sensitive manometer if we use a mineral oil like kerosine, but because kerosine is less dense than water the U-tube has to be inverted.

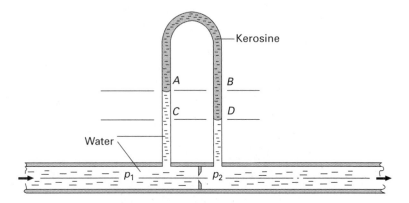

In the diagram above, what can we say about the pressures at points A and B, which lie at the same level in the same body of stationary fluid?

51

> The pressures are the same

Even though the U-tube is inverted, the principle is unchanged: at two points at the same level in the same body of stationary fluid, the pressures are the same.

(Remember that the water in the pipe is flowing. Points C and D are at the same level, and both in the same body of water, but because part of the body of water is moving we *cannot* say that the pressures at C and D are the same.)

Now, can you find the pressure difference $(p_1 - p_2)$, in terms of g, h, ρ and ρ_m?

52

$$(p_1 - p_2) = (\rho - \rho_m)gh$$

Working: the pressures at C and D are $p_C = p_A + \rho gh$ and $p_D = p_B + \rho_m gh$. Because A and B are at the same level in the same body of liquid we know that $p_A = p_B$.

Therefore $(p_C - p_D) = (\rho - \rho_m)gh$. Below the level of C and D both limbs are full of the same fluid (water) and so the pressure difference remains the same at any level. Thus

$$(p_1 - p_2) = (p_C - p_D)$$
$$= (\rho - \rho_m)gh$$

53

Sometimes the fluid whose pressure we wish to measure is a gas. The density ρ of a gas is so much smaller than the density of the liquid in the manometer tube that it is often reasonable to ignore it.

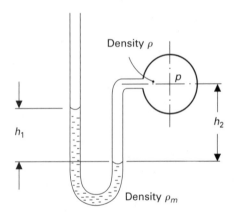

Returning to the equation we derived in Frames 40 and 41, the gauge pressure p in the pipe is given by

$$p = \rho_m gh_1 - \rho gh_2$$
$$= g(\rho_m h_1 - \rho h_2)$$

The density of liquids used in manometers ranges from around 800 kg/m³ upwards, while that of common gases is no more than 2 kg/m³, a ratio of 400:1 or more. In the great majority of cases the heights h_1 and h_2 are of comparable size.

Thus the second term ρh_2 in the bracket is usually less than 1/400 of the first.

Now go on to the next frame, where we shall do an example.

54

Example 4

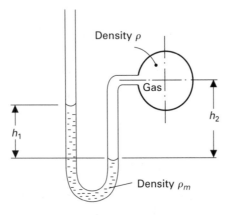

The manometer fluid is water, whose density is 1000 kg/m^3, and the gas in the pipe is carbon dioxide of density 1.9 kg/m^3.

If the heights are h_1 = 380 mm and h_2 = 570 mm, then in this case the gauge pressure in the pipe is

$$p = \rho_m g h_1 - \rho g h_2$$
$$= 1000 \times 9.81 \times 0.380 - 1.9 \times 9.81 \times 0.570$$
$$= 3728 - 10.6$$
$$= 3717 \text{ N/m}^2$$
$$= 3.72 \text{ kN/m}^2 \text{ (to 3 significant figures)}$$

The pressure difference across the height of the gas is 10.6 N/m^2, which is very much smaller than the overall pressure difference. This is largely because the density of carbon dioxide, even though this is one of the most dense of common gases, is only about 0.2% that of water. Since the margin of experimental error in using a simple U-tube manometer is generally much more than 0.2%, it is reasonable to ignore the pressure due to the column of gas (unless h_2 is much larger than h_1), and so to write

$$p = \rho_m g h_1$$

55

Here is a question for you to try: if, in the diagram above, the fluid in the manometer U-tube is kerosine, of density 880 kg/m^3, and the gas in the pipe is air, whose density is 1.26 kg/m^3, find the level difference h_1 that corresponds to air pressure 3.5×10^3 N/m^2.

56

$$\boxed{h_1 = 405 \text{ mm}}$$

Here is the working: we have air in the pipe, and above the kerosine in the manometer, and so the gauge pressure p in the pipe is given to sufficient accuracy by the equation $p = \rho_m g h_1$. Rearranging this, we have

$$h_1 = p/\rho_m g$$
$$= 3.5 \times 10^3/(880 \times 9.81)$$
$$= 0.405 \text{ m}$$
$$= 405 \text{ mm}$$

57

When measuring the pressure of a gas, we cannot achieve high sensitivity with a conventional U-tube, because all liquids are far more dense than any gas, so the difference in densities $(\rho_m - \rho)$ is not a small quantity.

An alternative approach is to use a manometer with one limb inclined instead of vertical:

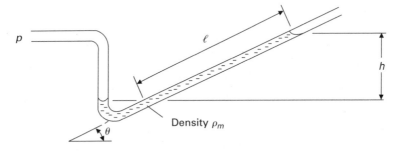

The pressure difference in the manometer liquid depends only on the height h, irrespective of the angle of the sloping limb, so the gauge pressure p of the gas is given by $p = \rho_m g h$ as usual.

If the angle between the sloping limb and the horizontal is θ, then the distance ℓ along the limb is given by $\ell = h/\sin\theta$.

The closer the sloping limb is to the horizontal, the smaller is the value of $\sin\theta$, and so the more sensitive the manometer becomes. (In practice an angle θ less than $10°$ is rare – with angles smaller than this it is hard to read the manometer accurately enough.)

In the next frame we shall do an example on this.

Example 5

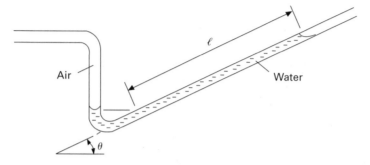

The angle θ of the sloping limb of the manometer is 20°, and the manometer is filled with water. The fluid whose pressure is being measured is air.

If the distance ℓ is 126 mm, what is the gauge pressure p in the air?

$$\boxed{423 \text{ N/m}^2}$$

Here is the working. If $\ell = 126$ mm, then $h = 126 \sin 20° = 43.1$ mm, so the gauge pressure is:

$$p = 1000 \times 9.81 \times (43.1 \times 10^{-3})$$
$$= 423 \text{ N/m}^2$$

With most manometers, finding the difference between the levels in the two limbs involves taking two readings and doing a subtraction; this is prone to error, and if there are many pressure values to measure it can become tedious.

Commercial inclined manometers are usually equipped with a large-diameter reservoir in the vertical limb (so that the level in this limb does not alter very much as the liquid moves), and the expanded graduations on the inclined limb are arranged to compensate for the small level changes in the vertical limb. The manometer is then read directly without any need for conversion from the inclined length ℓ to the height h.

60

Finally in this section, we must mention the mercury barometer, which is often used to measure atmospheric pressure in the laboratory.

The simplest form is just a glass tube closed at one end, filled with mercury and inverted so that its open end is below the surface of a bath of mercury.

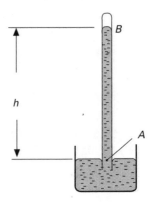

The pressure at the surface of the mercury in the open bath is atmospheric, so the pressure is also atmospheric at point A, at the same level in the same continuous, stationary body of mercury.

At the top of the mercury column, B, the pressure is almost zero – not quite, because a little mercury evaporates from the surface, so mercury vapour occupies the space above it, but the pressure of this vapour is very small indeed at normal temperatures.

The pressure difference is given by $p_A - p_B = \rho g h$ and since p_B is extremely small, $p_A = \rho g h$ approximately.

Thus the height h of the column of mercury is directly related to the atmospheric pressure.

Here is a simple question: if the height of the mercury column is 682 mm, what is the atmospheric pressure, in bar? The density of mercury is 13.6×10^3 kg/m^3, remember.

61

$$\boxed{0.91 \text{ bar}}$$

Working:

$$p = \rho g h$$
$$= (13.6 \times 10^3) \times 9.81 \times 0.682$$
$$= 90.99 \times 10^3 \text{ N/m}^2 \text{ or } 0.91 \text{ bar}$$

Next, to mark the end of the section on pressure, we have some revision examples.

Revision exercise: pressure and pressure measurement

1.

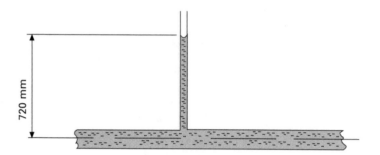

The liquid in the pipe is carbon tetrachloride, whose density is 1590 kg/m³. What is the pressure head at the centre-line of the pipe?

2. Pearl-fishers have been known to dive regularly to 12 m depth in the sea. If the density of the sea-water is 1020 kg/m³, what is the gauge pressure at this depth, measured in bar?

3. The jar shown below left is filled with air, and the manometer tube contains water (density 1000 kg/m³). If the pressure in the jar is to be reduced to 2000 N/m² below atmospheric, find the corresponding height h.

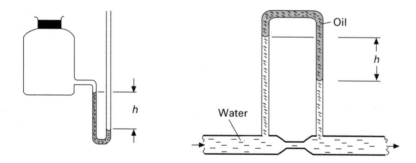

4. Water is flowing along the pipe (above right). The inverted U-tube contains oil of density 820 kg/m³ over the water. The level difference is $h = 223$ mm. What is the pressure drop across the restriction?

When you have completed all of these revision questions – and not before – check your answers with the solutions in Frame 63.

63

Solutions

1. The pressure head of the liquid is equal to the height the liquid can be raised by the action of the pressure alone. A piezometer indicates the pressure head directly: the density of the liquid does not come into it at all.

2. The gauge pressure p at a depth h below the surface of a liquid is given by

$$p = \rho g h$$

Here we have

$$p = 1020 \times 9.81 \times 12$$
$$= 1.2 \times 10^5 \text{ N/m}^2$$
$$= 1.2 \text{ bar}$$

3.
$$\rho g h = 2000 \text{ N/m}^2$$
$$h = 2000/(1000 \times 9.81)$$
$$= 0.204 \text{ m}$$
$$= 204 \text{ mm}$$

4. In a two-fluid manometer like this, we need to find the *difference* between the densities of the two fluids; then the calculation is just like that for a simple manometer:

$$\text{pressure drop} = (\rho_m - \rho)g h$$
$$= (1000 - 820) \times 9.81 \times 0.223$$
$$= 394 \text{ N/m}^2$$

64

Archimedes' Principle

Every body experiences an upthrust equal to the weight of fluid it displaces.

This is a statement of the Principle of Archimedes, the Greek mathematician and inventor who lived in Syracuse (in Sicily) in the 3rd century BC.

To demonstrate the principle, consider a 'lake' of stationary liquid in which a certain volume Q of liquid has been marked.

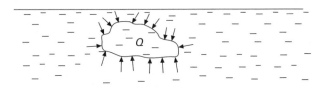

The pressure forces acting on Q are indicated by the arrows.

Can you think of another force that acts on the fluid in Q?

65

> Its weight

The only force acting, apart from the pressure forces, is that of gravity. There are no viscous forces because the fluid is all at rest.

The fluid in Q remains stationary, so the forces acting on it must be in equilibrium – in other words, the resultant of the pressure forces on Q must be equal and opposite to the weight of the fluid in Q. Since the weight is a downward force, the resultant of the pressure forces must be an upward force, which we shall call an upthrust.

If we imagine the fluid in Q replaced by a solid body of exactly the same shape, the pressure forces are unaltered, so the body experiences an upthrust equal and opposite to the weight of the fluid that was previously in the volume Q. This demonstrates the truth of Archimedes' Principle.

Here is a straightforward example for you to try: the volume of a small submarine is 30 m^3. When it is completely submerged in sea-water of density 1025 kg/m^3, what is the magnitude of the upthrust experienced by the submarine? The upthrust is equal to the *weight* of fluid displaced, remember.

66

$$\boxed{302 \text{ kN}}$$

Working:

$$
\begin{aligned}
\text{Upthrust} \ &= \text{weight of water displaced} \\
&= \rho_{\text{water}} \times g \times \text{(volume of water displaced)} \\
&= 1025 \times 9.81 \times 30 \\
&= 302 \times 10^3 \text{ N} \\
&= 302 \text{ kN}
\end{aligned}
$$

Archimedes' Principle applies just as well for bodies immersed in a gas. Here is an example.

A balloon filled with helium is to be used to lift a weather sensor/transmitter to the upper atmosphere. The balloon is approximately a sphere of diameter 1.5 m, and the total weight of the balloon and load is 12 N. What is the minimum air density if the balloon is to support the weight? The volume of a sphere is $(4/3)\pi r^3$, where r is the radius.

67

$$\boxed{0.69 \text{ kg/m}^3}$$

Working: the volume V of the sphere is $(4/3) \times \pi \times 0.75^3 = 1.77 \text{ m}^3$

If the balloon is to be able to support the total weight W, the upthrust must be at least equal to the weight, i.e.

$$\rho_{\text{air}} g V > W$$
$$\rho_{\text{air}} > 12/(9.81 \times 1.77)$$
$$\rho_{\text{air}} > 0.69 \text{ kg/m}^3$$

We have already seen (Frames 28 and 29) that atmospheric pressure decreases with height. The density of the air also diminishes as we ascend, so there is a limit to the height the balloon can achieve (although in practice a balloon may expand as the external pressure falls, which will partially compensate for the decreasing air density).

68

The upthrust on bodies that are only partially submerged in a liquid, such as ships floating on the sea, also obeys Archimedes' Principle. We can demonstrate this just as before.

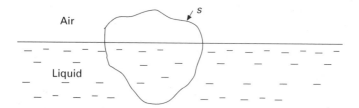

The diagram shows once again a 'lake' of liquid with a free surface. A volume S containing both liquid and air has been marked out. The air and liquid in the volume S is subject to gravity and pressure forces that are in equilibrium, so just as before the sum of the pressure forces on S must be an upthrust equal and opposite to the weight of the fluid – the air and liquid – in S. The weight of the air is usually so much smaller than the weight of the liquid that it can be ignored.

When an object is floating on the surface of a liquid, the upthrust exactly balances the weight of the object. Thus, a ship must displace an amount of water whose weight is equal to the weight of the ship.

Here is an example: a ship is found to displace a volume 4770 m^3 of sea-water, whose density is 1023 kg/m^3. What is the weight of the ship?

69

$$\boxed{47.9 \text{ MN}}$$

Solution: the ship floats in equilibrium, so it must be subject to an upthrust equal to its own weight. According to Archimedes' Principle, this upthrust is equal to the weight of fluid displaced. The weight of air displaced is negligible – so the ship must displace almost exactly its own weight of water. Therefore:

$$\text{weight of ship} = \text{weight of water displaced}$$
$$= 1023 \times 9.81 \times 4770$$
$$= 47.9 \times 10^6 \text{ N}$$
$$= 47.9 \text{ MN}$$

70

A given floating body will float at different heights in liquids of different densities.

For example, because the temperature and salinity of the sea varies from place to place, its density also varies, so a ship will float at different depths in different parts of the world. Plimsoll lines painted on the sides of ships, which mark the maximum depth of floating and so govern the load a ship can carry, have to set several depths for different locations for just this reason.

The depth at which a given body floats can be used to indicate the density of the liquid. An instrument which does this is called a *hydrometer*.

The hydrometer is usually shaped as shown in the diagrams below, weighted at the bottom so that it floats upright. The stem is graduated to indicate the density of the liquid.

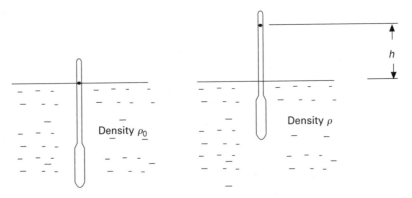

In the left-hand diagram the hydrometer is shown floating in a liquid of density ρ_0; a volume V_0 of the hydrometer is submerged, so that volume V_0 of liquid is displaced. When the hydrometer is floated in a liquid whose density ρ is greater, the hydrometer floats a distance h higher, so the submerged volume is now $(V_0 - Ah)$, where A is the area of cross-section of the stem.

The upthrust on the hydrometer must be equal and opposite to its weight W. Therefore

$$W = \rho_0 g V_0 = \rho g(V_0 - Ah)$$
$$\rho_0/\rho = 1 - Ah/V_0$$
$$h = \frac{V_0}{A}\left(\frac{\rho - \rho_0}{\rho}\right)$$

By making the area A rather small, that is, by making the stem narrow, we obtain a sensitive hydrometer – one which gives a large change in height h for only a small difference $(\rho - \rho_0)$ in densities.

Here is an example.

A hydrometer is required to give a height change of 100 mm for a density variation between 1000 and 1025 kg/m³. If the hydrometer has a submerged volume $V_0 = 100$ cm³ when floating in fresh water of density $\rho_0 = 1000$ kg/m³, what must be the area A of the stem?

Can you solve this one? It is not at all difficult, but take care not to get in a muddle with the units!

$$A = 24 \text{ mm}^2$$

Solution: the ratio

$$\left(\frac{\rho - \rho_0}{\rho}\right) = \left(\frac{1025 - 1000}{1025}\right) = \frac{1}{41}$$

Therefore

$$A = \frac{1}{41} \frac{V_0}{h}$$
$$= \frac{1}{41} \frac{100}{10} \text{ cm}^2 \; (h \text{ has been put into cm units})$$
$$= 0.24 \text{ cm}^2$$
$$= 24 \text{ mm}^2$$

A cylindrical stem 5.5 mm diameter will do nicely for this.

The ratio of the density of a given substance (liquid or solid) to the density of pure water is called the *relative density*, or sometimes the *specific gravity*, of the substance.

Here is a further example: the relative density of the electrolyte in an automotive lead–acid battery varies from about 1.10 when the battery is discharged up to 1.40 when fully charged. A small hydrometer is being designed for this range of relative densities, as a simple check on the condition of batteries.

If the height h to cover this range is to be 40 mm and the stem is to be a tube of 4 mm diameter, what should be the submerged volume V_0 of the hydrometer when floating in liquid of relative density 1.10?

73

$$\boxed{2.35 \text{ cm}^3}$$

Rearranging the equation from Frame 70:

$$V_0 = Ah\left(\frac{\rho}{\rho - \rho_0}\right)$$

The area of cross-section of the stem is

$$A = \pi d^2/4 = 12.56 \text{ mm}^2$$

The overall height variation is given as $h = 40$ mm and the fraction in the brackets is

$$\left(\frac{\rho}{\rho - \rho_0}\right) = \frac{1.4}{0.3} = 4.67$$

Substituting these values in the equation:

$$V_0 = 12.56 \times 40 \times 4.67$$
$$= 2345 \text{ mm}^3$$
$$= 2.35 \text{ cm}^3$$

to 3 significant figures.

Of course, the user of a hydrometer doesn't have to do this kind of calculation, because the stem of the instrument is graduated and the density can be read directly, but the designer of a particular hydrometer would have to.

Move on now to Frame 74, where we start the last section of this programme.

Surface tension

We all know that water emerging very slowly from a tap does not fall as a continuous stream. Instead it forms into a bulge which gradually grows until it can no longer support itself; then a drop of water is detached and falls, and the process starts once more.

This behaviour is due to intermolecular forces, which cause the water to be attracted inwards upon itself rather than flowing freely.

For the same reason, if we pour a glass of water very carefully we can fill it above the level of the brim.

A convenient way to represent what is happening is to imagine a tensioned membrane in the surface of the water, as if the water was surrounded by very thin and flexible balloon material. The tension is the same at all points in the membrane; that is, if we imagine a straight-line segment drawn in the surface, the tensile force across the line is the same wherever the line is placed. If we place two such line segments end to end, we get twice the force. Clearly the tension is proportional to the width across which it acts.

We define the *surface tension s* for a given situation as the tensile force acting per unit width of surface.

The value of s depends on the particular pair of fluids that are bounded by the surface, and also on their temperature. For example, water and air at 20 °C have surface tension $s = 74 \times 10^{-3}$ N/m.

In a water–air surface at 20 °C, what is the magnitude of the tensile force due to surface tension across a 25 cm width of surface?

$$\boxed{0.0185 \text{ N}}$$

The tensile force F is simply the product of the surface tension s and the width ℓ:

$$F = s \times \ell = 74 \times 10^{-3} \times 0.25$$
$$= 0.0185 \text{ N}$$

This is evidently a very small force. Indeed, in many engineering situations surface tension forces are negligibly small compared with the other forces that arise from gravity, pressure, inertia etc., but there are some situations where the surface tension forces are quite significant. This is why it is important to understand how surface tension forces arise, and how to calculate their magnitude.

76

When a surface is curved, the existence of the tension in the surface means that there must be a difference in pressure between one side of the surface and the other.

The diagram below represents a circular element of a spherical surface of radius R. The pressure outside the sphere is p, and the pressure inside is greater: we shall write it as $(p + \Delta p)$.

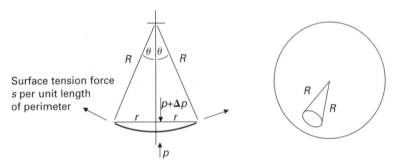

The resultant force due to pressure is $\Delta p \times \pi r^2$, downwards.

The horizontal components of the surface tension forces cancel each other out, but the vertical components add, to give a total of $s \times 2\pi r \times \sin \theta$ upwards.

So, for equilibrium

$$\Delta p \times \pi r^2 = s \times 2\pi r \times \sin \theta$$
$$\Delta p = (2s/r) \sin \theta$$
$$\Delta p = 2s/R$$

So the excess pressure Δp inside a spherical surface of radius R due to surface tension s is $(2s/R)$.

For the sake of interest, calculate the excess pressure inside a droplet of water of radius 0.4 mm when the temperature is 20 °C. ($s = 74 \times 10^{-3}$ N/m^2).

77

$$\boxed{370 \text{ N/m}^2}$$

The excess pressure is:

$$(2s/R) = 2 \times (74 \times 10^{-3})/(0.4 \times 10^{-3})$$
$$= 370 \text{ N/m}^2$$

This is a small, but by no means negligible, pressure.

You will have noticed that the excess pressure inside a spherical surface due to surface tension is inversely proportional to the radius. The smaller the radius becomes, the greater the excess pressure. (You may have noticed when blowing up a balloon that it quickly gets easier as the balloon gets bigger.)

On reflection, this is not very surprising, because the force due to surface tension depends on the *perimeter* of the surface, whereas the pressure force is proportional to the *area*. If we consider a smaller spherical surface, scaled down by some factor α, then the perimeter, and so the surface tension force, is also reduced in the ratio α, but the area is reduced in the ratio α^2. Thus the pressure has to *increase* by a factor α if equilibrium is to be maintained.

Now consider a cylindrical surface, which is the kind of shape that may arise in waves on the surface of water. Again there will be a pressure difference across the surface owing to the surface tension.

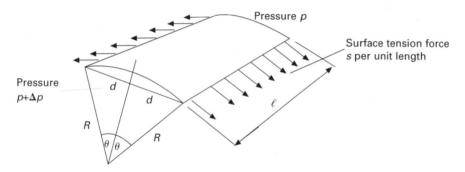

Can you now find an expression for the excess pressure Δp, in terms of the radius of curvature R and the surface tension s? The method can be very similar to that used in the previous example.

$$\boxed{\Delta p = s/R}$$

This time the pressure force is $\Delta p \times 2d \times \ell$, upwards.

The resultant force due to the surface tension is $2(s\ell \times \sin\theta)$, in which the factor 2 arises because there are two edges, each of length ℓ.

For equilibrium across the surface these two forces must be equal and opposite, so

$$\Delta p \times 2d \times \ell = 2(s\ell \times \sin\theta)$$

and, since $d/R = \sin\theta$, $\Delta p = s/R$.

Once again we see that the excess pressure on the inner (concave) side of the surface is inversely proportional to the radius of curvature.

When large waves occur on the surface of water, the forces due to gravity are large but, because the radius of curvature is large, the pressure due to surface tension is small. With large waves the effect of surface tension is negligible.

With small waves, however, the gravity forces are small and give rise to only small pressure differences, while the surface tension causes relatively significant pressures. Thus small ripples are influenced strongly by surface tension.

Another case where the effect of surface tension becomes more significant as dimensions get smaller is in tubes such as piezometers and manometers.

Usually the surface of liquids meets a solid boundary at an angle which is not a right angle, owing to the interplay of the intermolecular forces in this region. For example, the surface of water meets glass as shown in diagram (a) below. The precise value of the angle θ depends very much on how clean the glass is, but for water it is always less than $90°$.

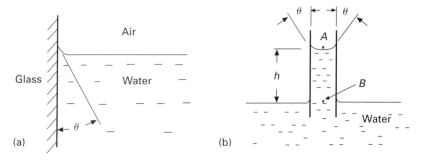

Consider the vertical glass tube containing a column of water, shown in diagram (b). The surface of the water meets the glass at angle θ.

Owing to surface tension the column of water rises a distance h up the tube. The pressure at point B within the tube (at the same level as the water in the reservoir) is atmospheric, as is the pressure at point A above the surface of the water in the tube. Thus the pressure forces on the top and the bottom of the water between A and B in the tube are equal and opposite. The remaining forces on this water, namely the weight and the force due to the surface tension, must be in equilibrium.

If the density of the water is ρ, what is the weight of a cylindrical column of water of diameter d and height h?

$$\rho(\pi d^2 h)g/4$$

Working: the volume of the column of water is $\pi(d/2)^2 h$, so its weight is $\rho\pi(d/2)^2 hg$.

In fact, the surface of the water is curved, so the height h does not include quite all the water, and this value for the weight is not exact. If the diameter of the tube is small, the error is not large. The curved surface of the liquid in a tube is called a *meniscus*.

The upward force due to the surface tension is readily calculated by considering the forces at the perimeter of the meniscus (the calculation is similar to that done in Frame 76). The resultant upward force is $s \times \pi d \times \cos\theta$.

Equating:

$$\rho\pi(d/2)^2 hg = s \times \pi d \times \cos\theta$$

$$h = \frac{4s \times \cos\theta}{\rho g d}$$

We see that, as expected, the height the column of water is raised by surface tension is inversely proportional to the diameter d of the tube.

Suppose a clean glass tube of 1 mm bore is dipped into a beaker of water. The temperature is 20 °C, and so the surface tension of water is 74×10^{-3} N/m. If the angle of contact is $\theta = 15°$, how far up the tube does the water rise?

$$29 \text{ mm}$$

Working: using metre units,

$$h = \frac{4 \times (74 \times 10^{-3}) \times \cos 15°}{1000 \times 9.81 \times 0.001}$$

$$= 0.029 \text{ m}$$

This phenomenon, whereby liquid can rise quite substantial distances up a narrow-bored tube, can cause significant errors when using such tubes to measure pressures etc. This is one reason why tubes as narrow as 1 mm bore are only rarely used, but even with the more common sizes of 6 mm diameter upwards the error can be as much as 5 mm, which is still serious.

83

Fortunately, a U-tube manometer in which the two legs of the tube are identical is free from this error because both legs are similarly affected, so the difference between the two levels is the same as if surface tension were not present.

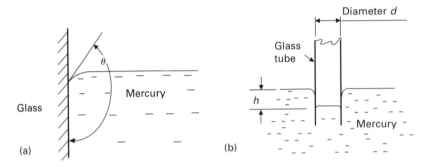

The surface of mercury meets glass at an angle greater than 90° (diagram (a) above) so mercury in a glass tube is depressed *below* the level it would have in the absence of surface tension, as shown in diagram (b). The distance h is calculated in exactly the same way as for water or any other liquid.

Here is an example: the surface tension of a mercury/air interface at 20 °C is 465 μN/mm, and the angle of contact is $\theta = 130°$. Calculate the depth h to which the mercury is depressed in a glass tube of diameter $d = 2$ mm. The density of mercury is 13.6×10^3 kg/m^3.

84

$$\boxed{h = 4.5 \text{ mm}}$$

To obtain this result, all we need to do is to substitute in the formula we derived for h:

$$h = \frac{4s \times \cos \theta}{\rho g d}$$
$$= \frac{4 \times (465 \times 10^{-3}) \times \cos 130°}{(13.6 \times 10^3) \times 9.81 \times 0.002}$$
$$= -4.48 \times 10^{-3} \text{ m}$$
$$= -4.5 \text{ mm approximately}$$

This brings us to the end of this programme, except for the test exercise. Before you tackle that, read through the summary of the principal results of the programme, which follows in Frame 85, and revise any points where you do not feel completely confident. Then turn over and work through the questions on the test exercise: by now they should seem quite straightforward.

Revision summary

1 In Newtonian fluids (which include water, mercury, many other liquids and all the common gases) the shear stress in the fluid is proportional to the velocity gradient:

$$\tau = \mu \left(\frac{du}{dy} \right)$$

where μ is a constant called the *viscosity* of the fluid.

2 The pressure at a point in a fluid at rest is the same in all directions.

3 The pressure is always the same everywhere on a horizontal plane in a body of fluid at rest.

4 The pressure difference between two points in a stationary fluid whose density ρ is constant is $\rho g h$, where h is the difference in height of the two points.

5 The difference between the absolute pressure p and the atmospheric pressure p_0 is called the *gauge pressure*.

6 The *pressure head* at a point in a liquid is equal to the height the liquid can be raised above the point by the action of the pressure alone.

7 A manometer is often used to measure a difference between two pressures. There are many types: in every case the pressure difference may be found by applying principles 3 and 4 above.

8 Archimedes' Principle: every body experiences an upthrust equal to the weight of fluid it displaces.

9 The ratio (ρ/ρ_0) of the density of a given substance to that of pure water is called the *relative density* of the substance. It is also sometimes called the *specific gravity*.

10 The intermolecular forces which cause a fluid to be attracted inwards upon itself are usually represented by a tension in an imaginary membrane in the surface of the fluid. The tension per unit width of surface is called the *surface tension* of the fluid.

86

Test exercise

1 Water is drawn from a well by a pump which is situated 6.5 m above the surface of the water. By how much is the pressure at the pump less than atmospheric? (Neglect any losses due to friction.)

2 A manometer containing oil is used to measure the pressure of air in a pipe (see the diagram on the left below). The density of the oil is 850 kg/m³. Find the gauge pressure of the air.

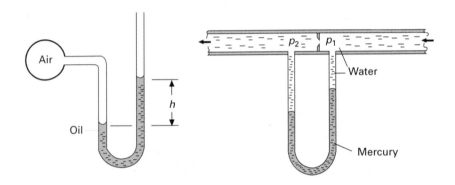

3 A mercury manometer is used to monitor the pressure difference across an orifice in a pipe (right-hand diagram above). The pipe contains water, and the liquid in the manometer U-tube is mercury. What pressure difference is indicated when the levels differ by 42 mm? (The density of mercury is 13.6×10^3 kg/m³.)

4 At the surface of part of the wing of an aircraft the velocity gradient in the air is 150×10^3 s⁻¹. If the viscosity of the air is 1.8×10^{-5} N s/m², what is the viscous shear stress at this point?

5 The block shown below, made of teak of density 850 kg/m³, floats with a depth $h = 34$ cm beneath the surface. Find the density of the liquid.

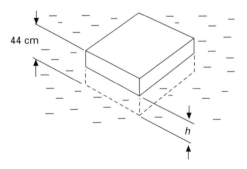

6 The surface tension of water at 70 °C is 64.4×10^{-3} N/m. If the angle of contact with a glass tube is 12° and the tube diameter is 3 mm, how far up the tube will the water be drawn by capillary action?

Further problems

1 Calculate the gauge pressure at a depth of 2000 m below the surface of the sea, taking the density of sea-water as 1026 kg/m^3.

2 A cylindrical plug 70 mm long and 35 mm diameter fits closely into a fixed cylindrical shell. The radial gap of 0.02 mm between the two members is filled with a viscous liquid. When a constant axial force of 5 N is applied, the plug moves steadily at a speed 43 mm/s. Estimate the viscosity of the liquid.

3 A steel pipeline conveying gas has outside diameter 1.25 m and internal diameter 1.20 m. The pipeline is laid across the bed of a river, completely immersed in water and anchored at intervals of 3 m along its length. Calculate the buoyancy force on the pipe per metre length. Given that the density of steel is 7800 kg/m^3, estimate the upward force on each anchorage.

4 A hydrometer is to be designed. The length of the stem is to be 200 mm between the lowest and the highest graduations, and the hydrometer is to be used for liquids whose relative densities are between 0.95 and 1.25. The volume of the large bulb B (below the lowest graduation on the stem) is 12.2 cm^3. The total mass of the hydrometer is to be adjusted by including a weight at the bottom of the bulb. What should the total mass be? What would be a suitable diameter for the stem?

5 A mercury–water manometer is to be used as a means of measuring the pressure of water in a pipe. The diameter of the tube forming the manometer U-tube is 3 mm. The angle of contact at the mercury–air interface is 130°, and at the mercury–water interface is 140°. What difference in height between the two mercury levels would you expect due to surface tension alone? (Use figures for density and surface tension from the tables on p. 400. Take the surface tension of mercury in contact with water as 0.375 N/m.)

Programme 2

FLUID STATICS AND
HYDROSTATIC FORCES

1

Introduction

In the previous programme the largest section was devoted to the subject of pressure in fluid at rest. You will remember, no doubt, that the force δF due to pressure p acting on a small area δA is given by $\delta F = p\,\delta A$.

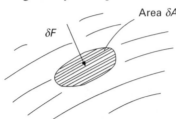

To find the total force exerted due to pressure over a larger area A, we have to sum the contributions δF over all the elements of the area. When the pressure is uniform over the whole of a flat area, this process is very straightforward: the total force is F, where

$$F = p\delta A_1 + p\delta A_2 + p\delta A_3 + \dots$$
$$= p(\delta A_1 + \delta A_2 + \delta A_3 + \dots)$$
$$= pA$$

Thus, when the pressure is uniform over the whole area, the total force is just the product of ...?

2

The pressure and the area

Here is an example.

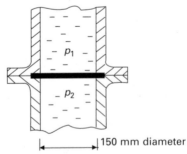

150 mm diameter

The cylindrical pipe shown contains two liquids, one above the separator plate and one below. The internal diameter of the pipe is 150 mm. The pressures are p_1 above and p_2 below the plate.

If $p_1 = 1.2\ \text{MN/m}^2$, what force is exerted on the plate from above by the pressure? ($1\ \text{MN} = 10^6\ \text{N}$)

3

$$\boxed{21.2 \text{ kN}}$$

Working: the area exposed to the pressure is

$$\pi r^2 = \pi \times 0.075^2$$
$$= 17.7 \times 10^{-3} \text{ m}^2$$

so the force exerted is

$$1.2 \times 10^6 \times 17.7 \times 10^{-3} = 21.2 \times 10^3 \text{ N}$$
$$= 21.2 \text{ kN}$$

Now, if the pressure p_2 below the plate is 0.8 MN/m², what is the resultant force on the plate due to the two pressures?

4

$$\boxed{7.1 \text{ kN}}$$

The upward force exerted on the underside of the plate is once again the product of the pressure and the area; that is

$$0.8 \times 10^6 \times 17.7 \times 10^{-3} = 14.1 \times 10^3 \text{ N}$$
$$= 14.1 \text{ kN}$$

Since the two pressure forces act in opposite directions, the resultant is the difference between them, that is $(21.2 - 14.1) = 7.1$ kN.

As you will probably have realised, we could have obtained this result more directly by finding the *difference* in pressure between the two sides and multiplying this by the area.

Here is another example.

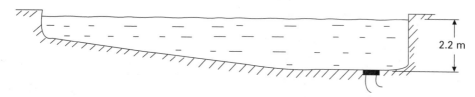

A swimming pool is 2.2 m deep at its deepest point. We wish to find the gauge pressure at the bottom of the pool at this point. First of all, just make sure you remember the definition of gauge pressure: gauge pressure is the difference between the absolute pressure and ...?

5

| Atmospheric pressure |

So, what is the gauge pressure at the bottom of the 2.2 m deep swimming pool?

6

| 21.6 kN/m² |

Here is the working: the surface of the water in the swimming pool is exposed to the atmosphere, and so the pressure at the surface is atmospheric pressure. Thus the gauge pressure at the bottom of the pool is just the difference between the pressure at the bottom and the pressure at the surface, i.e.

$$\text{gauge pressure} = \rho g h$$
$$= 1000 \times 9.81 \times 2.2$$
$$= 21.6 \times 10^3 \text{ N/m}^2$$
$$= 21.6 \text{ kN/m}^2$$

At this deepest point there is a drain so that the pool can be emptied. The entrance to the drain is blocked with a flat cover 200 mm square, the space below the cover being at atmospheric pressure. What is the net force on the cover due to pressure forces?

7

| 864 N |

The net force is the product of the area and the pressure difference between the two sides of the cover. Since the underside of the cover is at atmospheric pressure, the pressure difference is equal to the gauge pressure at the bottom of the pool. Therefore the net force is

$$0.2^2 \times (21.6 \times 10^3) = 864 \text{ N}$$

The examples we have done so far have all been of pressure forces on horizontal surfaces, where the pressure is uniform over the whole area. Before going on to cases where the pressure is *not* uniform, we must turn our attention to the idea of the centroid of an area, so *carry on now to the next frame.*

Centroid of a plane area

8

The centroid of an area is a point which may be defined in a rather similar way to the centre of gravity of a body.

The centre of gravity is the point through which the weight of the body can always be taken to act: it is a point about which the weight has no moment.

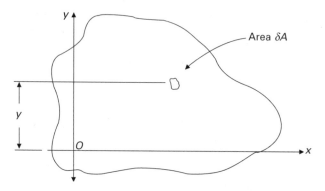

We are less used to taking moments of areas than of forces, but it is equally possible. In the diagram above, the total moment of the area about the axis Ox is found by summing all the contributions $y\delta A$ due to elements δA of area; if the total moment $\Sigma \, y\delta A$ comes to zero, then axis Ox must pass through the centroid C of the area.

If we can find two axes about both of which the moment of the area is zero, then the centroid C must lie at their point of intersection.

Consider a circular area, as shown below:

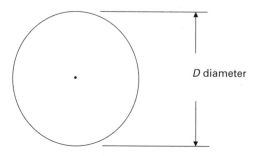

Where do you think the centroid of this area will lie?

9

This may seem just common sense, but it can readily be proved, as follows. A diameter of the circle is an axis of symmetry, so the moment about the diameter of the area on one side of it must be equal to the moment of the area on the opposite side. The resultant moment of the area about the diameter is zero, and C must lie on the diameter.

Since this is true for *any* diameter, the centroid C of the circle lies at the centre.

Indeed, whenever an area has an axis of symmetry, the centroid C of the area must lie on the axis.

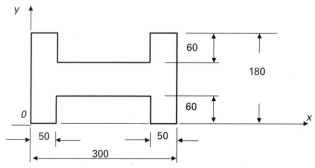

What are the coordinates $(\bar{x}, \bar{y})$ of the centroid for the area shown above?

10

$\bar{x} = 150, \bar{y} = 90$

The area has two axes of symmetry; the centroid C lies at their point of intersection.

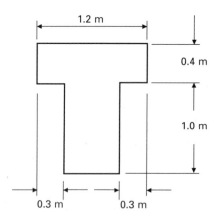

How many axes of symmetry does this shape have?

11

One

It has only one axis of symmetry, the vertical axis. The centroid C must lie on this axis, but in order to find its location on this axis we shall have to take moments.

In this case we can divide the figure conveniently into two rectangles:

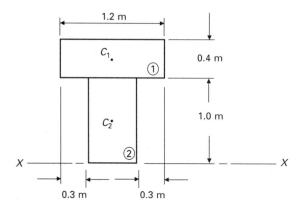

Their areas A_1 and A_2 are ...?

12

$$A_1 = 0.48 \text{ m}^2; A_2 = 0.6 \text{ m}^2$$

... and the centroids C_1 and C_2 of the two rectangles are located at their geometric centres of course, by symmetry.

The moment of the area of rectangle 1 about an axis can be found simply by multiplying together the area A_1 and the distance between the centroid C_1 and the axis – in just the same way as we regard the weight of a body as acting through its centre of gravity when calculating the moment of the weight about an axis.

So, what is the moment of the area of rectangle 1 about the axis $X-X$?

13

$$0.576 \text{ m}^3$$

The moment is just the product (area A_1) × (distance between C_1 and axis $X-X$). Likewise, for rectangle 2 the area moment is (0.6×0.5) m^3, or 0.30 m^3. Thus the total area moment is ...?

14

$$\boxed{0.876 \text{ m}^3}$$

... simply by adding up the moments of the separate rectangles.

This total moment of area about the axis $X-X$ must be equal to the total area A multiplied by the distance $\bar{y}$ from the centroid C to the axis. Thus

$$A\bar{y} = 0.876$$
$$(0.48 + 0.60)\bar{y} = 0.876$$

So the distance $\bar{y}$ is ...?

15

$$\boxed{0.811 \text{ m}}$$

Now, here is another example:

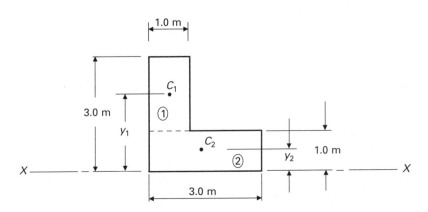

We wish to find the y-coordinate of the centroid of this L-shaped area. Regarding it as composed of rectangles 1 and 2 as shown, first of all find the y-coordinates y_1 and y_2 of the centroids C_1 and C_2 of the two rectangles.

16

$$\boxed{y_1 = 2.0 \text{ m}; \quad y_2 = 0.5 \text{ m}}$$

The centroids are at the centres of the two rectangles, by symmetry.

Now, by taking moments about the axis $X-X$, find the y-coordinate, $\bar{y}$, of the centroid C of the L-shaped area.

17

$$\boxed{\bar{y} = 1.1 \text{ m}}$$

Here is the working: the sum of the moments of the two rectangular areas about axis $X-X$ is

$$A_1y_1 + A_2y_2 = 2.0 \times 2.0 + 3.0 \times 0.5$$
$$= 5.5 \text{ m}^3$$

and this total moment is equal to the whole area A multiplied by the y-coordinate $\bar{y}$ of the overall centroid, C. Thus

$$A\bar{y} = 5.5$$

The area of the whole figure is $A = 2.0 + 3.0 = 5.0 \text{ m}^2$, so

$$5.0\,\bar{y} = 5.5$$
$$\bar{y} = 1.1 \text{ m}$$

Occasionally, if rarely, we come across a shape which cannot be composed from areas whose centroids are already known, and we are then compelled to calculate from first principles. An example of this is done in the next frame.

18

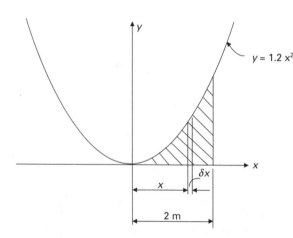

We consider the shaded area, which is 2 m wide, 4.8 m high, and bounded by the curve $y = 1.2x^2$. We shall find the x-coordinate of the centroid of this area.

The area of the narrow vertical strip shown is

$$\delta A = y\delta x$$
$$= 1.2x^2\delta x$$

The total area is the integral

$$A = \int_0^2 1.2x^2 \mathrm{d}x$$

which is equal to ...?

19

$$\boxed{A = 3.2 \text{ m}^2}$$

This integral should be quite straightforward:

$$\int_0^2 1.2x^2 \mathrm{d}x = 1.2 \times \left[x^3/3\right]_0^2$$
$$= 1.2 \times [8/3]$$
$$= 3.2 \text{ m}^2$$

The moment of the area of the strip about the y-axis is

$$\delta M = (1.2x^2 \delta x) \times x$$

To get the total moment, we integrate:

$$M = \int_0^2 1.2x^3 \mathrm{d}x$$

which comes to ...?

20

$$\boxed{4.8 \text{ m}^3}$$

Here is the working:

$$\int_0^2 1.2x^3 \mathrm{d}x = 1.2 \times \left[x^4/4\right]_0^2$$
$$= 1.2 \times [4]$$
$$= 4.8 \text{ m}^3$$

This total moment is equal to $A\bar{y}$, where the total area $A = 3.2$ m^2. Thus

$$3.2 \times \bar{y} = 4.8$$
$$\bar{y} = 1.5 \text{ m}$$

It is not often necessary to calculate the position of the centroid from first principles in this way – usually we can divide our area into parts whose properties are available from tables – but when this is the only possible way the method is as set out above.

Now we must return to the calculation of forces on surfaces subject to fluid pressure.

21

The hydrostatic force on an inclined plane area

In both the examples we did earlier about pressure forces, the flat surface on which the pressure acted was horizontal, so the pressure was uniform over the whole surface. If the surfaces had been inclined, the pressure would have varied with height, and would not have been uniform over the surface.

When the fluids concerned are gases, their density is so small that the pressure varies very little over a typical area, and it is usually sufficiently accurate to treat the pressure as uniform even if the surface *is* inclined, or even vertical.

Here is an example: a flat, circular inspection cover, 450 mm diameter, is fitted in the side of a cylindrical steam vessel, as shown in the diagram below.

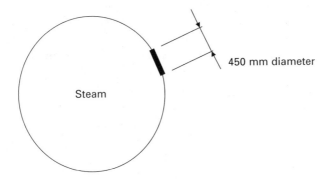

When the steam pressure in the vessel is 8 bar (gauge), what is the resultant force exerted on the inspection cover by the pressure?

22

$$\boxed{127 \text{ kN}}$$

Working: the area of the cover is $\pi \times 0.45^2/4 = 0.159$ m^2 and the pressure difference between the inside and the outside of the vessel is the gauge pressure, that is 8×10^5 N/m^2.

The resultant force is the area times the pressure difference:

$$\text{Resultant force} = 0.159 \times 8 \times 10^5$$
$$= 127 \times 10^3 \text{ N}$$
$$= 127 \text{ kN}$$

We may also wish to know exactly where on the surface the force can be considered to act. We already know that the pressure is virtually uniform over the area of the circular cover. Can you suggest where the resultant force due to the pressure will act?

23

This may seem fairly obvious, but perhaps we ought to justify it: we can argue in the same way as we did in Frame 9 of this programme, where we were finding the centroid of a circular area. We consider a diameter of the circle. The pressure forces are distributed symmetrically each side of the diameter, so there is no resultant moment about the diameter: the resultant force must intersect the diameter.

Since this is true for *any* diameter, the resultant force must act through the centre of the circle.

The point where the resultant pressure force acts on the surface is called the *centre of pressure*.

Usually the centre of pressure is not the same point as the centroid of the area. It is only in a case like this, where the pressure is uniform over the whole area, that the centre of pressure is at the centroid of the area.

Now we turn to the case of a rectangular tank, and estimate the force exerted by the water on the end of the tank, whose width B is 1.3 m. The depth H of the water is 1.8 m.

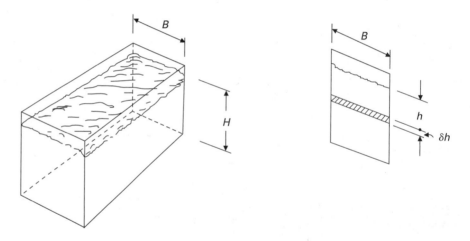

We can think of this force as the resultant of the pressure forces on all the little elements of area that together make up the end of the tank. Let us consider first a narrow horizontal strip (shown shaded in the diagram above), on which the pressure is effectively uniform. The depth to the strip is h; its area is $B\,\delta h$.

Using the symbol ρ for the density of the liquid, what is the force exerted on the strip by the pressure of the liquid?

FLUID STATICS AND HYDROSTATIC FORCES

$$\boxed{\rho g h B \delta h}$$

Working: the gauge pressure at depth h is $\rho g h$, and the area of the strip is $B\,\delta h$. The force exerted is the product of the pressure and the area. (We use the gauge pressure because it is the *difference* between the pressure on the inside surface and the atmospheric pressure on the outer surface that produces the force.)

To find the total resultant force on the end of the tank, we need to sum up the forces on *all* such strips, so that the whole area is included.

$$\text{Total force} = \Sigma\ \rho g h\ B\ \delta h$$
$$= \rho g B\ \Sigma\ h\ \delta h$$

since ρg and B are constants. This sum is most easily found by making the Σ into an integral:

$$\text{Total force} = \rho g B \int_0^H h\ \mathrm{d}h$$
$$= \rho g B \left[h^2/2\right]_0^H$$
$$= \rho g B H^2/2$$

Now substitute for ρ (1000 kg/m³), g (9.81 m/s²), B (1.3 m) and H (1.8 m), and obtain the total force.

$$\boxed{20.7 \text{ kN}}$$

Let's look again at the result of the integration:

$$\text{Total force} = \rho g B\ H^2/2$$

This can be written as $(\rho g H/2) \times (BH)$. We recognise the product (BH): it is the area of the end of the tank. The other factor $(\rho g H/2)$ is a pressure.

What depth of liquid does this pressure correspond to?

26

$H/2$, half the depth of the tank

So, for the rectangular tank with rectangular ends, the force on the end of the tank is given by the area of the end multiplied by the pressure at the half depth.

Now let us take a different case – a tank with vertical triangular ends.

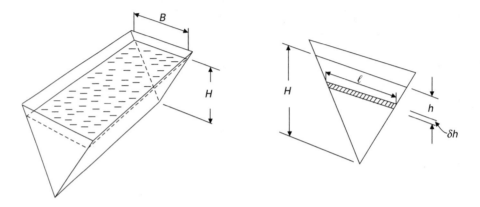

To find the pressure force on the end of the tank, we can use a very similar method. Once again we shall begin by taking a narrow horizontal strip at depth h. The length of the strip, across the tank, varies according to the depth: at the surface, when $h = 0$, the width is B, but at the bottom of the tank, when $h = H$, the width is zero. Can you write down an expression for the length ℓ of the strip in terms of B, H and h?

$$\ell = B(1 - h/H)$$

Working:

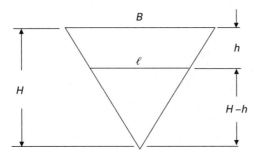

The larger triangle and the smaller triangle in the diagram are similar, that is, they have the same angles and are exactly the same shape. The ratios of the base to the height must therefore be the same. Thus

$$\ell/(H - h) = B/H$$
$$\ell = B(1 - h/H)$$

Following the same process as in the last example, we find the force on the shaded strip, which is

$$\rho g h B(1 - h/H)\delta h$$

or

$$\rho g B(h - h^2/H)\delta h$$

The total force on the end of the tank is the sum of the forces on all these strips, which as before we can write either with a Σ sign, or more helpfully as an integral:

$$\text{Total force} = \rho g B \int_0^H (h - h^2/H)\mathrm{d}h$$
$$= \rho g B[h^2/2 - h^3/3H]_0^H$$
$$= \rho g B(H^2/2 - H^3/3H)$$
$$= \rho g B H^2/6$$

The end of the tank is a triangle, so its area is $BH/2$. In our last example we rewrote the expression for the force as a product of a pressure and the area of the end of the tank.

Now rearrange the expression above for the total force in the same way.

28

$$\boxed{\text{Total force} = (\rho g H/3) \times (BH/2)}$$

This time, with our triangular-section tank, we see that the pressure, $(\rho g H/3)$, corresponds to a depth $H/3$.

It may possibly have occurred to you that in each of these cases the depth ($H/2$ in the case of the rectangle, $H/3$ with the triangle) is the distance down to the centroid of the area. We shall see shortly that it is true in every case that the force due to pressure on a plane surface submerged in a fluid is given by the area of the surface multiplied by the pressure at the centroid of the area.

To see this in general, we turn to the case of an inclined plane area submerged in a liquid of density ρ; the liquid is at rest, but because the plane area is not horizontal, the pressure varies from place to place over the area.

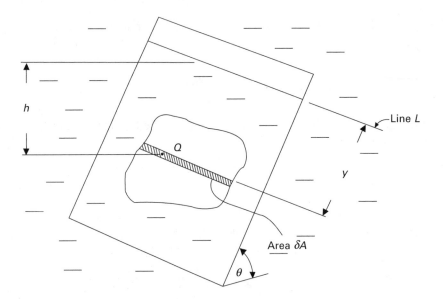

The area concerned is marked out on a rectangular plate mounted in the liquid at angle θ to the horizontal, as shown above. We wish to find the force F exerted by pressure on the marked area.

Consider one point within the area, say Q. This point is at depth h below the surface of the liquid, and so the gauge pressure at point Q is ...?

$$\boxed{\rho g h}$$

... in the usual way. All points on the horizontal line through Q are also at depth h; the gauge pressure is $\rho g h$ all the way along this line.

If we take a narrow horizontal strip of area δA, the force on this strip is the pressure times the area, i.e.

$$(\rho g h) \times \delta A$$

or

$$(\rho g \times y \sin \theta) \times \delta A$$

where y is the sloping distance down the plane from the surface to the horizontal line through Q, as shown.

Now, to obtain the total force F we must sum the forces over the whole area, strip by strip:

$$F = \Sigma(\rho g \times y \sin \theta \times \delta A)$$

Since ρ, g and $\sin \theta$ are all constants and do not vary over the area, we can take them outside the summation sign and obtain

$$F = \rho g \sin \theta \, \Sigma(y \delta A)$$

The expression $\Sigma(y \delta A)$ should be quite familiar: it is the sum of the 'moments' of all the areas δA about the line L where the plane meets the liquid surface, and it may conveniently be written as $A\bar{y}$, where $\bar{y}$ is the distance from the line L to the centroid of the area A.

Thus we have

$$F = \rho g A \bar{y} \sin \theta$$
$$= \rho g A \bar{h}$$

where $\bar{h}$ is the depth from the surface of the liquid to the centroid of the area.

Now $\rho g \bar{h}$ is the gauge pressure at the centroid of the area, and so we find that what we saw in the two earlier examples is always true:

the total force F on a plane submerged area is equal to its area multiplied by the pressure at the centroid of the area.

30

Example

A flat circular window 350 mm diameter as shown below is fitted in the curved base of a tank, which is filled with sea-water to a depth of 6.5 m above the centre of the window. The density of the sea-water is 1024 kg/m³. We wish to find the force exerted on the window by the water.

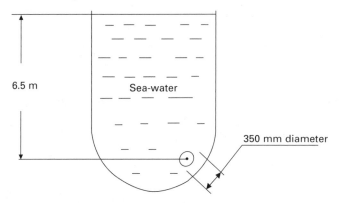

The window in the tank is circular, and so the centroid of the area of the window is located ...?

31

> at the centre of the window

The centroid of the window is 6.5 m below the surface of the water. The gauge pressure at this depth is

$$p = \rho g h$$
$$= 1024 \times 9.81 \times 6.5$$
$$= 65.3 \times 10^3 \text{ N/m}^2$$

The force F exerted on the window is the product of this pressure and the area of the window, i.e.

$$F = 65.3 \times 10^3 \times \pi \times (0.35/2)^2$$
$$= 6280 \text{ N}$$

In this example, the outer surface of the window is exposed to atmospheric pressure. Thus the resultant force on the window due to the pressures on the two sides is given by the area of the window multiplied by the difference between the absolute pressure on the inside and that on the outside: multiplied by the gauge pressure, in other words. Using the gauge pressure will always yield the *net* force on the surface, as if the other side was exposed to atmospheric pressure.

The next frame contains another example, this time for you to do.

32

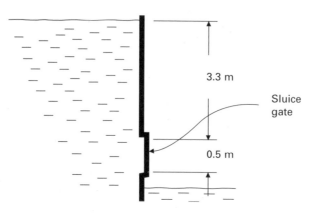

3.3 m

Sluice gate

0.5 m

A rectangular sluice gate is used to control water flow at a lock on a canal. The sluice gate is 0.4 m wide by 0.5 m tall, and when the gate is closed its top edge is 3.3 m below the water surface as shown. Find the resultant force due to pressure on the sluice gate.

33

6.97 kN

Working: the depth to the centroid of the rectangular gate is $3.3 + 0.25 = 3.55$ m, so the gauge pressure at that point is

$$p = \rho g h$$
$$= 1000 \times 9.81 \times 3.55$$
$$= 34.8 \times 10^3 \text{N/m}^2$$

The area of the gate is $0.5 \times 0.4 = 0.2$ m^2.

Thus the resultant force F on the gate is given by

$$F = 34.8 \times 0.2 \text{ kN}$$
$$= 6.97 \text{ kN}$$

What we are doing here, in effect, is to find the total force by multiplying the area of the surface by an *average* pressure; as we have already shown, this average pressure is simply the pressure at the centroid of the area.

34

Now here is a slightly different case: the same rectangular sluice gate is now submerged on both sides, as shown below.

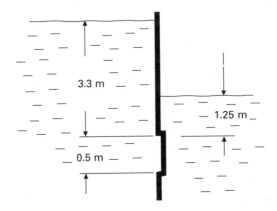

3.3 m

1.25 m

0.5 m

Can you now find the resultant force on the gate due to water pressure?

35

> 4.02 kN

Working: the area exposed to pressure is 0.2 m² on both sides.

The gauge pressure at the centroid on one side is $p_1 = 34.8 \times 10^3$ N/m², as before. On the other side the depth to the centroid is $(1.25 + 0.25) = 1.50$ m, so the gauge pressure there is p_2, where

$$p_2 = 1000 \times 9.81 \times 1.50$$
$$= 14.7 \times 10^3 \text{ N/m}^2$$

The resultant force F on the gate is given by

$$F = (p_1 - p_2)A$$
$$= (34.8 - 14.7) \times 0.2 \text{ kN}$$
$$= 4.02 \text{ kN}$$

Here the resultant force due to pressure is the product of the area and the pressure *difference* between the two sides of the sluice gate. In this case it is clearly satisfactory to use gauge pressures, because the pressure difference has the same value whether we use gauge pressures or absolute pressures.

Before going on to the next section of the programme, we have a few revision questions, just to make sure that you have fully understood what we have covered so far.

36

Revision exercise

1 What are the coordinates of the centroid of the area shown on the left in the diagram? (Divide the shape into three rectangles, and then you shouldn't have to calculate.)

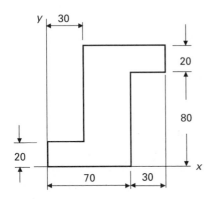

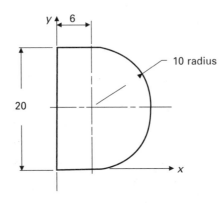

2 What are the coordinates of the centroid of the shape shown on the right? (Divide this into a rectangle and a semicircle. The position of the centroid of the semicircle is $4r/3\pi$ to the right of the centre of curvature of the semicircular arc, where r is the radius.)

3 The upper part of the end of a water tank is rectangular, and the lower part is triangular, as shown. What force does the water exert on the end of the tank? (Hint: find the forces on the rectangular part and on the triangular part separately, then add them together. The centroid of a triangle is 1/3 of the height away from the base – which in this case is at the top, of course.)

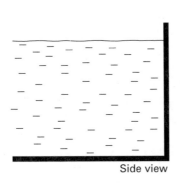

Side view

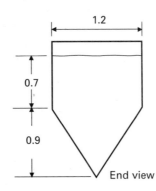

End view

37

Solutions

1 This S-shaped area looks as if it has some sort of symmetry, but in fact it does not have symmetry about any *axis*. However, common sense probably suggests that the point labelled C in the diagram below must be the centroid – all we need is to justify this.

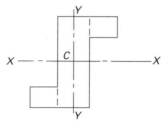

One way to do this is to regard the area as three rectangles. About the axis labelled $X-X$, the large rectangle is symmetrical and has no moment, and the two small rectangles have equal and opposite moments. Thus the centroid must lie on $X-X$. A similar argument applies for moments about $Y-Y$. Thus C must lie at their intersection: $x = 50$, $y = 50$.

Alternatively, we may observe that any line drawn through point C cuts the edges of the figure in points that are equidistant either side of C. Thus the moments of areas about an axis through C *perpendicular to the plane of the paper* must sum to zero, so C must be the centroid.

2 In this case there is a horizontal axis of symmetry, on which the centroid must lie, but to find out exactly where on this axis it lies we have to take moments. The area of the semicircle is A_1, where $A_1 = \pi \times 10^2/2 = 157$ mm^2, and the area of the rectangle is $A_2 = 120$ mm^2.

The centroid of the semicircle is distance 4.24 mm from the centre, so, taking moments about the y-axis,

$$(157 + 120)x = 157 \times (6 + 4.24) + 120 \times 3$$
$$277x = 1968$$
$$x = 7.10 \text{ mm}$$

3 For each part, the force exerted is equal to (area) $\times$ (gauge pressure at the centroid), where we use gauge pressure because atmospheric pressure acts on the outside of the tank end.

For the rectangular part,

$$\text{force} = (1.2 \times 0.7) \times (1000 \times 9.81 \times 0.35) \text{ N}$$
$$= 2.88 \text{ kN}$$

For the triangular part,

$$\text{force} = (\tfrac{1}{2} \times 1.2 \times 0.9) \times (1000 \times 9.81 \times (0.7 + 0.9/3)) \text{ N}$$
$$= 5.30 \text{ kN}$$

Thus the resultant force on the tank end is $(2.88 + 5.30) = 8.18$ kN.

The centre of pressure

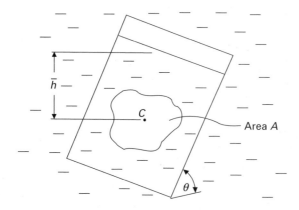

Now we consider once again an area A marked out (as shown above) on a plane submerged in a liquid of density ρ. Point C is the centroid of the area.

First of all, what is the magnitude of the force F exerted on the area A by the pressure? (Use the gauge pressure in this calculation.)

$$F = A\,\rho g \bar{h}$$

Just as before, the force is equal to the product of the area and the pressure at the centroid.

We may also wish to find out where this resultant force acts on the panel. Do you recall the name we give to the point of the surface where the resultant pressure force acts?

40

The centre of pressure

This idea was introduced back in Frame 23, where we discussed, briefly, the point where the pressure force acts on a circular panel. In that case the pressure was uniform all over the panel, so the resultant pressure force acted through the centroid of the area.

In this case, though, the pressure is not uniform: it increases with the depth. So the part of the surface *below* the centroid must experience more force than the part above. This means that the centre of pressure must be at a greater depth than the centroid.

41

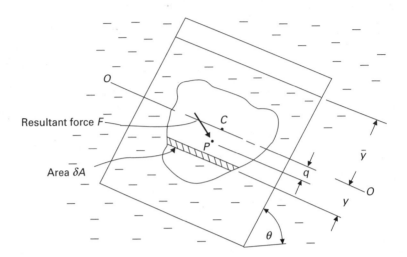

We shall take the centre of pressure P to be a distance q lower down the plane than the centroid C of the area: to find the value of this unknown distance q, we have to take moments. We can take moments about any axis we care to choose: let us choose the horizontal axis $O-O$ through C. The gauge pressure at the centroid C we shall call p_C.

The moment of the resultant force F (acting at the centre of pressure P) about axis $O-O$ is then $F \times q$; this must be the same as the sum of the moments of the pressure forces on all the elements of the area.

As we have already done several times, we consider a narrow horizontal strip across the panel. The strip is a distance y below the centroid C, and its area is δA. The gauge pressure at the strip is equal to the pressure at the centroid, p_C, plus the extra pressure because the strip is deeper by a distance $y \sin \theta$, i.e. the gauge pressure is $p_C + \rho g y \sin \theta$. If the area of the strip is δA, what is the magnitude of the pressure force on the strip?

42

$$\boxed{\text{Pressure force} = p_C \delta A + \rho g y \sin \theta \delta A}$$

The pressure force is just the product of the area and the pressure.

The moment of this force about the axis $O-O$ is

$$\delta M = p_C y \, \delta A + \rho g \, y^2 \sin \theta \delta A$$

in which p_C, y, ρ and $\sin \theta$ are all constants.

(continued on p. 79)

Summing all these moments over the whole area A, we must get a result equal to the moment of the resultant force F acting at the centre of pressure P: thus

$$F \times q = p_C \, \Sigma \, y \, \delta A + \rho g \, \sin \theta \, \Sigma y^2 \, \delta A$$

Now, the quantity $\Sigma \, y \, \delta A$ is the sum of the moments of all the elements of area about the axis $O-O$ through the centroid, C. By the definition of the centroid C, the value of this sum is ...?

43

> Zero

By definition, the centroid of the area is the point about which the area has no moment, so the value of the total area moment $\Sigma \, y \, \delta A$ must be zero. This leaves

$$F \times q = \rho g \sin \theta \, \Sigma y^2 \delta A$$

Substituting for F the expression we found in Frame 39, $F = A\rho g \overline{h}$:

$$A \rho g \overline{h} \times q = \rho g \sin \theta \, \Sigma y^2 \delta A$$

so

$$q = \frac{\sin \theta \, \Sigma y^2 \delta A}{A \, \overline{h}}$$

and, since $\overline{h} = \overline{y} \sin \theta$,

$$q = \frac{\Sigma y^2 \delta A}{A \, \overline{y}}$$

Finally, the quantity $\Sigma \, y^2 \, \delta A$ is of a type that crops up quite often in engineering. It is called a *second moment of area* – 'second' because the small area δA is multiplied by y^2, the square of the moment arm, rather than by y itself as in ordinary moments. The second moment of area is usually denoted by the symbol I, and where (as here) the moment is taken about the axis $O-O$ we can specify this by writing the symbol as I_C.

On now to the next frame, where we shall work through an example.

44

Example

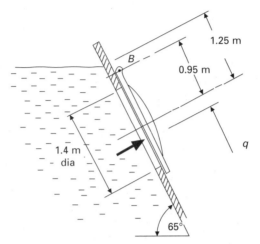

A circular opening 1.4 m diameter in the sloping side of a water tank is to be closed by a heavy cast-iron cover. The centre of the opening is a distance 1.25 m from the surface, as shown above.

Let us imagine ourselves to be the designers of the cover. We shall need to estimate (a) the force on the cover; (b) the position of the centre of pressure, P; and (c) the moment exerted about the hinge B.

(a) The outer side of the cover is subject to atmospheric pressure, so we can find the resultant pressure force F on the cover directly by using the gauge pressure in the calculation. This force is simply the area multiplied by the pressure at the centroid, C; so F is equal to ...?

45

$$\boxed{17.1 \text{ kN}}$$

Working:

$$F = \pi r^2 \times \rho g h$$
$$= (\pi \times 0.7^2) \times (1000 \times 9.81 \times 1.25 \, \sin 65°)$$
$$= 17.1 \times 10^3 \text{ N}$$

(b) The centre of pressure P is below the centroid C by distance q, where

$$q = I_C / A\bar{y}$$

The second moment of area, I_C, for a circle is given by $I_C = \pi d^4/64$ (This expression is quoted widely in tables, including the one on p. 401.)

What is the value of the distance q in this case?

46

$$\boxed{98 \text{ mm}}$$

The area of the circle is $A = \pi r^2 = \pi d^2 / 4$, so we get

$$q = \frac{\pi d^4}{64} \times \frac{4}{\pi d^2} \times \frac{1}{\bar{y}} = \frac{d^2}{16 \bar{y}}$$

Putting in the values, we get

$$q = \frac{1.4^2}{16 \times 1.25} = 0.098 \text{ m, or 98 mm}$$

(c) Finally, we wish to find the moment of the pressure force about the hinge, B. This is simply the product of the force F and the distance of its line of action from B.

$$\text{The distance } PB = (PC + CB)$$
$$= 0.098 + 0.95$$
$$= 1.048 \text{ m}$$

so the moment of the force is . . .?

47

$$\boxed{17.9 \text{ kN m}}$$

The moment is

$$(\text{force} \times \text{distance}) = (17.1 \times 10^3) \times 1.048$$
$$= 17.9 \times 10^3 \text{ N m}$$

Armed with these results, we, the designers, will be able to work out the forces on the fastenings of the cover, and so determine how large they need to be. Now, here is an example for you to do on your own:

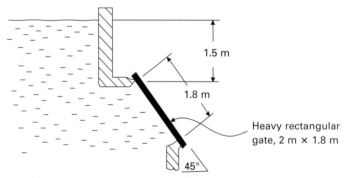

Once again we have an opening in a water tank that is closed by a heavy gate. This time the gate is rectangular, 2 m × 1.8 m: the other dimensions are given in the diagram. First of all, what is the resultant pressure force on the gate?

48

> 75.4 kN

The force is the product of the area and the gauge pressure at C, as usual:

$$F = (2 \times 1.8) \times (1000 \times 9.81 \times (1.5 + 0.9/\sin 45°))$$
$$= 75.4 \times 10^3 \text{ N}$$

Now, what is the distance q between the centroid of the area of the gate and the centre of pressure? (The second moment of area of a rectangular area is given in the table on p. 401.)

49

> 89 mm

Here is the working: first, to find the second moment of area of the rectangular gate about the horizontal axis $O-O$ through the centroid of the area. The breadth of the panel is $b = 2$ m, and the depth is $d = 1.8$ m, so the second moment of area is

$$I_C = 2 \times 1.8^3/12$$
$$= 0.972 \text{ m}^4$$

Next, the area of the panel is

$$A = (2 \times 1.8) = 3.6 \text{ m}^2$$

and distance $\bar{y}$ from the centroid to the surface along the inclined direction of the surface of the gate is $1.5\sqrt{2} + 0.9 = 3.02$ m. Thus,

$$q = I_C/A\bar{y} = 0.972/(3.6 \times 3.02)$$
$$= 0.089 \text{ m}$$
$$= 89 \text{ mm}$$

All this is quite straightforward when the area concerned is just one of the standard shapes for which the formula is quoted in tables – a circle, rectangle or triangle. When the area is a different shape, it can often be broken down into simple standard ones.

We shall be looking at an example of this in the next frame, so move on now.

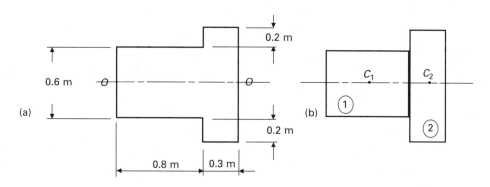

(a)

(b)

The area shown in diagram (a) above can be made up from two rectangles 1 and 2 as shown in diagram (b). The centroids of both rectangles lie on the axis $O-O$, so we can quote their second moments about $O-O$ at once:

$$\text{for rectangle 1 it is } (0.8 \times 0.6^3)/12 = 0.014 \text{ m}^4$$
$$\text{and for rectangle 2 it is } (0.3 \times 1.0^3)/12 = 0.025 \text{ m}^4$$

Since the second moment of area is made up by summing all the contributions $y^2\delta A$ over all the elements of the area, we can simply add together these second moments about the axis $O-O$ to obtain the total second moment for the whole figure, which is ...?

51

$$\boxed{I_C = 0.039 \text{ m}^4}$$

This is just addition of two numbers – not too difficult!

If second moments of areas can be added when areas are put together, they can equally well be subtracted when one area is taken away from another.

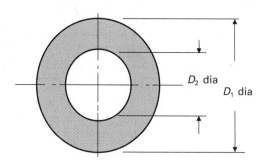

Can you find the second moment of area I_C for the annular area shown in the diagram? (Refer to p. 401 for the second moment about an axis passing through the centre of the circle.)

52

$$I_C = \pi(D_1{}^4 - D_2{}^4)/64$$

The second moment of area for the whole of the larger circle is equal to that for the smaller circle plus that for the annular area. Thus, the second moment for the annulus is equal to the difference between the second moments for the larger circle and for the smaller circle.

Writing this out in algebra, we have that I_C for the annulus is given by

$$I_C = \pi D_1{}^4/64 - \pi D_2{}^4/64$$

53

In both of the previous two examples the axis $O-O$ passed through the centroids of all the areas, that is of the two areas added or subtracted, and of the resulting area which was the sum or difference.

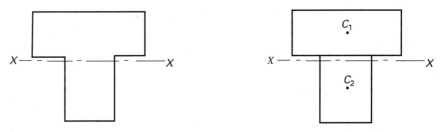

In the T-shaped area shown here the area can be composed from two rectangular shapes as indicated in the right-hand diagram. Just as before, we can find the second moment of area of the whole figure by adding up the second moments of the component parts:

$$I_{X(\text{whole figure})} = I_{X(\text{rectangle 1})} + I_{X(\text{rectangle 2})}$$

However, neither of the centroids C_1 and C_2 of the two rectangles lies on the axis $X-X$ which passes through the centroid C of the composite T-shaped area; so we cannot simply add up values calculated from standard expressions for second moments, because each of these expressions is for a second moment about an axis that does pass through the centroid of the area.

It is actually not at all difficult to work out the second moment of an area about an axis displaced from its centroid C, as we shall see in the next frame.

The parallel axis theorem

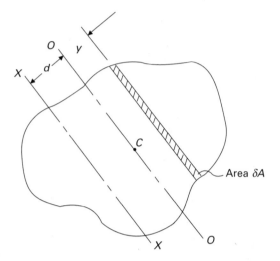

Consider an area as shown above. Suppose we know the second moment of area I_C about the axis $O-O$ which passes through C, and we wish to calculate the second moment I_X about the parallel axis $X-X$. I_X is defined in the usual way as the sum of all the contributions of second moments from strips of area δA parallel to the axis $X-X$. The moment arm in each case is $(y + d)$. Thus

$$I_X = \Sigma(y+d)^2\,\delta A$$
$$= \Sigma(y^2 + 2yd + d^2)\,\delta A$$
$$= \Sigma y^2\,\delta A + 2d\Sigma y\,\delta A + d^2\Sigma\,\delta A$$

where the constants 2, d and d^2 have been brought in front of the summation signs.

Looking at these terms in turn, $\Sigma y^2\,\delta A$ is simply I_C, the second moment about axis $O-O$; $\Sigma y\,\delta A$ is the *first* moment of the area about the centroid C, and this is zero by definition of C. The third term is equal to Ad^2, because $\Sigma\delta A$ is just the total area. After all this we have:

$$I_X = I_C + Ad^2$$

This important result is known as the *parallel axis theorem*. It states that, if we know the second moment of area I_C of a certain plane area about an axis through the centroid C, then the second moment I_X about another axis $X-X$ parallel to the first is equal to $(I_C + Ad^2)$, where A is the total area and d is the distance between the two axes.

Turn over now to the next frame, where we will try a simple example.

55

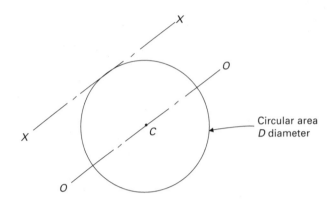

For the circular area shown, the second moment about an axis $O-O$ through C is $I_C = \pi D^4/64$. What is the second moment of area about the axis $X-X$?

56

$$\boxed{I_X = 5\pi D^4/64}$$

Here is the working:

$$I_X = I_C + Ad^2$$

from the parallel axis theorem. We know that $I_C = \pi D^4/64$. To this we must add Ad^2; the area of a circle is $A = \pi D^2/4$, and the 'transfer distance' between the two axes $O-O$ and $X-X$ is $D/2$. This gives

$$I_X = \pi D^4/64 + (\pi D^2/4) \times (D/2)^2$$
$$= 5\pi D^4/64$$

Now for another example:

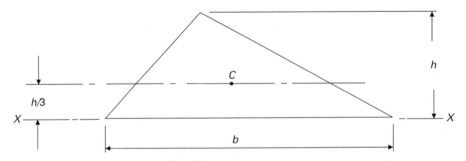

The second moment of area of the triangle shown about the axis $X-X$ is $(bh^3/12)$. Find the second moment of area about the parallel axis through the centroid C of the area, which is a distance $h/3$ away. (Use the parallel axis theorem, but take care to substitute the terms in the right places!)

$$\boxed{bh^3/36}$$

This question is the opposite way round from the previous one, in that we are wishing to find the second moment of area about an axis through the centroid C, given the second moment about a parallel axis. The parallel axis theorem is

$$I_X = I_C + Ad^2$$

and, turning this round,

$$I_C = I_X - Ad^2$$

The area A of the triangle is $bh/2$, so

$$\begin{aligned}
I_C &= bh^3/12 - (bh/2) \times (h/3)^2 \\
&= bh^3/12 - bh^3/18 \\
&= bh^3/36
\end{aligned}$$

The second moment of area about an axis through the centroid is always less than the second moment about any parallel axis. This fact is made clear by the parallel axis theorem: since Ad^2 is always a positive quantity if the axis $X-X$ does not pass through the centroid, I_X is always greater than I_C.

We are now in a position to find the second moment of area for shapes like the one in Frame 53, and indeed to solve problems about the force and moment due to pressure on areas of virtually any shape.

In the next frame we tackle an example of this type.

58

Example

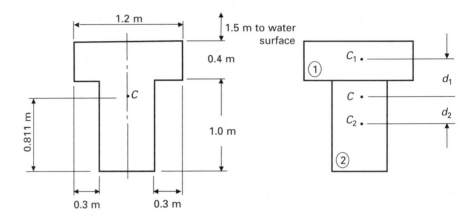

An object immersed in water is closed by a vertical end-plate shaped as shown in the diagram, the top edge of the the plate being 1.5 m below the water surface. We wish to find the magnitude and the position of the line of action of the force exerted on the plate by the water pressure.

We have already worked out (Frames 10–14) that the centroid of the area is located 0.811 m above the lower edge of the plate, and it lies on the vertical centre-line, by symmetry.

So, using gauge pressure, the magnitude of the pressure force on the end-plate is ...?

59

$$\boxed{22.1 \text{ kN}}$$

Working: force $F =$ (pressure at the centroid) × area. The depth to the centroid is

$$h = (1.5 + 1.4 - 0.811)$$
$$= 2.089 \text{ m}$$

so the gauge pressure is

$$p = 1000 \times 9.81 \times 2.089 \text{ N/m}^2$$
$$= 20.5 \text{ kN/m}^2$$

The area of the plate is 1.08 m². Therefore the force is $(20.5 \times 1.08) = 22.1$ kN. Now we must find the position of the centre of pressure.

60

The centre of pressure is below the centroid C by a distance $I_C/A\bar{y}$, and we already know the area A and the depth $\bar{y}$ to the centroid. It remains to find the second moment of area about the horizontal axis through C.

Consider first the upper rectangular part of the shape, labelled 1 on the right-hand diagram. About the horizontal axis through its own centroid C_1 the second moment of area is

$$I_{C1} = 1.2 \times 0.4^3/12 = 6.4 \times 10^{-3}\ \text{m}^4$$

To find the second moment of area about the horizontal axis through the overall centroid C, we must add on the transfer term $A\,d_1^2$, where d_1 is the distance $C_1 C$ and A is the area of rectangle 1. The transfer term is

$$A\,d_1^2 = 0.48 \times 0.389^2 = 72.6 \times 10^{-3}\ \text{m}^4$$

so the total is

$$(6.4 + 72.6) \times 10^{-3} = 79.0 \times 10^{-3}\ \text{m}^4$$

Now, can you find the second moment of area for rectangle 2 about the horizontal axis through the overall centroid?

61

$$\boxed{108 \times 10^{-3}\ \text{m}^4}$$

The method is just the same:

$$I_{C2} = 0.6 \times 1.0^3/12 = 50 \times 10^{-3}\ \text{m}^4$$

For rectangle 2:

$$Ad_2^2 = 0.6 \times 0.311^2 = 58 \times 10^{-3}\ \text{m}^4$$

Adding these, we get $108 \times 10^{-3}\ \text{m}^4$.

The total second moment about the horizontal axis through the centroid C is thus

$$I_C = (79 + 108) \times 10^{-3}\ \text{m}^4 = 187 \times 10^{-3}\ \text{m}^4$$

Substituting this into our expression for the depth of the centre of pressure below the centroid, we get

$$I_C/A\bar{y} = (187 \times 10^{-3})/(1.08 \times 2.089)\ \text{m} = 82.9\ \text{mm}$$

Thus the centre of pressure is a distance 82.9 mm lower than the centroid C of the area.

Now try the revision questions in the next frame.

62

Revision exercise

Throughout this exercise you may need to refer to the tables on p. 401 for geometrical properties of plane figures.

1 (a) Find the depths $\bar{y}_1$ and $\bar{y}_2$ to the centroids C_1 and C_2 of the rectangle and triangle shown in the diagram below, and (b) find the depth $\bar{y}$ to the centroid C of the whole figure.

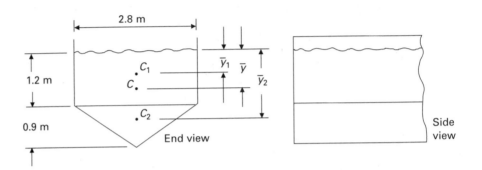

End view   Side view

2 The plane figure shown forms the vertical end of a water tank. What is the magnitude of the force exerted on the plane by the water?

3 Find the second moment of area of the figure about the horizontal axis $O-O$ through the centroid C. (This will involve use of the parallel axis theorem for both the triangle and the rectangle – be systematic about this and you should have no trouble.)

4 Finally, find the position of the centre of pressure P of the complete figure.

Solutions

1 (a) $\bar{y}_1 = 0.6$ m ; $\bar{y}_2 = 1.2 + 0.9/3 = 1.5$ m
   (b) The areas are $A_1 = 3.36$ m^2; $A_2 = 1.26$ m^2; so the total area is $A = 4.62$ m^2.
   Now, taking moments about the top edge,

$$4.62\,\bar{y} = 3.36 \times 0.6 + 1.26 \times 1.5$$
$$\bar{y} = 0.845 \text{ m}$$

2   The magnitude of the force $=$ area $\times$ gauge pressure at centroid
$$= 4.62 \times (1000 \times 9.81 \times 0.845) \text{ N}$$
$$= 38.3 \text{ kN}$$

3 For the rectangle, $I_C = bd^3/12 = 2.8 \times 1.2^3/12 = 0.403$ m^4. The transfer distance d_1 between the centroid C_1 of the rectangle and the centroid C of the whole figure is $d_1 = 0.845 - 0.6 = 0.245$ m .
   Therefore $A_1 d_1^2 = 3.36 \times 0.245^2 = 0.202$ m^4.
   Then for the triangle, $I_C = bd^3/36 = 2.8 \times 0.9^3/36 = 0.057$ m^4.
   The transfer distance is $d_2 = 1.5 - 0.845 = 0.655$ m, and therefore $A_2 d_2^2 = 1.26 \times 0.655^2 = 0.541$ m^4.
   Totalling all the contributions: $I_C = 1.203$ m^4.

4 Finally, the distance q between the centroid C and the centre of pressure P is given by

$$q = \frac{I_C}{A\bar{y}} = \frac{1.203}{4.62 \times 0.845} = 0.308 \text{ m}$$

These questions should not have caused you any real difficulty, but if you did come across any problems just refer back to the relevant section (Frames 38–61) and make quite sure you have mastered it. Then turn on to the final section of this programme.

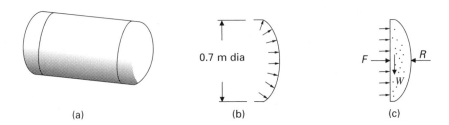

64

The hydrostatic force on a curved surface

We have seen how to calculate the force exerted by stationary liquid on a flat surface, but these methods are of no immediate use when fluid is pressing against curved surfaces, like the inside of a pipe, or the curved surface of a dam, or the inside of a cylindrical pressure vessel – such as the one shown in diagram (a) below.

0.7 m dia

F R

W

(a)   (b)   (c)

The pressure vessel is a steel cylinder containing compressed air. We wish to calculate the force acting on the dished end of the vessel due to the pressure.

We might consider doing this by summing all the pressure forces acting on elements of the curved end (diagram (b)), but because of the curvature the forces act in differing directions and cannot readily be added.

A much easier approach is to look at the equilibrium of the air contained between the curved end and an imaginary plane surface, as shown in diagram (c). The forces acting on this air consist of its own weight W; the pressure force F exerted by the remainder of the compressed air on the flat circular area; and the force R exerted by the inner surface of the dished end. No other forces act on the air, and so these three forces are in equilibrium. It is usually not very difficult to calculate the weight W and the pressure force F, so we can now find the third force R.

In accordance with Newton's third law, the force exerted by the air on the dished end is equal and opposite to R: we thus have the answer to the original question.

First, if the gauge pressure of the air in the vessel is 6 bar, what is the magnitude of the force F (using gauge pressure)?

231 kN

The working for this should be very familiar now: the force exerted on the plane area is just the product of the pressure and the area.

$$F = (6 \times 10^5) \times (\pi \times 0.7^2/4)$$
$$= 231 \times 10^3 \text{ N}$$

We use gauge pressure rather than absolute pressure because the dished end of the vessel is subject to atmospheric pressure on the outside, and it is the difference between the pressures inside and outside that gives rise to the force on the end.

Now we need to know the weight W of the air in our volume. What can we say about this? Is the weight comparable with the force F that we have already calculated?

W is very much smaller than F

Because the fluid contained is air – a gas – its density is very small, and so in this case the weight of fluid W is relatively small and can be ignored.

Thus there are effectively only two forces on the contained air, F and R, and for equilibrium they must be equal and opposite. This means that the resultant force exerted by the air on the dished end of the vessel is *equal* to the force F, in both magnitude and direction.

The method we have used in this example, of considering the equilibrium of a volume of fluid that is pressing against the curved surface in question, can be used in virtually every case. The next frame contains another example, so turn over now.

67

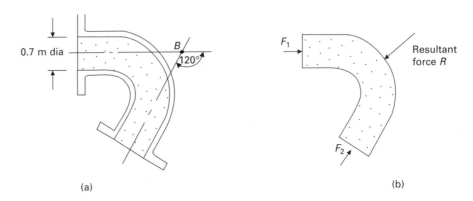

(a)   (b)

The 120° pipe elbow shown in (a) above contains stationary gas at gauge pressure 500 kN/m^2, and we wish to find the force exerted by the gas on the elbow. The inner surface of the pipe elbow is certainly curved, so we shall use the same technique as before, namely, to select a certain volume of fluid that is in contact with the pipe elbow and write down the conditions for its equilibrium.

The most suitable volume of gas to select is that contained within the pipe elbow and between two plane surfaces, one each end; this volume is drawn in (b) above.

What is the magnitude of the force F_1 due to pressure on the left-hand end of the volume of fluid?

68

$$F_1 = 8.84 \text{ kN}$$

Just pressure multiplied by area, as usual, and again we are using gauge pressure because the pipe elbow is surrounded by air at atmospheric pressure.

The force F_2 acting on the other end has the same magnitude, of course.

The weight of the gas is relatively small and can be ignored, so there are effectively just three forces acting – F_1, F_2 and R – and they are in equilibrium. We can therefore draw a closed triangle whose sides represent, in magnitude and direction, the three forces.

So, what must be the magnitude of the force R?

15.3 kN

From the triangle of forces:

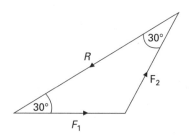

We see that

$$R = F_1 \cos 30° + F_2 \cos 30°$$
$$= 2 \times (8.84 \ \cos 30°)$$
$$= 15.3 \text{ kN}$$

From the diagram, the direction of force R is at 30° to both F_1 and F_2. In order to describe the force R completely, we need to know the position of the line of action of this force, as well as the magnitude and direction. The position must give complete equilibrium, that is, no resultant force or moment.

The lines of action of forces F_1 and F_2 intersect in a point labelled B on diagram (a) in Frame 67. What is the resultant moment of F_1 and F_2 about point B?

Zero

The lines of both forces pass through point B, so neither has any moment about B.

The three forces must have zero resultant moment – so what do we know about the line of action of force R?

It must also pass through point B

Three forces in equilibrium must all pass through a single point – if the line of action of one of the forces did not pass through the intersection of the other two, then there would be a moment about that point, and equilibrium would not be satisfied.

72

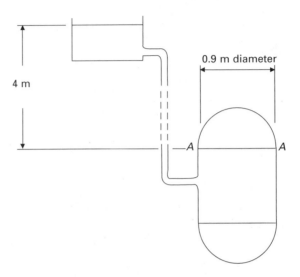

So far we have been dealing with gases, whose density is so small that their weight can be ignored. Now, here is an example where this is not the case, because the fluid is a liquid.

A water tank with hemispherical ends is filled from a second, higher tank as shown. What is the weight of the water contained between the upper hemispherical end and the plane $A-A$? (The volume of a sphere of radius r is $4\pi r^3/3$.)

73

1.87 kN

The weight W is given by $W = \rho g V$, where V is the volume, so the calculation should not be at all troublesome.

Now find the upward force due to the *gauge* pressure acting on the water above the plane $A-A$. (Gauge pressure is used for the usual reason: that the resultant force on the end of the tank depends on the difference between the pressure inside and the pressure outside, which is atmospheric.)

$$\boxed{25.0 \text{ kN}}$$

Working: the gauge pressure p at the level of plane A–A is given by

$$p = \rho g h$$
$$= 1000 \times 9.81 \times 4.0 \text{ N/m}^{-2}$$
$$= 39.2 \text{ kN/m}^2$$

so the upward force F on the water above plane A–A is

$$F = p \times A$$
$$= 39.2 \times (\pi \times 0.45^2)$$
$$= 25.0 \text{ kN}$$

There are only three forces acting on the water contained between the hemispherical end of the tank and the plane A–A: the weight W of the contained water, the upward force F exerted by the water below A–A, and the force R exerted by the inner hemispherical surface of the end. These three forces must be in equilibrium.

So, what is the force R? And what force is exerted on the end of the tank?

$$\boxed{R = 23.1 \text{ kN downwards; force on tank end is } 23.1 \text{ kN upwards}}$$

The weight W and the pressure force F are both vertical forces, one downward and the other upward. The force R which brings the situation to equilibrium must also be vertical, and its magnitude is just the difference between that of F and that of W, i.e. 23.1 kN.

Finally, the force on the tank end exerted by the water is equal and opposite to force R.

The example in the next frame is of a case where the pressure is not uniform.

76

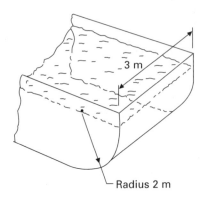

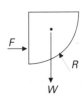

Radius 2 m

The ends of a water tank are in the form of circular quadrants, of radius 2 m and 3 m long. We wish to determine the force exerted by the water on one end of the tank.

As usual, attempts to calculate the force by direct summation or integration are laborious; it is far simpler to choose a suitable volume of liquid (one pressing against the end of the tank and otherwise bounded by planes) and write down the conditions of equilibrium for it.

We take the quadrant-shaped volume of water shown on the right in the diagram. The forces on this water consist of its weight W, the force F acting on the vertical plane which forms the left-hand boundary of the prism due to the water beyond, and the force R exerted by the inner surface of the tank wall.

First, what is the volume of water in the quadrant-shaped end of the tank?

77

$$9.42 \text{ m}^3$$

The area of the quadrant is $\frac{1}{4}\pi r^2$, and to find the volume we multiply this by the length.

So the weight W of this water is ...?

78

$$92.5 \text{ kN}$$

Next we must find the force F acting on the left of this volume of water. This is equal to the area of the vertical plane multiplied by the pressure at which point?

The centroid of the area

So (using gauge pressure) what is the magnitude of the force F?

58.9 kN

Working: the area of the vertical plane is $A = (2 \times 3) = 6 \text{ m}^2$. We multiply this by the (gauge) pressure p at the centroid C, which is at the centre of the rectangle. This pressure is given by

$$p = \rho g h$$
$$= 1000 \times 9.81 \times 1 \text{ N/m}^2$$
$$= 9.81 \text{ kN/m}^2$$

Thus, using gauge pressure, we have

$$F = 6 \times 9.81$$
$$= 58.9 \text{ kN}$$

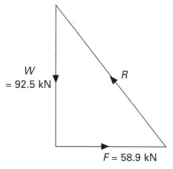

Above is the triangle of forces. Since the weight W is vertical and the pressure force F is horizontal, we can see straight away that the horizontal and vertical components of the force R are ...?

58.9 kN to the left; 92.5 kN upwards

The remaining unanswered question is, 'Where does the force R act?'. We tackle this in the next frame.

82

As we already know, three forces in equilibrium must pass through a single point.

The weight W acts through the centre of gravity of the volume of water, and we can look up its position in tables (for example on p. 401 of this book). It lies a distance $(4r/3\pi)$ from each of the two planes, and in the centre of the 3 metre length.

$$4r/3\pi = 4 \times 2/3\pi$$
$$= 0.849 \text{ m}$$

The pressure force F acts through the centre of pressure on the vertical plane, which lies below the centroid C by a distance q, where

$$q = I_X/A\bar{y}$$

What is the value of this distance q?

83

<table>
<tr><td>0.33 m</td></tr>
</table>

The area of the vertical plane is a rectangle, so the second moment of area about the horizontal axis through the centroid is

$$I_X = b \times d^3/12$$
$$= 3 \times 2^3/12$$
$$= 2.0 \text{ m}^4$$

Thus

$$q = 2.0/(6 \times 1)$$
$$= 0.33 \text{ m}$$

These two dimensions give the coordinates of the point of intersection of forces W and F, and thus of a point on the line of action of force R.

Finally, the force exerted on the wall of the tank by the pressure of the water against it is of course equal and opposite to the force R exerted *on* the water *by* the wall of the tank.

You may have noticed in the previous frame that the centre of pressure of the rectangular area is a distance below the top edge equal to two thirds of the height of the rectangle. This is always the case for a rectangle whose top edge lies in the liquid surface, and it is often convenient to be able to recall this; but remember also that it is true *only for this special case*.

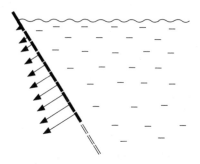

Here we have an edge view of a rectangular area whose top edge is at the liquid surface. The variation of (gauge) pressure with depth is shown by the arrows.

If we divide the rectangle up into a number of strips of equal area (shown edge-on in the diagram) the force on these strips is proportional only to the pressure acting, i.e. it varies linearly with depth, in the same way as the pressure itself varies. Thus, the distribution of the force on the rectangular area with depth can be represented by a triangular graph. The centre of pressure is then at the level corresponding to the centroid of the triangle, that is, two thirds of the way down from the surface.

It is often useful to draw a graph like this, showing the distribution of pressure over the surface. Remember, though, that the distribution of force is *not* the same shape as the distribution of pressure unless the width of the plane is constant, in other words, unless it is a rectangle.

Turn over now to the next frame.

85

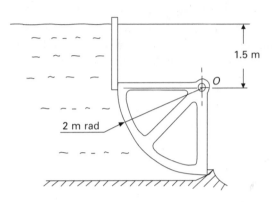 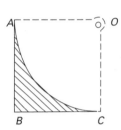

The diagram shows a radial sluice gate, used to control substantial flows of water. The radius of the curved surface of the gate is 2 m, and it is 3.0 m wide.

We wish to find the force on the gate due to water pressure, and we shall tackle this, as usual, by writing down the conditions for equilibrium of a suitable volume of water. This volume must be pressing against the gate, so we shall choose the volume shown in the second diagram (the end is shown shaded). It is bounded by planes on which the pressure forces acting are easily calculated. It extends the full width of the gate, of course.

We must make sure we include all the forces that act on this volume. One is the weight of the water contained within it. What other forces act on it?

86

> Pressure forces on the planes AB and BC, plus
> the reaction R exerted by the cylindrical surface of the gate

First of all, calculate the weight W of water contained in the volume. It is ...?

25.3 kN

Here is the working: the shaded area is

$$A = 2 \times 2 - \tfrac{1}{4}(\pi \times 2^2) = 0.858 \text{ m}^2$$

so the volume is

$$V = 3 \times 0.858 = 2.58 \text{ m}^3$$

and the weight is

$$W = 1000 \times 9.81 \times 2.58 \text{ N} = 25.3 \text{ kN}$$

Now calculate the pressure force F_{AB} exerted on the vertical rectangular plane whose edge is marked AB. (Use gauge pressure, of course.)

147 kN

Working: the area of the face AB is 6 m^2, and the depth to the centroid of the area is 2.5 m. Thus the force exerted by hydrostatic pressure is

$$F_{AB} = 6 \times (1000 \times 9.81 \times 2.5) \text{ N} = 147 \text{ kN}$$

Finally we must calculate the upward force F_{BC} exerted on the horizontal plane area marked BC. This is . . .?

206 kN

The pressure on this area is uniform, because it is horizontal. Thus the force exerted is

$$F_{BC} = (2 \times 3) \times (1000 \times 9.81 \times 3.5) \text{ N} = 206 \text{ kN}$$

It is useful to state the reaction force R exerted on the water by the surface of the sluice gate in the form of its horizontal and vertical components. You should now be able to calculate what these are.

Horizontal: 147 kN; vertical: 181 kN

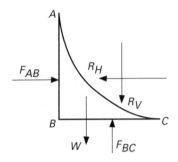

The free-body diagram (that is, a diagram showing the volume element concerned separated off from its surroundings, with all the forces exerted on it by the surroundings clearly shown) indicates immediately that, for equilibrium, the horizontal component force

$$R_H = 147 \text{ kN}$$

and the vertical component

$$R_V = 206 - 25.3$$
$$= 181 \text{ kN}$$

Lastly, we have not yet worked out the position of the line of action of the force R. This is not quite as simple as in the previous case, because there are now four forces involved, and furthermore, because the top edge A does not lie in the liquid surface, F_{AB} does not act two thirds of the way down face AB. However, in this case we can use a different method.

Consider any element of the surface of the radial sluice gate. The pressure force on the area element must be normal to the area, so it acts along the radius, passing through the axis of the hinge, O. Since this is so for *all* such forces, the resultant of them must also pass through the axis. Indeed, this is one of the advantages of the radial gate: because the pressure force on the gate has no moment about the axis of rotation, the mechanism of the gate has to overcome only the weight of the gate itself, plus any friction.

In this example, we have calculated the horizontal and vertical components of R as 147 kN and 181 kN respectively. At what angle to the horizontal is the resultant of these two forces?

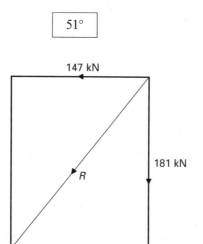

The force R can be derived from its horizontal and vertical components, as shown in the diagram above. Thus the angle between the force R and the horizontal is

$$\tan^{-1}(181/147) = \tan^{-1} 1.231 = 51°$$

Since the force R must pass through the centre O of the cylindrical surface, and the angle of its line of action has been calculated, its position is completely defined.

You have now completed this programme, apart from doing the test exercise. Before you do that, read through the revision summary in the next frame, and make sure you are quite confident of your understanding of all the material.

92

Revision summary

1 The force exerted by fluid pressure on a plane surface is equal to the area of the surface multiplied by the pressure at the centroid of the area. This holds true whatever the angle of inclination of the plane.

2 The centroid C of a plane area is the point such that the moment of the area about any axis through C is zero.

3 If a plane area has an axis of symmetry, the centroid of the area lies on that axis.

4 The point through which the resultant pressure force on a surface acts is called the centre of pressure.

5 For a plane surface submerged in a liquid, the centre of pressure is lower than the centroid by a distance down the plane $(I_C/A\bar{y})$, where A is the area, $\bar{y}$ is the distance down the plane from the surface to the centroid, and I_C is the second moment of area about the horizontal axis in the plane through C.

6 If I_C is the second moment of a certain plane area about an axis in the plane through the centroid C, then the second moment I_X about another axis parallel to the first is equal to $(I_C + Ad^2)$, where A is the total area and d is the distance between the two axes.

7 The hydrostatic force on a curved surface is usually most easily found by considering the equilibrium of a volume of fluid bounded by the curved surface itself and by planes chosen such that the pressure forces on the planes are readily calculated.

Test exercise

1 A tank contains oil whose density is 880 kg/m³. A circular opening in the tank, 460 mm diameter, is covered by a door (see the left-hand diagram below). Find the resultant pressure force on the door.

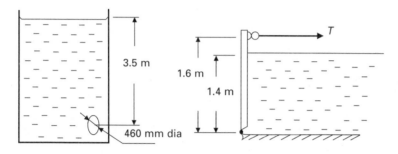

2 A rectangular channel 3 m wide contains water 1.4 m deep. The end of the channel is closed by a gate, which is hinged about the axis *B* at the level of the bottom of the channel, and is held in place by a cable at the top as shown in the right-hand diagram above. What is the tension in the cable?

3 An opening shaped as shown below left in the vertical side of a tank is covered by a heavy door. If the water surface is 1 m above the top of the door, calculate (a) the hydrostatic force on the door, (b) the depth from the surface to the centre of pressure, and (c) the tension in the fastening bolt *B*.

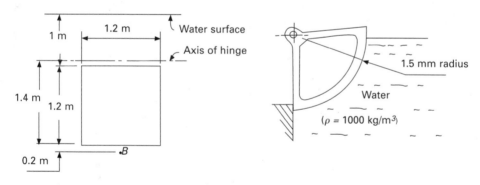

4 Calculate the horizontal and vertical components of the hydrostatic force on the sluice gate shown in the diagram on the right. The gate is 3 m wide.

94

Further problems

1   We all know from weather maps that atmospheric pressure varies from time to time and from place to place. If the difference in atmospheric pressure between one place and another over the sea is 120 millibars (1 bar $= 10^5$ N/m²), what difference in sea level results, in addition to any other differences in level due to tides, etc.? (Take $\rho = 1025$ kg/m³.)

2   A flat plate in the form of a right-angled triangle is submerged in water w ith one side, 3 m long, lying in the water surface, and with the plate at 30° to the horizontal (see the left-hand figure below). What is the hydrostatic force on one side of the plate?

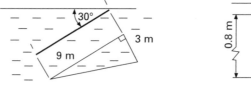
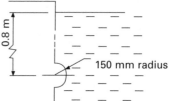

3   Underwater lighting in a swimming pool is provided by hemispherical lamp fittings, as shown in the right-hand figure above. Find the magnitude and direction of the resultant force on the lamp glass due to water pressure.

4   The gate shown in the left hand diagram below, hinged at B, is 2 m wide normal to the plane of the diagram. Find the force F required to hold the gate closed. (Neglect the weight of the gate.)

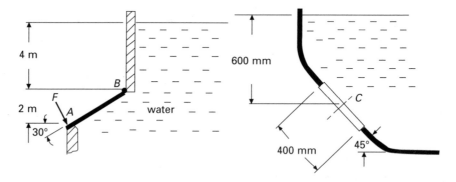

5   A circular window in the side of a large aquarium tank is 400 mm in diameter and is at an angle of 45° to the horizontal, as shown in the right-hand diagram above. The centre C of the window is 600 mm vertically below the surface of the fresh water in the tank. Find the force on the window and the distance from the centre C to the point at which it acts.

Programme 3

BUOYANCY AND STABILITY

OF FLOATING BODIES

1

This programme is mostly about ships and boats: how they manage to float upright, and why they sometimes do not.

First let us consider the equilibrium of a stationary floating object, such as a ship.

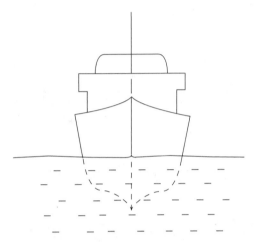

Two forces act upon it: its own weight W acting vertically downwards, and an upthrust vertically upwards exerted by the surrounding fluid.

The upthrust is governed by Archimedes' Principle, which we covered in Programme 1.

Just check that you remember it:

Every body experiences an upthrust equal to ...?

2

the weight of fluid displaced by the body

Here is a complete statement of Archimedes' Principle: *every body experiences an upthrust equal to the weight of fluid that it displaces.*

You may have used slightly different words, but that doesn't matter provided the idea is the same. After all, Archimedes wrote in ancient Greek, so we have the latitude allowed by translation into English, at least.

To make sure you are quite familiar with the application of Archimedes' Principle, the next frame contains an example for you to try.

Example

3

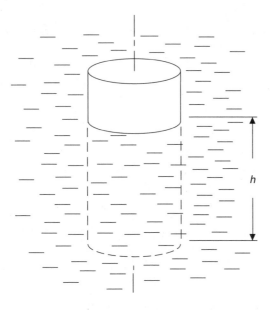

A cylindrical drum with flat ends, whose diameter is 600 mm, floats in fresh water with its axis vertical. If the total mass M of the drum (including contents) is 225 kg, to what depth h will it be submerged?

4

796 mm

Working: since the cylinder is floating in equilibrium, its weight must be exactly balanced by the upthrust, and this is equal to the weight of water displaced.

$$\text{weight of cylinder} = \text{weight of water displaced}$$
$$Mg = \rho_{\text{water}} \times (\text{volume displaced}) \times g$$
$$225 \times g = 1000 \times (\pi \times 0.3^2 \times h) \times g$$
$$h = 0.796 \text{ m or } 796 \text{ mm}$$

If this is not completely familiar, turn back to Programme 1 and go over Frames 64 to 73 once more.

When you feel quite confident about Archimedes' Principle, turn over to the next frame.

5

Centre of buoyancy

In the example we have just done, the upthrust on the cylinder will act along the vertical centre-line – because of the symmetry of the cylinder about the centre-line, it would be unreasonable to expect it to act anywhere else.

Now consider a ship, such as the one shown below: a much more complex shape. The side view shown has no symmetry, so we cannot easily tell where the line of action of the upthrust will be.

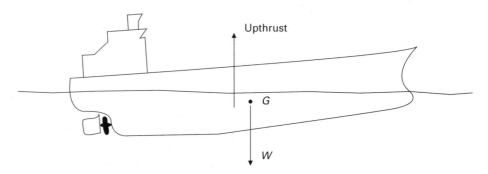

Suppose that the weight W of the ship and the upthrust acting on it are of equal magnitude and opposite in direction, but act along different lines, as shown in the diagram. Is the ship then in equilibrium?

6

$$\boxed{\text{No}}$$

No, although there is no resultant force on the ship, it is still subject to a resultant moment, or couple. If we take moments about any point, such as G, the centre of gravity of the ship, we can see there is a clockwise moment acting.

The ship can be in equilibrium only if the weight and the upthrust are equal and opposite, *and also act along the same vertical line*.

Thus we cannot be confident that an object subject to an upthrust is in equilibrium unless we know the position of the line of action of the upthrust, as well as its magnitude.

We deal with this topic in the next few frames.

7

When we discussed Archimedes' Principle in Programme 1, we used the example of a volume Q of fluid in a 'lake' of stationary fluid. We argued that, when all is in equilibrium, the weight of the fluid in Q is balanced by an upthrust from the surrounding fluid, so this upthrust must be equal and opposite to the weight of fluid.

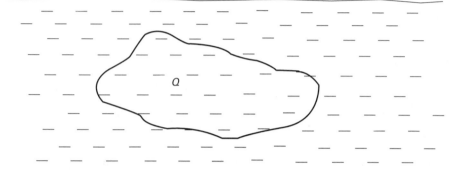

There is a single point through which the weight of any body or collection of matter may be considered to act. This point is called ...?

8

The centre of gravity

As we have just seen in the case of the ship, equilibrium is achieved only when the two forces, weight and upthrust, are equal and opposite, and also act along the same line.

The weight of the fluid in Q acts through the centre of gravity of the fluid. All the fluid is stationary and in equilibrium, so the line of action of the upthrust on Q must also pass through the centre of gravity of the fluid in Q.

If now the fluid in Q is replaced by a solid body of exactly the same shape, the upthrust is unaltered: its magnitude is unchanged, and it continues to act through the same point.

Thus the upthrust on a body always acts through the centre of gravity of the fluid displaced by the body. This point is called the centre of buoyancy.

9

Let's look first at a simple shape – a cylindrical body with flat ends, completely submerged in water.

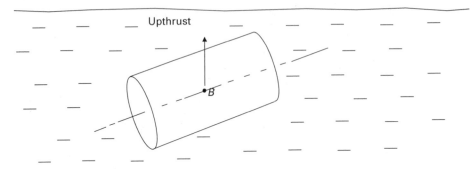

The upthrust acts through the centre of gravity of the water displaced; that is, of the water that would otherwise occupy the space. The density of the water is uniform, so common sense, or considerations of symmetry, tell us that the centre of gravity of this cylindrical volume of water lies on the axis of the cylinder, mid-way between the flat ends. As we have seen, this point is called the *centre of buoyancy*, labelled *B* on the diagram.

10

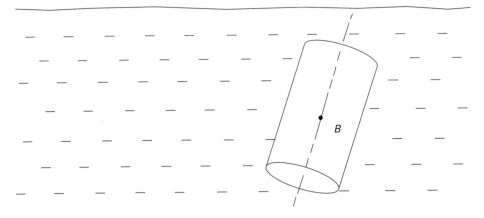

Now the body is moved to a new fully submerged position as shown above. Does the upthrust now act through the same point *B* on the axis of the cylinder, or somewhere else?

11

The same point, B

The centre of gravity of the water displaced by the cylinder is still at the geometric centre of the cylinder.

Here is another example: we wish to find the centre of buoyancy B of a T-shaped object with flat ends, submerged in a liquid (diagram (a) below): so we need to find the centre of gravity of the liquid displaced by the object.

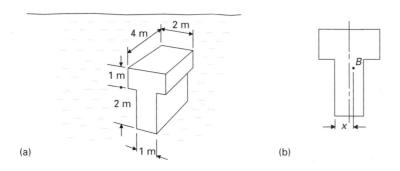

(a)   (b)

First we look at the displaced liquid from one end (diagram (b)), remembering that B is its centre of gravity. What would you expect the dimension x to be?

12

0.5 m

The T-shaped object is symmetrical about the centre-line shown, so the centre of gravity of the liquid displaced by it must lie on the centre-line.

In fact this centre-line is a view of the edge of a *plane* of symmetry which runs right down the middle of the object. We can save ourselves a lot of effort by using the symmetry of this object to help us find the centre of gravity of the displaced fluid.

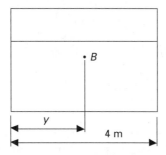

If we look at the object from the side, there will be another plane of symmetry. So, what will be the distance y?

13

$$\boxed{y = 2 \text{ m}}$$

By using the symmetry of the object we have been able to find two of the three coordinates of the centre of buoyancy. Now we need to find the third coordinate, the height z from the base of the object to the centre of buoyancy.

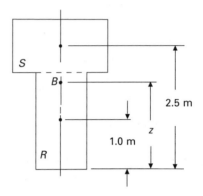

There is no horizontal plane of symmetry, so to find z we have to take moments. (This is just the same process as we used in the last programme, Frames 8 to 17, for finding the centroid of an area.) Probably the simplest way to do the calculation is to regard the object as made up of two rectangular blocks, R and S. The mass of the liquid displaced by each block can be thought of as concentrated at the centre of gravity of the block shape.

Have a go now at the calculation of z – what do you get?

14

$$\boxed{z = 1.75 \text{ m}}$$

Here is the working. If we call the length of the object L and the density of the liquid ρ, the moment of the mass of block R about the base level is $\rho \times (2 \times 1 \times L) \times 1$, which is equal to $2\rho L$. Likewise, the moment of the mass of block S is $\rho \times (1 \times 2 \times L) \times 2.5$, which equals $5\rho L$. Equating the sum of these to the total moment:

$$2\rho L + 5\rho L = \rho \times (2L + 2L) \times z$$
$$z = 1.75 \text{ m}$$

(Of course, we need not have included ρ or L in our calculation, because they are both common factors in all terms in the equation, and so cancel out.)

Now, consider another submerged object: this time it is a child's toy submarine. The weight of the submarine is equal in magnitude to the upthrust on it, but the mass is not uniformly distributed, so the centre of gravity G does not coincide with the centre of buoyancy.

15

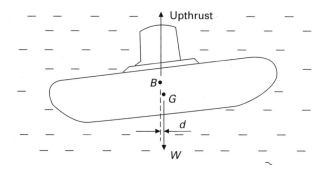

Although the upthrust and the weight have the same magnitude, the submarine is not in equilibrium. What resultant is acting on it?

16

A clockwise couple of magnitude $W \times d$

If no other forces act, this couple, or moment, causes the submarine to turn in the clockwise direction, so bringing G more nearly below B. When G is exactly below B, the submarine will be in equilibrium, with no resultant forces or moments (left-hand diagram below).

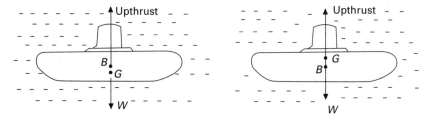

What about the situation shown in the right-hand diagram? The centre of buoyancy B is unchanged, because it is determined by the shape of the body; but the mass has been redistributed, perhaps by shifting some cargo, so the centre of gravity is higher. Is this also equilibrium?

17

> Yes

Indeed it is. But suppose the submarine is disturbed ever so slightly from this position, as in the diagram below.

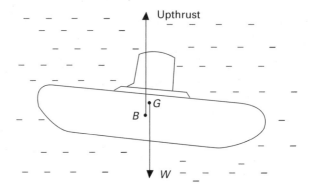

What happens now?

18

> The submarine will begin turning clockwise so as to bring *G* below *B*

The submarine will not reach equilibrium again until *G* is directly below *B*. It will probably oscillate for a while (like a pendulum) either side of this position, but eventually it will settle down there.

The position of equilibrium with *G* above *B* we call *unstable*, because even a small disturbance will cause the submarine to move towards a different equilibrium position. This position is like that of an upside-down pendulum: the slightest disturbance is enough to cause the pendulum to accelerate away from its inverted position.

With *G* below *B* the position is one of *stable* equilibrium – if displaced slightly, the submarine returns towards this position, like a more conventional pendulum.

All this remains true for *any* completely submerged body. To summarise:

The equilibrium of a body completely submerged in a single fluid is stable provided the centre of gravity *G* is below the centre of buoyancy *B*.

19

An airship in flight is of course completely surrounded by a single fluid – air – and depends on the buoyancy force, or upthrust, to keep it aloft. The centres of buoyancy B and of gravity G of a helium-filled airship are shown in the diagram below.

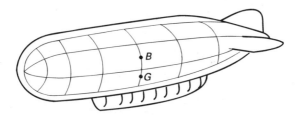

Is this a position of stable equilibrium or unstable equilibrium?

20

Stable equilibrium

The centre of gravity G is below the centre of buoyancy B, so the equilibrium is stable. With an airship, the gas envelope represents the great majority of the volume, so the centre of buoyancy is close to the geometric centre of the envelope. Because a large proportion of the total weight is concentrated in the pod mounted beneath the envelope, containing the crew, payload, fuel, engines etc., the centre of gravity is well below the centre of the gas envelope. The equilibrium is therefore stable.

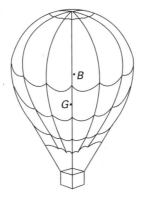

A hot-air balloon or a helium-filled balloon also has its relatively weighty payload suspended beneath, so again G is below B and equilibrium is stable.

The next frame contains a few revision questions, just to make sure you can be quite confident about the material we have covered so far.

21

Revision exercise

(Perhaps you should cover up the opposite page while you solve these questions)

1 The object shown below is submerged in water. What is the coordinate $\bar{x}$ of its centre of buoyancy? (The volume of the bar connecting the two blocks is small enough to be neglected.)

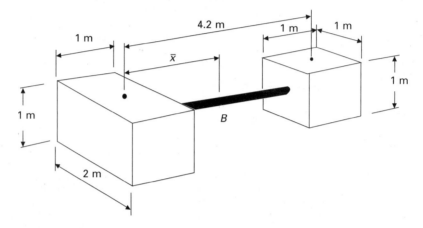

2 Find the coordinate $\bar{y}$ of the centre of buoyancy B of the object shown in the diagram below, which is completely submerged in water.

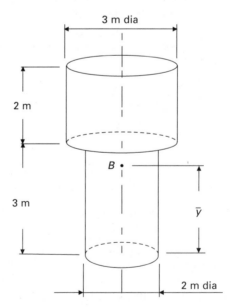

3 The centre of gravity of the object of Question 2 is 2.6 m above the base. Is the equilibrium of the object stable or unstable in the position shown?

Solutions

22

1 The volume of the larger of the two blocks is 2 m^3, and that of the smaller block is 1 m^3.

Taking moments about the centre of the larger block

$$1 \times 4.2 = (2 + 1) \times \bar{x}$$
$$\bar{x} = 4.2/3 = 1.4 \text{ m}$$

2 As in the example we did in Frames 11–14, we can regard this object as composed of two parts. In this case each part is a cylinder, whose volume is easily calculated.

The volume of the upper cylinder is $\pi \times 1.5^2 \times 2 = 4.5\pi$ m^3 and the volume of the lower cylinder is $\pi \times 1^2 \times 3 = 3\pi$ m^3. Taking moments about the bottom of the object,

$$3\pi \times 1.5 + 4.5\pi \times 4 = (3 + 4.5)\pi \times \bar{y}$$
$$\bar{y} = 22.5/7.5$$
$$= 3.0 \text{ m}$$

3 We have just shown that the centre of buoyancy B of the two-cylinder object is 3.0 m above the bottom of the object. If the centre of gravity G is 2.6 m above the bottom, then G is below B, and the equilibrium is stable.

Move on now to the next frame.

23

Floating bodies – metacentric height

Now we come to the case of a floating object. Here is a simple one – a thick wooden board floating in water.

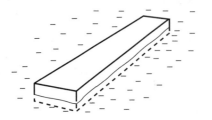
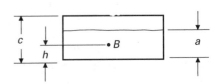

As always, the upthrust acts through the centre of buoyancy, which is at the centre of gravity of the fluid displaced.

The fluid displaced includes both the air displaced by the upper part of the board and the water displaced by the lower part. When calculating the upthrust and finding the centre of buoyancy, we usually ignore the displaced air and consider only the liquid. The liquid is so much more dense than the air that this introduces only a very small error.

So, making this slight approximation, what is the height h of the centre of buoyancy B above the base of the board?

24

$$\boxed{h = a/2}$$

The board is of uniform material, so it is easy to tell where its centre of gravity is. What is the height of the centre of gravity above the base?

$$\boxed{c/2}$$

Now here is a diagram of the situation:

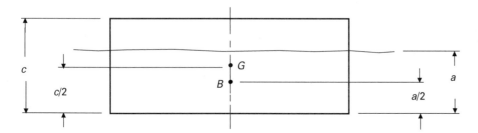

It is well known that a wooden board will float stably in the position shown in the diagram; most of us will have seen one floating just like this. Yet we see that the centre of buoyancy is *below* the centre of gravity.

All the cases we considered earlier were of bodies fully submerged in one fluid. Now we have the quite different situation of a floating object – partly submerged in a liquid, with the remainder sticking out into air. To see how it can float stably even with B below G, consider the situation where the plank has been turned through an angle θ:

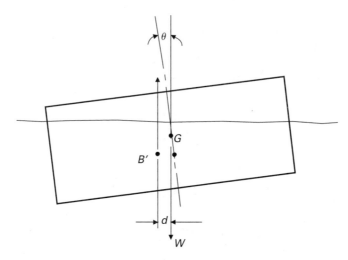

The shape of the submerged part is now a trapezium, not a rectangle. The volume of the portion to the left of the centre-line is clearly greater than that to the right, so the centre of buoyancy will now be to the left also. Its new position is B', as shown.

What is the resultant couple, or moment, acting on the board? (Give the sense as well as the magnitude.)

26

> The couple is $W \times d$, clockwise

The couple tends to restore the board to its original position.

Thus the equilibrium of the board is stable, even though B is *below* G in this case.

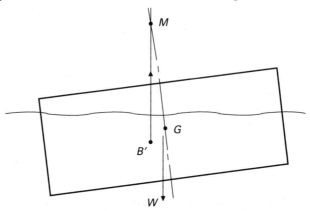

In this diagram the line of the upthrust (passing through the centre of buoyancy, of course) has been extended so that it intersects the central plane of symmetry in a point M.

This point M, where the line of the upthrust intersects the central plane, is given a special name: the *metacentre*.

27

In the diagram in Frame 26, where the metacentre M is above G, there is a restoring moment on the board when it is disturbed.

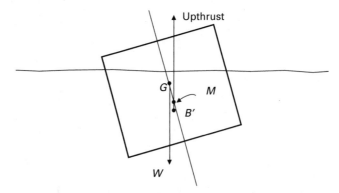

In this diagram, the board is narrower. When the board is turned through an angle, the difference between the volumes each side of the centre-line is smaller and so the line of the upthrust does not move so far off centre. With a narrow board such as this we shall find that the metacentre M is *below* G. In which direction is the moment on the board now, clockwise or anticlockwise?

28

Anticlockwise

The moment is now acting to *increase* the angle θ, so the equilibrium is unstable.

Thus, the equilibrium of a floating body is *stable* when the metacentre M is *above* the centre of gravity of the body, G; when M is *below* G the equilibrium is unstable.

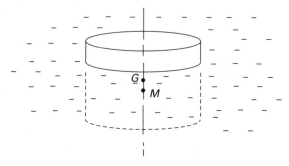

The diagram above is of a cylinder floating on water, with the centre of gravity G and the metacentre M shown on the diagram. Is the cylinder stable in the position shown?

29

No, it is unstable

The cylinder has its metacentre M below the centre of gravity G, so we know that the situation must be one of unstable equilibrium.

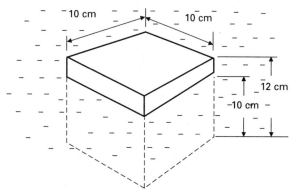

This diagram shows a block of wood 10 cm square and 12 cm long floating in water with 10 cm of its length submerged. The metacentre is 5.8 cm above the base of the block. If the material of the wood is of uniform density, is this a position of stable equilibrium?

30

> No, it is unstable

The centre of gravity G is 6 cm above the base of the block, so M is below G, and the position is one of unstable equilibrium.

Clearly the relative positions of the metacentre M and the centre of gravity G are of very great importance for ships and other such floating bodies. The height of M above G is given a special name: the *metacentric height*. It is often represented by the symbol $\overline{GM}$.

We have not said anything so far about how the position of the metacentre M changes as the angle θ varies. In fact, for small angles θ – up to 10°, say – the position of M on the vertical centre-line hardly alters at all as θ varies, so the metacentric height $\overline{GM}$ is virtually constant.

Now, here is a cross-section of a ship, viewed from one end.

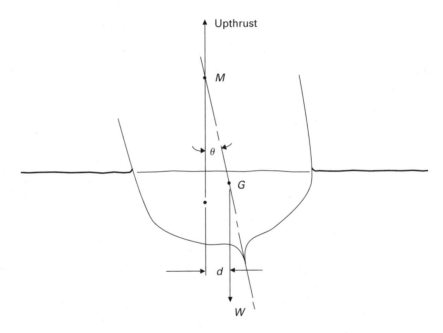

The moment arm d of the restoring couple on the ship is directly related to the distance $\overline{GM}$ (the metacentric height) and the angle θ. Can you write down the relationship? It is a straightforward matter of trigonometry.

$$d = \overline{GM} \sin \theta$$

The restoring couple, or moment, acting on the floating object is equal to $W \times d$, and so

$$\begin{aligned}
\text{restoring moment} &= W \times d \\
&= W \times \overline{GM} \times \sin \theta \\
&= W \times \overline{GM} \times \theta
\end{aligned}$$

approximately, if θ is small and is expressed in radians.

Since both W and $\overline{GM}$ are constants, the restoring moment is directly proportional to the angle θ.

This expression comes in useful if we wish to measure the metacentric height of a ship experimentally. The procedure adopted is to move a heavy object across the deck of the ship, and measure the angle through which the ship turns as a result.

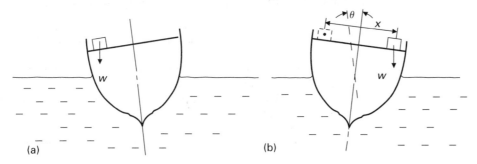

(a)   (b)

Diagram (a) shows the ship with the heavy object of weight w on the deck, and diagram (b) shows the situation when the object has been moved a distance x across the deck. Naturally, the ship heels over a little.

The change in position of the object has in effect produced a change of turning moment on the ship, equal to $w \times x$. The ship is maintained in equilibrium by the restoring moment, given as before by $W \times \overline{GM} \times \theta$.

Equating these,

$$W \times \overline{GM} \times \theta = w \times x$$
$$\overline{GM} = \frac{w \times x}{W \times \theta} = \frac{m \times x}{M \times \theta}$$

where m is the mass of the heavy object and M is the mass of the ship.

The next frame contains an example of the application of this result.

32

Worked example

In an experiment to determine the metacentric height for a passenger liner of displacement 28 000 tonne (i.e. its mass is 28 000 tonne), an object of mass 8 tonne is moved a distance 10 m across the width of the ship. The ship is observed to turn through an angle of 0.38°. Find the metacentric height $\overline{GM}$.

Here is the working. First convert the angle: $0.38° = 0.38 \times (\pi/180)$ rad $= 6.6 \times 10^{-3}$ rad.

$$\overline{GM} = \frac{m \times x}{M \times \theta}$$
$$= \frac{8 \times 10}{28\,000 \times 6.6 \times 10^{-3}}$$
$$= 0.43 \text{ m}$$

which probably seems quite a small distance for so large a ship. We shall see later that passenger ships usually have fairly small metacentric heights, or else the passengers may have an uncomfortable voyage. Now, here is an example for you to try:

33

The crew of a small motor cruiser all move to one side of the vessel to wave to a passing boat. The displacement of the cruiser is 40 tonne. The combined mass of the crew is 400 kg, and they are initially distributed evenly over the width of the boat, which is 4 m.

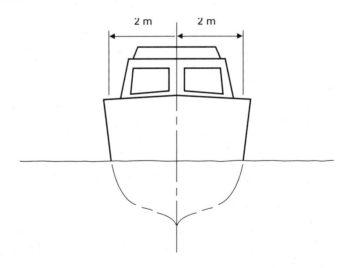

If the metacentric height of the boat is 0.25 m, through what angle does it turn when the crew all move to one side?

$$\boxed{4.6°}$$

Working: as before,

$$\theta = \frac{m \times x}{M \times \overline{GM}}$$

Now putting in the values:

$$\theta = \frac{400 \times 2}{40\,000 \times 0.25}$$
$$= 0.08 \text{ radians}$$
$$= 4.6°$$

When a ship heels over to left or right (to port or starboard), the motion is called *rolling*. Motion in roll is rotation about a longitudinal fore-and-aft axis.

When the bows of the ship rise and the stern moves down, or vice versa, the motion is called *pitching*; this is rotation about a transverse axis.

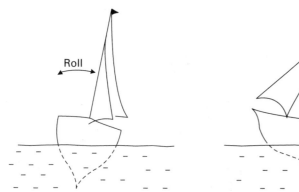
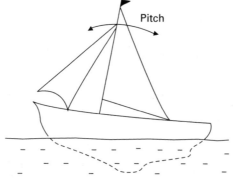

A ship will have different metacentric heights for motion in pitch and in roll: the metacentric height for pitching motion can be investigated experimentally in a similar way to that for roll.

Returning to our experiments with the passenger liner of Frame 32, if the object of mass 8 tonne is moved a distance 30 m longways along the deck, the ship turns through a pitch angle of 0.11°. Remembering that the mass of the ship is 28 000 tonne, what is the metacentric height for pitch? The calculation is done in exactly the same way as before.

35

$$\boxed{4.46 \text{ m}}$$

As before, we first convert to radians: $0.11° = 1.92 \times 10^{-3}$ rad. Then

$$\overline{GM} = \frac{m \times x}{M \times \theta} = \frac{8 \times 30}{28\,000 \times 1.92 \times 10^{-3}} = 4.46 \text{ m}$$

In this case the metacentric height in roll was 0.43 m; the metacentric height in pitch is about ten times as great. Of course, the ratio of the two metacentric heights will not have exactly this value in every case, but it is typical for a ship's metacentric height in pitch to be much the greater.

When designing a ship, naval architects have to calculate the metacentric heights – most particularly the metacentric height in roll – to ensure that the ship will be safely stable. In the next frames we derive a simple formula which allows the metacentric height to be calculated.

36

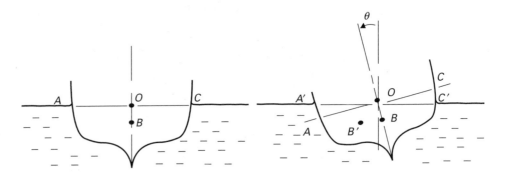

The diagrams above show a floating vessel, first in its normal equilibrium position, and second when rotated through an angle θ. The initial centre of buoyancy is B, but it moves to a new position B' when the vessel is rotated.

You will recall that the centre of buoyancy is the point through which the upthrust on the vessel may be considered to act. It is the centre of gravity of ...?

> The centre of buoyancy is the centre of gravity of the displaced fluid

It has moved to a new position because the shape of the fluid displaced has altered: the wedge-shaped volume of fluid OAA' has been added, and the wedge-shaped volume OCC' has been removed.

It can be shown by a few lines of theory (which we shall skip for the moment) that the distance BB' moved by the centre of buoyancy is given by

$$BB' = \theta(I/V)$$

where V is the submerged volume of the vessel, i.e. the volume of liquid displaced, and I is a second moment of area.

We have come across second moments of area before, in connection with the position of the hydrostatic force acting on a submerged flat object; they also appear in calculations on the bending of beams. Here is yet a third situation where the second moment of area crops up: this time the area concerned is the area of the waterline plane, that is, the area of liquid surface penetrated by the vessel. To find the metacentric height in roll, we need to use the second moment of area about the axis of roll, O.

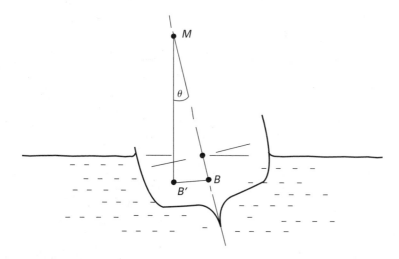

Provided θ is small and is expressed in radians, we see from the triangle $BB'M$ that $BB'/BM \approx \theta$.

The equation at the top of the page tells us that $BB' = \theta(I/V)$.

What is the distance BM, expressed in terms of I and V?

38

$$\boxed{BM = I/V}$$

The distance BM by which the metacentre M is above the centre of buoyancy B is called the *metacentric radius*; it is calculated just by finding the ratio of the second moment of the water-line area about the roll axis, I, to the submerged volume, V. Notice that M is always above B, never below.

From now on we shall use the symbol $\overline{BM}$ for metacentric radius, to remind us that M stands for the metacentre, not the mass. Do not confuse the metacentric radius $\overline{BM}$ with the metacentric height $\overline{GM}$. It is the metacentric *height* that determines the degree of stability of the floating vessel.

If we are able to calculate the metacentric radius $\overline{BM}$, and we also know the positions of the centre of buoyancy B and the centre of gravity G, it is straightforward to find the metacentric height $\overline{GM}$, and hence to determine the margin of stability of the floating vessel.

Here is a worked example.

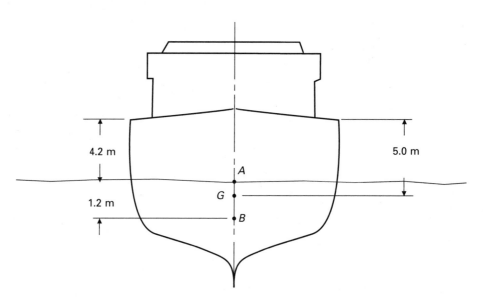

The ship shown above has a fully laden displacement of 350 tonne. In this condition its centre of gravity G is 5.0 m below the deck. It is floating in sea-water of density 1025 kg/m^3, the deck is 4.2 m above the surface of the water, and the centre of buoyancy B is 1.2 m below the surface of the water. The second moment of the waterline area about the longitudinal axis through A is $I = 228$ m^4. We wish to find the metacentric height.

The working is given in the next frame, but you can start by calculating the submerged volume V yourself.

$$\boxed{341 \text{ m}^3}$$

The volume of water displaced by the ship is $V = 350/1.025 = 341$ m^3.

The metacentric radius is then given by $\overline{BM} = I/V = 228/341 = 0.67$ m, and M is always above B, remember.

It is usually best now to sketch the positions of the important points on a simple diagram:

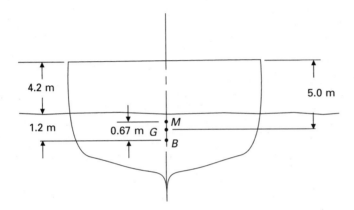

From this, we can see that G is above B by a distance

$$BG = (4.2 + 1.2 - 5.0) = 0.4 \text{ m}$$

so the metacentric height is $\overline{GM} = 0.67 - 0.40 = 0.27$ m. M is above G, so the ship is stable.

Now it is time for you to do an example, so turn to the next page.

40

We wish to investigate the stability of a uniform rectangular block floating with 0.4 m depth submerged.

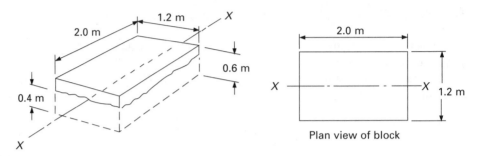

Plan view of block

As always, the block is more likely to be unstable in roll, i.e. turning about the longitudinal axis X–X, than in pitch.

First we must find the metacentric radius, $\overline{BM}$, in roll. Remembering that the second moment of area of a rectangular area is given by

$$I = bd^3/12$$

where b is measured parallel to the axis and d perpendicular to it, calculate the value of I for the waterline area in this case.

41

$$\boxed{I = 0.288 \text{ m}^4}$$

Working:

$$I = \frac{bd^3}{12} = \frac{2 \times 1.2^3}{12} = 0.288 \text{ m}^4$$

Note that the distance b is measured parallel to the axis, and is 2 m in this case; dimension d, measured perpendicular to the axis, is 1.2 m.

It is straightforward now to calculate the metacentric radius, $\overline{BM}$. What result do you get?

42

$$\boxed{\overline{BM} = 0.3 \text{ m}}$$

Working: the metacentric radius is

$$\overline{BM} = \frac{I}{V} = \frac{0.288}{2 \times 1.2 \times 0.4} = 0.3 \text{ m}$$

Now draw a simple diagram – an end view of the block is best – to show the relative positions of B (centre of buoyancy), G (centre of gravity) and M (metacentre); then calculate the metacentric height $\overline{GM}$.

43

$$\boxed{\overline{GM} = 0.2 \text{ m}}$$

Your diagram should have looked something like this:

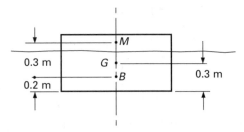

From the diagram it is easy to see that M is *above* G, so the block is able to float stably in the position shown.

It is time now to review what we have covered in the past few frames, so turn over to the revision exercise on the next page.

44

Revision exercise

1 To find the metacentric height in roll of his 3.3 tonne vessel, an amateur yachtsman uses a heavy container of mass 50 kg. When placed at one side of the deck, the container causes the yacht to heel by 3.7°. The container is then moved across the deck to the opposite side, and produces a heel of 3.7° the other way. The overall width of the deck is 3.1 m.

What is the metacentric height in roll?

2 A block in the form of a cube of side 3.0 m floats with half its height submerged, as shown. The mass of the block is not uniformly distributed: the centre of gravity G is below the geometrical centre by a distance y.

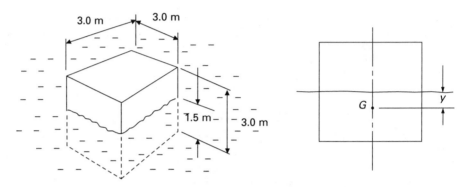

(i) What is the height of the centre of buoyancy B above the bottom of the block?

(ii) Find the value of the metacentric radius, $\overline{BM}$, and so find the height of the metacentre M above the bottom of the block.

(iii) If the block is to float stably as shown, what is the minimum distance y by which the centre of gravity G is below the geometric centre of the block?

Solutions

1 By equating the disturbing moment due to the displacement of the heavy container to the restoring moment which results from the shift in the position of the centre of buoyancy, we obtained the result

$$\overline{GM} = \frac{m \times x}{M \times \theta}$$

The total angle θ through which the yacht turns is 7.4°. This angle θ must be expressed in radians, of course. Converting:

$$7.4° = 7.4 \times \pi/180 \text{ rad}$$
$$= 0.129 \text{ rad}$$

Now all we need do is to substitute in the equation, and we get

$$\overline{GM} = \frac{50 \times 3.1}{3300 \times 0.129} = 0.36 \text{ m}$$

so the metacentric height in roll of the yacht is 0.36 m.

2   (i) The centre of buoyancy B of the block is at the centre of gravity of the liquid displaced, as always; so B is distance 0.75 m above the bottom of the block.

(ii) We can calculate the metacentric radius, $\overline{BM}$, from the equation $\overline{BM} = I/V$. The submerged volume V is equal to $3 \times 3 \times 1.5$ m³ $= 13.5$ m³.

The second moment of area of the waterline plane, I, about a transverse axis is given by

$$I = bh^3/12$$

so in this case

$$I = 3 \times 3^3/12$$
$$= 27/4$$
$$= 6.75 \text{ m}^4$$

Therefore

$$\overline{BM} = 6.75/13.5 \text{ m}$$
$$= 0.5 \text{ m}$$

Thus the position of the metacentre M is $(0.75 + 0.5)$ m $= 1.25$ m above the bottom of the block, or 0.25 m below the geometrical centre.

(iii) For stability, G must be lower than this, i.e. the distance y must be at least 0.25 m.

46

We now return briefly to the equation $BB' = \theta(I/V)$, first introduced in Frame 37, to see how it is derived. In particular, why does the equation include the *second moment of area* of the waterline plane?

The equation tells us how far the centre of buoyancy B moves when a floating object is tilted through an angle θ. Remembering that the centre of buoyancy is at the centre of gravity of the liquid displaced, we can find how far it shifts in position by taking moments.

Consider a small area δa of the waterline plane, at a distance x from the axis: when the vessel is tilted this area sweeps through a distance $\theta \times x$ (see the diagrams below). The weight of liquid in the volume swept out is $\rho g\,(\theta \times x)\,\delta a$, and the *moment* of this weight about the axis is the product of the weight and the distance, $\rho g\theta\, x^2\, \delta a$.

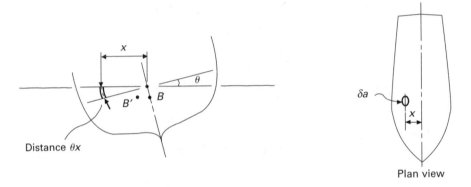

Distance θx

δa

Plan view

The distance x comes into this quantity once through being the moment arm, and again because the weight is proportional to the distance x, so the moment involves the factor x^2; i.e. it is a second moment.

Summing up the effects of all these weights over the whole waterline area, we get

$$\text{total moment} = \rho g\theta\, \Sigma x^2\, \delta a = \rho g\theta I$$

where I is the second moment of area.

Looking at the matter in another way, the upthrust originally acted through B but now acts through B', the shifted centre of buoyancy. The corresponding moment is equal to the upthrust multiplied by the distance BB'.

The weight of fluid displaced is $\rho g V$, and for small angles θ this is virtually constant. Thus, the moment is equal to $BB' \times \rho g V$. Now, equating the two moments:

$$BB' \times \rho g V = \rho g\theta I$$

Hence

$$BB' = \theta(I/V)$$

Effect of a liquid cargo on stability

47

The engines of many seagoing vessels use liquid fuel. The supply of liquid fuel, which is stored in a tank in which it can move about, has an adverse effect on the stability of the ship.

Oil tankers are similarly affected, and so sometimes are ships carrying grain, which can move about almost like a liquid.

Even a ship that is not intended to contain any liquid may, through damage or accident, take in sea-water. Ship designers and safety authorities have to be able to work out what the result of such accidents might be, and try at the design stage to minimise the risk of catastrophe.

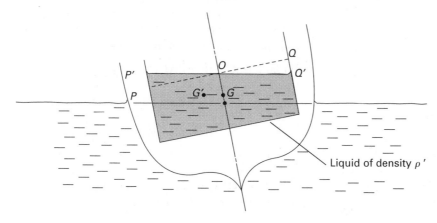

The sketch above shows a ship in which there is a tank containing a liquid of density ρ'. The second moment of area of the surface of the liquid about the axis of roll is I'.

When the ship heels over as shown, the centre of gravity of the liquid in the tank moves from its initial position G to a new position G'. Just as before, this occurs because the wedge-shaped volume of liquid OPP' has been added, and the wedge-shaped volume OQQ' has been removed.

Referring back to Frame 46, can you say what total moment (in terms of ρ', g, θ and I') is exerted by the weight of the liquid in these wedges?

48

$$\boxed{\text{Total moment} = \rho' g \theta \times I'}$$

The calculation is just the same as in Frame 46, but using the different density ρ' and second moment of area I' that apply to the liquid in the tank.

In Frames 30 and 31 we saw that, when a floating object such as a ship is turned through an angle θ from its equilibrium position, it is subject to a restoring couple, or moment, given by

$$\text{restoring moment} = W \times \overline{GM} \times \theta$$

approximately, if θ is small and is expressed in radians.

When a tank of liquid is introduced into the ship, the moment due to the liquid in the tank acts in the sense that tries to increase θ, so it reduces the restoring moment. The difference between these is the net restoring moment, given by

$$\text{net restoring moment} = W \times \overline{GM} \times \theta - \rho' g \theta \times I'$$
$$= W \times \theta \times \left(\overline{GM} - \frac{\rho' g I'}{W} \right)$$
$$= W \times \theta \times \left(\overline{GM} - \frac{\rho' I'}{M} \right)$$

where M is the mass of the ship.

We see from the terms in the brackets that the effect of the tank of liquid is to reduce the metacentric height $\overline{GM}$ by a distance

$$\frac{\rho' I'}{M}$$

The metacentric radius BM is reduced by the same distance.

To see how these results are used in practice, carry on to the next frame where we work through a numerical example.

Worked example

49

A ship of displacement 3500 tonne carries oil fuel in four tanks 5 m long and 2.5 m broad, the tanks arranged with their length in the fore-and-aft direction. The specific gravity of the oil is 0.84, and the density of the sea-water in which the ship is floating is 1020 kg/m^3. By how much is the metacentric height of the ship reduced by the oil contained in the tanks?

Here is the working: the mass of the ship is equal to the mass of water displaced: this is what is meant by the term *displacement*. The second moment of area of one of the tanks about its own axis is I', given by

$$I' = \frac{bd^3}{12} = \frac{5 \times 2.5^3}{12} = 6.51 \text{ m}^4$$

Thus each tank reduces the metacentric height $\overline{GM}$ by a distance

$$\frac{\rho' I'}{M} = \frac{(0.84 \times 1000) \times 6.51}{3500 \times 1000} = 1.56 \times 10^{-3} \text{ m}$$

Since there are four tanks, the metacentric height is reduced by four times this amount, i.e. by 6.24 mm.

For a ship of this size, the metacentric height may be 500 mm or more, so a reduction of 6 mm or so is not serious.

In the expression $(\rho' I'/M)$, the mass of the ship, M, is equal to the density of the water in which it is floating multiplied by the volume of water displaced:

$$M = \rho V$$

Sometimes the liquid inside the ship is also water, having found its way in through gradual leakage or accident: its density ρ' is then equal to ρ.

If the second moment of area of the surface of the water inside the ship is I' (as before), the reduction of the metacentric height of the ship caused by the water contained within it can be expressed in terms of I' and V only.

Now derive this expression, by substituting for M and ρ' in the fraction $(\rho' I'/M)$.

50

$$\boxed{\text{Reduction in } \overline{GM} \text{ is } (I'/V)}$$

Since M, the mass of the ship, is equal to ρV, and $\rho' = \rho$, the reduction in the metacentric height due to the water contained inside the ship is given by

$$\text{reduction in } \overline{GM} = \frac{\rho' I'}{\rho V} = \frac{I'}{V}$$

Now try this example: a car ferry has a displacement of 8000 tonne. The car deck is approximately rectangular, 15 m wide × 110 m long, and the metacentric height in roll is 0.73 m. If sea-water of density 1025 kg/m³ is accidentally taken into the car deck, in quantity sufficient to cover the deck even when the boat heels, will the vessel remain stable?

51

$$\boxed{\text{No, it will become unstable}}$$

Here is the working: the volume of sea-water displaced is given by

$$V = 8000/1.025$$
$$= 7805 \text{ m}^3$$

The second moment of area of the water in the car deck about the longitudinal axis (the roll axis) is

$$I' = \frac{110 \times 15^3}{12}$$
$$= 30940 \text{ m}^4$$

Therefore the reduction in the metacentric height due to the water in the ship is given by

$$\frac{I'}{V} = \frac{30940}{7805}$$
$$= 3.96 \text{ m}$$

This is much greater than the metacentric height of the ship without any water inside, so it is clear that the ship will be unstable if a substantial amount of sea-water finds its way into the car deck.

52

Indeed, most drive-on ferries are very susceptible to any intake of water to the car decks, because these decks are such large open areas. A small amount of water is tolerable, because with only a small angle of heel the water all moves to one side, where its area becomes insignificant. A large volume of water taken in may cause instability over a large angle of heel, however.

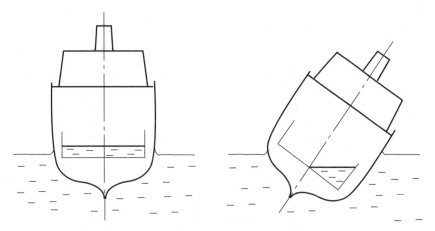

With a large angle of heel, the water inside the ship all moves to one side, so the centre of gravity is no longer on the central plane; and the shape of the submerged volume may change significantly (see the diagram above). The ship may then be in a very dangerous condition. (Of course, our calculation of the reduction of metacentric height applies only while the liquid fills the whole width of the tank or car deck, so it refers to the *initial* stability of the ship.)

Were it not so inconvenient for loading, an obvious solution to the vulnerability of car ferries to intake of water would be to divide the car deck into compartments. With the car ferry of Frame 50, if the car deck were divided down the middle, into two areas each of 110 m × 7.5 m, would the vessel still be unstable if one of these areas took in water?

53

> No, the car ferry would then be stable

Working: for this area $I' = 110 \times 7.5^3/12 = 3870$ m^4. If water is taken in, reduction in $\overline{GM}$ is 3870/7805 m, or 0.50 m. This is less than the initial metacentric height, so the vessel remains stable.

Move on now to our final topic for this programme.

54

Period of rolling

Our final topic is the rate at which a floating object, such as a ship, oscillates to and fro in roll or pitch. This is a matter of great interest to travellers who suffer from seasickness, and also to naval designers who may wish to be able to launch projectiles from a moving ship.

Just a few frames ago (Frame 48) we referred to the restoring moment that acts on a floating object when it is turned through an angle θ from its equilibrium position:

$$\text{restoring moment} = W \times \overline{GM} \times \theta$$

Both W and $\overline{GM}$ are constants, so the restoring moment is directly proportional to the angle θ.

You have probably come across other situations where the restoring force is proportional to the deflection from the equilibrium position – the motion of a mass governed by a spring, for example, or of a simple pendulum. Do you know what we call the kind of motion that occurs in such a system?

55

| Simple harmonic motion |

So when a floating object is deflected from its equilibrium position and then released, its ensuing motion is simple harmonic, or sinusoidal, oscillation.

We are assuming here that, apart from the restoring force that is proportional to the deflection, all other forces and moments are relatively small. In reality, there is always a friction or damping effect which causes the oscillation to decrease unless there is an energy input from outside (e.g. from waves on the surface of the water), but nonetheless the oscillation is close to simple harmonic.

The oscillatory motion of a ship obeys virtually the same equation as that of a pendulum, which is covered in the next frame.

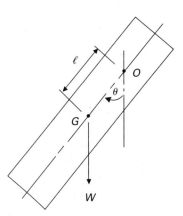

The pendulum shown consists of a rigid bar of weight W suspended at a pivot O. The centre of gravity G is a distance ℓ from O.

The period T of oscillation of such a pendulum is given by

$$T = 2\pi\sqrt{\frac{J}{W\ell}}$$

where J is the moment of inertia of the pendulum about the axis of rotation through the pivot O.

In a very similar way, the period of oscillation of a ship in roll is given by

$$T = 2\pi\sqrt{\frac{J}{W \times \overline{GM}}}$$

where now J represents the moment of inertia of the ship about the longitudinal axis through the centre of gravity G. (The friction forces have been ignored, but in fact they have little effect on the period.)

We can see from this that, if the weight W of the ship and its moment of inertia J remain constant, the period of roll is proportional to $1/\sqrt{\overline{GM}}$.

Here is an example: for a certain passenger ship the period of roll is 5 s, and the passengers complain that this is uncomfortable. The operators wish to increase the roll period to 7.5 s. If the metacentric height is initially 1.1 m, to what must its value be altered to give the desired new roll period?

57

$$\boxed{\text{New } \overline{GM} = 0.49 \text{ m}}$$

Working: the ratio of the new period to the old period is 7.5/5.0.

We have seen that the period is proportional to $1/\sqrt{GM}$, so $\overline{GM}$ must alter in the ratio

$$(5.0/7.5)^2$$

Therefore the new metacentric height is given by

$$\overline{GM} = 1.1 \times (5.0/7.5)^2$$
$$= 0.49 \text{ m}$$

The weight of a ship, its moment of inertia and its metacentric height are all calculated by naval architects at the design stage, so the period of roll is readily found at this stage. Any later modifications to the ship have to be carefully considered, especially if they involve alterations to the way the weight is distributed, in case the period of roll and, more importantly, the stability of the ship are affected.

This brings this programme to an end, apart from the test exercise. On the next page is the revision summary of the principal results, which you should read carefully before you go on to the test exercise to make sure you have fully understood everything we have done in the programme.

Revision summary

58

1 The upthrust on a body acts through the centre of gravity of the fluid displaced by the body. This point is called the centre of buoyancy.
2 For a body completely submerged in a single fluid, such as a submarine or a hot-air balloon, the equilibrium is stable provided the centre of gravity is *below* the centre of buoyancy.
3 When a body floating on the surface of a liquid is rotated through a small angle, the point where the line of the upthrust intersects the central plane is called the *metacentre*.
4 A body will float stably on the surface provided the metacentre is *above* the centre of gravity of the body. The height of the metacentre M above the centre of gravity G is called the *metacentric height*, $\overline{GM}$.
5 The metacentric height of a floating body of mass M, such as a ship, can be found experimentally by moving a heavy object of mass m a distance x across the deck of the ship. If the ship turns through an angle θ as a result, then

$$\overline{GM} = \frac{m \times x}{M \times \theta}$$

θ must be expressed in radians.
6 The metacentric radius, $\overline{BM}$, is the height from the centre of buoyancy B to the metacentre M. It is given by

$$\overline{BM} = I/V$$

where I is the second moment of the waterline area about the axis in question, and V is the submerged volume.
7 A liquid cargo with a free surface, such as oil fuel, has an adverse effect on the stability of a ship. Likewise, any water inside the ship makes it less stable. If the density of the liquid is ρ' and the second moment of the area of its free surface is I', then the effect of the liquid is to reduce the metacentric height of the ship by a distance $(\rho' I'/M)$, where M is the mass of the ship.
8 The period T of roll of a ship is given by $T = 2\pi\sqrt{J/(W \times \overline{GM})}$, where W is the weight of the ship and J is the moment of inertia of the ship about the longitudinal axis through the centre of gravity G.

59

1 The metacentric height in roll of a ship of displacement 500 tonne is to be investigated by an experiment. When a 6.5 tonne crate is moved a distance 5.8 m across the deck, the ship heels over through 5.2°. What is the metacentric height?

2

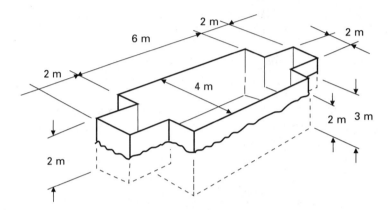

The vessel shown, which is symmetrical both side-to-side and end-to-end, floats in fresh water with its base 2.0 m below the surface. What is the height of the centre of buoyancy above the base?

3 The centre of gravity of the vessel of Question 2 is 1.2 m above the base. Find the metacentric height in roll (i.e. in rotation about the long axis), and determine whether the vessel will float stably in the position shown.

4 Referring again to the vessel of Question 2, determine by how much the metacentric height is reduced if a quantity of rainwater accumulates in the lower part of the vessel. Is the vessel now stable?

Further problems **60**

1 A floating body consists of two cylindrical parts, the upper one of diameter 1.0 m and the lower of diameter 0.707 m. It floats in a liquid as shown. Find the depth H to the centre of buoyancy.

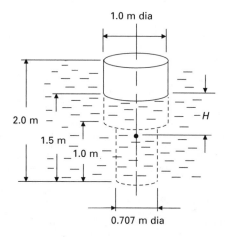

2 The centre of mass G of the body of Question 1 is 0.75 m above the bottom. Find the metacentric height for the body when it floats as shown.

3 A uniform rectangular body, of specific gravity 2/3, has length a, width b and height c, where $a > b > c$. Find the maximum value of c if the body is to float stably in this position in water.

4 A rectangular pontoon, 12 m long by 4 m wide and weighing 300 kN, floats in freshwater (see the diagram below). A steel tube 12 m long and weighing 40 kN is placed on the deck along the longitudinal axis of the pontoon. The centre of gravity of the loaded pontoon is 250 mm above the water surface. Determine the metacentric height and the maximum distance the tube may be rolled across the deck if the angle of heel is not to exceed 5°.

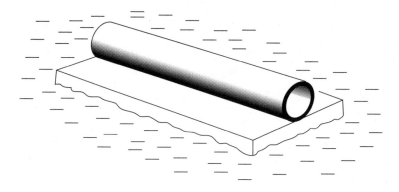

Continued on next page

5 Because of the weight of extra equipment fitted to an 85 000 tonne aircraft carrier since it was originally built, two light buoyancy tanks are to be attached to the sides of the ship. The left-hand diagram below shows the ship before the tanks have been fitted. The centre of buoyancy is B_1, the metacentric height is 0.28 m and the period of roll is 20 s. The plan area of the ship at the waterline is 9000 m^2.

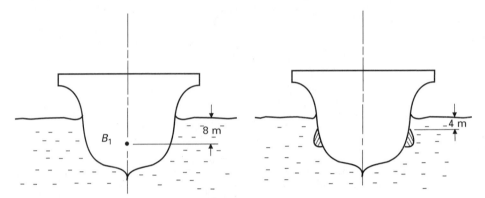

The tanks, each of which has a volume of 1050 m^3, are to be fitted so that their centroids are 4 m below the new waterline, as shown in the right-hand diagram. Assuming that the plan area of the ship is virtually unchanged as it rises in the water, and taking the density of sea-water as 1025 kg/m^3, estimate

(a) how far the ship will rise in the water when the tanks are fitted
(b) the new position of the centre of buoyancy
(c) the new metacentric height
(d) the new period of roll of the ship.

Programme 4

FLUID DYNAMICS:

CONTINUITY PRINCIPLE AND

BERNOULLI'S EQUATION

1

Steady flow, streamlines and streamtubes

We now come to the subject of fluid dynamics: the study of fluids in motion.

We only need to think of the swirling flow that can be seen in the spray behind a road vehicle travelling in wet weather to realise that the motion of fluids can be very complex. Flow of this kind is virtually impossible to analyse in detail.

Fortunately there are many common situations in which analysis is possible because the flow is *steady*; that is, the parameters of the flow at any point (the speed and direction of motion, the pressure, the density etc.) do not vary with time. Flow of liquid along a pipe, of air over the wing of aircraft or of water through a pump are just a few of the many cases which can be treated by steady-flow analysis.

For each of the following cases, do you think the flow is likely to be steady or unsteady?

(a) Flow of water through the nozzle of a fire-hose
(b) Flow of air over a waving flag
(c) Flow of natural gas along a pipeline

2

(a) steady; (b) unsteady; (c) steady

In most instances the rate of flow of water through a fire-hose or of gas along a pipeline is probably roughly constant, so the flow will be steady. In the case of the flag, even though the speed of the wind may be constant, the flow around the waving flag is continuously varying as the shape of the flag changes, so the flow is unsteady.

In this book we shall be confining our attention to instances of steady flow.

Whether the flow is steady or unsteady, it is often useful to draw a diagram of the pattern of flow of a fluid. A common way to do this is to draw lines which at every point have the direction of the fluid velocity. These lines are called *streamlines*.

A typical diagram is shown in the next frame.

3

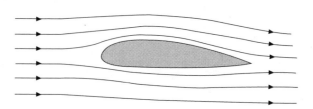

The diagram above shows an aerofoil (a shape like the wing of an aircraft or the blade of a turbine), with the flow around it illustrated by streamlines. A picture like this is very helpful when we wish to visualise the flow.

When fluid is flowing past a solid boundary, such as the surface of an aerofoil or the inner surface of a pipe, obviously the fluid cannot flow into or out of the wall, so its velocity close to the boundary wall must be parallel to the wall.

So, close to the solid boundary, is it possible to have streamlines that are not parallel to the boundary?

4

| No, the streamlines must be parallel to the boundary wall |

At every point the streamlines have the direction of the fluid velocity: this is how they are defined. Close to the boundary the velocity is parallel to the wall, so the streamlines must be parallel to the wall also. (There is only one exception to this: close to a point where the velocity of the fluid is zero, the streamlines may not be parallel to the wall – but this is a special case. Apart from this, the streamlines close to a wall are always parallel to it.)

Because the fluid is everywhere moving in the same direction as the streamlines, fluid can never cross a streamline.

Do you think it is possible for streamlines to intersect one another? (What is the direction of motion of the fluid at the point where the lines cross?)

5

No, streamlines cannot intersect one another

If two streamlines were to cross, then at the point of intersection a particle of fluid would have to be moving in two directions at once, which is of course impossible.

It is often useful to consider a part of the total flow in isolation from the rest. A common way of doing this is to imagine a tubular surface, formed by streamlines, along which the fluid flows. This tubular surface is called a *streamtube*.

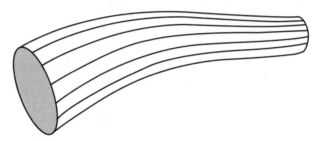

The diagram above shows a streamtube. Remembering that the 'wall' of the tube is formed of streamlines, can fluid flow through the wall of the tube?

6

Fluid cannot flow through the 'wall' of a streamtube

We have already seen that flow is always along and never across a streamline, so the fluid cannot escape through a streamtube's wall, which is entirely composed of streamlines. In this respect a streamtube is just like a solid-walled pipe.

It differs from a pipe in that if the flow is not steady the streamlines will not always be in the same place; but when the flow conditions at each point do not vary with time the positions of the streamlines do not vary, so the walls of the streamtube are effectively fixed. When the flow does not vary with time we call it . . .

7

Steady flow

Throughout this book we shall only be considering cases where the fluid flows steadily, that is, where the position of the streamlines does not change with time.

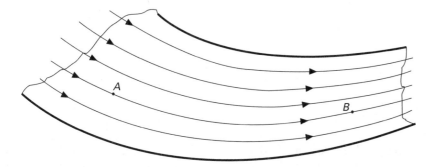

Consider the diagram above, in which flow along a curved passage is shown by means of the streamlines. A particle of the fluid is initially at point *A*. If the flow is steady, so that the position of the streamlines does not change, does the particle remain on the same streamline as flow takes place, or does it end up on a different streamline?

8

It remains on the same streamline

Because flow is steady, the streamline is effectively fixed in position. The velocity of the particle is always along the streamline, so the particle must stay on the same streamline. Sooner or later, it will pass through the point *B* on the streamline.

Thus, in steady flow, the streamlines show us the actual paths followed by the particles. Remember, in this book we shall only be looking at situations where the flow is steady.

In unsteady flow, the position of the streamlines is not constant, so the streamlines only indicate the instantaneous directions of motion of the particles, but not their paths over an extended time interval.

9

Continuity: conservation of matter

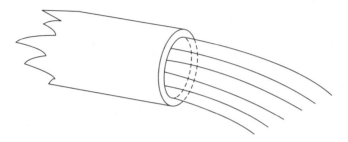

The diagram shows the open end of a section of pipe carrying water. We may wish to find out the rate at which the water is flowing along the pipe.

A simple and effective method is to catch the water for a timed period in a container such as a bucket. By weighing the bucket before and afterwards and subtracting, we can find out the mass of water coming out of the pipe during the timed period.

For example, suppose the mass of an empty bucket is 0.8 kg, the timed period is 8 s and the mass of the bucket together with the water at the end of the 8 s period is 7.2 kg. What mass of water has flowed out of the pipe per second, on average?

10

$$\boxed{0.80 \text{ kg/s}}$$

Working: the bucket's mass is 0.8 kg empty. Together with the water, the mass is 7.2 kg. So the mass of water is (7.2 − 0.8), or 6.4 kg.

The water has taken 8 s to flow along the pipe, so, if the water flows at a constant rate, in 1 s the amount of water will have been (1/8) × 6.4, or 0.80 kg.

The mass of fluid flowing per unit time is called the *mass flow rate*, and here it is 0.80 kg/s.

Now try another problem: the mass of an empty container is 3.8 kg, and it is filled with liquid at a flow rate 1.1 kg/s. How long will it take before the total mass, container plus liquid, is 17.0 kg?

12 s

Here is the working: the mass of liquid in the container finally is $(17.0 - 3.8)$, or 13.2 kg.

The time needed for this to flow is then $(13.2/1.1)$, or 12 s.

We may need to know not only the *mass* flow rate, but also the *volume* flow rate of a fluid, often called the *discharge*. The volume flow rate is the volume of fluid flowing per unit time: multiply it by the density of the fluid, and we get the mass flow rate.

If the density of the fluid flowing at 1.1 kg/s in Frame 10 is 880 kg/m^3, what is the discharge?

1.25 l/s

If your answer for the discharge was 1.25×10^{-3} m^3/s, you were quite right, but it is often more helpful to choose units which give us quantities that are easy to visualise. You can probably imagine what a litre looks like, so $1\frac{1}{4}$ of them will immediately mean something tangible to you, whereas 1.25×10^{-3} m^3 is much harder to think of.

In case your answer wasn't either of these, here is the working. The mass flow rate of the liquid is 1.1 kg/s, and the density is 880 kg/s.

The volume of 1.1 kg of liquid is $(1.1/880)$ m^3, or 1.25×10^{-3} m^3. 1 m^3 is equal to 1000 l, so the volume flow rate, or discharge, is 1.25 l/s.

13

If we know the size of the pipe, we can now deduce the mean velocity of the fluid in the pipe.

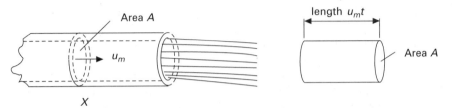

Suppose the area of cross-section of the pipe at point X is A, and the mean velocity of the fluid past point X is u_m. Then in a time t a quantity of fluid of cross-sectional area A and length $u_m t$ will flow past point X. The volume of this quantity of fluid is $(A\, u_m t)$, and so the volume per unit time, denoted by the symbol Q, is given by

$$Q = A\, u_m$$

So if the area of cross-section is 0.5×10^{-3} m^2 and the discharge Q is 1.25 l/s, what is the mean velocity of the fluid?

14

$$\boxed{\text{mean velocity } u_m = 2.5 \text{ m/s}}$$

Working: the equation $Q = A\, u_m$ can be rearranged to give $u_m = Q/A$. Putting in the values of Q and A, the mean velocity is

$$u_m = \frac{(1.25 \times 10^{-3} \text{ m}^3/\text{s})}{(0.5 \times 10^{-3} \text{ m}^2)} = 2.5 \text{ m/s}$$

You may be wondering why we are being careful to call this the *mean* velocity, rather than just the velocity. This is because the velocity of the fluid along a pipe is not the same everywhere across a section. The velocity is greatest at the centre of the pipe, and decreases as the wall is approached, tending to zero at the wall. A typical velocity distribution is as shown below:

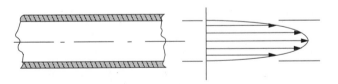

The principle of continuity allows us to deduce only the *mean* velocity over the whole area, but not the local velocity at some point on the section.

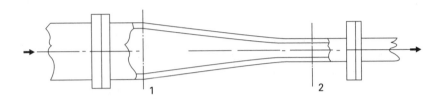

This diagram shows a *contraction* in a pipeline, that is, a length of pipe in which the area of cross-section decreases. A liquid is flowing from left to right through the contraction.

We know that the mass flow rates must be the same at points 1 and 2; furthermore, a liquid being virtually incompressible (i.e. its density is nearly constant, irrespective of pressure), the volume flow rates at 1 and 2 must also be the same. So the speed of the liquid at 2, where the area is smaller, must be greater than the speed at 1.

The volume flow rate at point 1 is $A_1 u_1$ (where we have used the symbol u_1 to denote the mean velocity at 1). Likewise at 2 the discharge, or volume flow rate, is $A_2 u_2$, and these two rates must be equal:

$$A_2 u_2 = A_1 u_1$$

(Remember that this applies only when the fluid density does not change between points 1 and 2.)

If water is flowing through a contraction whose geometry is

$$A_1 = 8 \times 10^{-3} \text{ m}^2 \qquad\qquad A_2 = 2 \times 10^{-3} \text{ m}^2$$

and the upstream mean velocity is $u_1 = 1.6$ m/s, what is the downstream mean velocity, u_2?

16

$$\boxed{u_2 = 6.4 \text{ m/s}}$$

Working:

$$u_2 A_2 = u_1 A_1$$
$$u_2 \times (2 \times 10^{-3}) = 1.6 \times (8 \times 10^{-3})$$

so

$$u_2 = \frac{1.6 \times 8}{2} = 6.4 \text{ m/s}$$

17

In these situations, where we are comparing the velocities of the fluid at two points in a tube, it is only the *ratio* of the areas that matters, not their individual values. In the example we have just done the ratio of the areas at points 1 and 2 is $A_1/A_2 = 4$, so the ratio of the velocities at points 2 and 1 is also 4: $u_2/u_1 = 4$. Make sure to remember that, if A_1 is greater than A_2, then u_2 must be greater than u_1 and not the other way round!

What is more, if the pipe is circular in section, and the diameters are known – say, d_1 and d_2 – then

$$\frac{A_1}{A_2} = \frac{\pi d_1^2/4}{\pi d_2^2/4} = \frac{d_1^2}{d_2^2} = \left(\frac{d_1}{d_2}\right)^2$$

so the ratio of the areas is the *square* of the ratio of the diameters.

Now you try using this method:

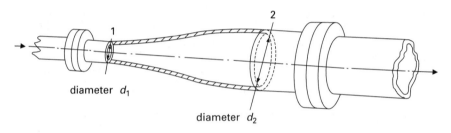

diameter d_1

diameter d_2

The diagram shows a *diffuser* – a diverging section of pipe. The diameters are $d_1 = 24$ mm and $d_2 = 36$ mm. If the mean velocity of the liquid flowing through the pipe at point 1 is 4.5 m/s, find the mean velocity at point 2.

18

$$\boxed{u_2 = 2.0 \text{ m/s}}$$

Here is the working:

$$u_2 A_2 = u_1 A_1$$
$$u_2 = u_1 A_1/A_2 = u_1 (d_1/d_2)^2$$
$$= 4.5 \times (24/36)^2$$
$$= 2.0 \text{ m/s}$$

It is very easy to forget to square the diameters when comparing velocities at different points in round pipes, so be careful!

19

There are many cases of fluid flow – water in a river estuary, air flow around a moving vehicle or aircraft etc. – where the fluid is not confined by a solid boundary.

We can still apply the continuity principle in these cases if we use the idea of the streamtube, which we introduced in Frame 5 of this programme. Just to remind you, a streamtube is an imaginary tube whose walls are formed from a bundle of neighbouring streamlines. Fluid flow is always along and never across the streamlines, so no fluid can enter or escape through the walls of the streamtube.

Remember that we are considering only steady flow conditions, in which case the streamlines which form the wall of the streamtube are fixed in position and the volume of the streamtube does not vary with time.

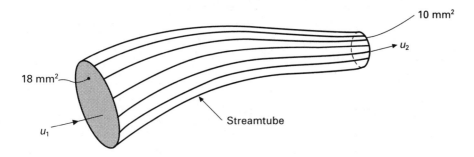

A steady flow of water is passing along a curved passage, and part of the flow is represented by the streamtube shown in the diagram. If the mean outlet velocity from the streamtube is $u_2 = 0.45$ m/s, what is the mean inlet velocity u_1?

20

$$\boxed{u_1 = 0.25 \text{ m/s}}$$

Working:

$$A_1 u_1 = A_2 u_2 = Q, \text{the discharge}$$

Therefore

$$u_1 = (A_2/A_1) \times u_2$$
$$= (10/18) \times 0.45$$
$$= 0.25 \text{ m/s}$$

21   Control surfaces

So far, in every case where we have used the principle of continuity, there has been just a single inlet and a single outlet, but the principle applies equally well when there are several inlets and several outlets. In these instances we often find it helpful to introduce a *control surface*.

A control surface is simply an imaginary surface drawn around some part of the system, through which fluid can enter at some points and leave at others. The purpose of the control surface is to define a certain volume of the system for use in our analysis.

Sometimes the whole of the control surface is imaginary, but quite often part of the control surface will coincide with a real boundary.

We have already used a control surface (without actually calling it that) in Frame 17. Here the control surface consisted of the inner surface of the diverging pipe, together with a circular area of diameter d_1 at point 1, and a circular area of diameter d_2 at point 2.

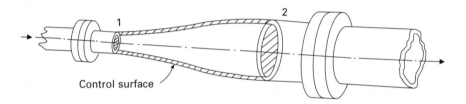

Liquid entered through the circular area at 1, and left through the circular area at 2.

We did the same thing in Frame 15, so the idea is not really unfamiliar. Now let's see how it applies when there is more than just a single inward flow path and a single outward flow path.

22

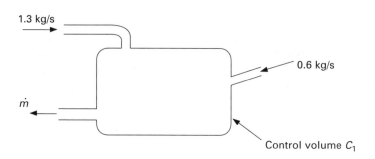

Conditions in the control volume C_1 are steady, so the total mass contained in the volume is constant. The mass flow rates into the control volume are shown in the diagram.

For the outward mass flow rate we have used the symbol $\dot{m}$, which is a shorthand for dm/dt. What is the value of this outward mass flow rate?

23

$$\dot{m} = 1.9 \text{ kg/s}$$

Conditions are steady, the mass inside the control surface is constant, so the algebraic sum of all the flows must be zero. In other words, the sum of all the inward flows must be equal to the sum of all the outward flows.

The sum of the inward flows is $(0.6 + 1.3) = 1.9$ kg/s.

There is only one outward flow, and this must therefore be $\dot{m} = 1.9$ kg/s.

Now try a slightly different one: in the control volume C_2 shown below, conditions are steady, so the mass of fluid contained in the control volume is constant.

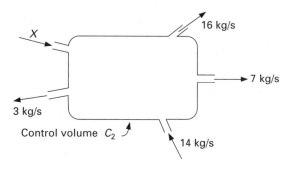

Find the unknown mass flow rate X.

24

$$\boxed{X = 12 \text{ kg/s}}$$

Here is the working. All the outward flows are known: the total is $(16 + 3 + 7) = 26$ kg/s. Conditions are steady, so the total inward flow must also come to 26 kg/s.

So

$$(X + 14) = 26$$

and

$$X = 12 \text{ kg/s}$$

25

The idea of a control surface can be applied to solids, or to mixtures of solids with fluids, as well as to fluids on their own. As long as conditions within the control volume are steady and the total mass contained is constant, the sum of the mass flows into the control volume must be equal to the sum of the mass flows outwards. Consider this example:

The process of mixing a certain biscuit dough involves the continuous supply into a mixer of

> 30 kg/min of flour
>
> 40 kg/min of fat
>
> 0.1 l/s of water

The dough leaves the mixer and passes in a continuous stream to the biscuit moulding machine.

What weight of dough is received by the moulding machine each minute? (One litre of water has a mass of 1 kg, remember.)

26

$\boxed{76 \text{ kg/min}}$

Working: the mass flow rate of the mixed dough from the mixer must be the same as the total mass flow rate of the ingredients into the mixer.

The mass flow rate of water into the mixer is 0.1 kg/s, or 6 kg/min. Thus the total mass flow rate inwards is (30 + 40 + 6), or 76 kg/min, so the mass flow rate of dough from the mixer to the moulding machine must be 76 kg/min also.

Here is another problem, this time involving mass flows into and out of a large coal-fired boiler.

Pulverised coal is blown into the boiler continuously at a rate of 5000 tonne/h. The air supply rate is 4800 kg/s.

If ash accumulates below the furnace at a rate of 1200 tonne/h, what is the mass flow rate of exhaust gases and products up the flue?

27

$\boxed{21\ 080 \text{ tonne/h}}$

In this problem the boiler can be treated as a control surface, in which conditions are steady. Matter does not accumulate within the furnace itself, so the relatively small mass contained in the furnace is constant.

The rate of inflow of air is 4800 kg/s: 4.80 tonne/s, or 17 280 tonne/h.

Thus, the total rate of inflow of matter is (5000 + 17 280), or 22 280 tonne/h, this rate being the combined flow of air and pulverised coal.

There are two outward flows from the boiler: ash, at 1200 tonne/h, and products of combustion passing up the flue. By subtraction, the mass flow rate of combustion products up the flue must be 21 080 tonne/h.

The next frame is a revision exercise about the contents of this programme so far. The solutions to the questions are on the right-hand page, so ideally you should cover up that page until you have solved all the problems. They are all quite straightforward.

28

Revision exercise

1 Water is flowing from left to right through the tapered pipe shown below. The mean velocity of the water at the outlet is 4.8 m/s. What is the mean velocity of the water at the inlet?

65 mm dia

25 mm dia

2 Liquid of density 920 kg/m³ is flowing along a cylindrical pipe of internal diameter 70 mm. A container of mass 1.4 kg is used to catch the liquid emerging from the pipe. After a period of 16.0 s the total mass of the container and the liquid is 29.7 kg. Find:
(a) the mass flow rate of the liquid
(b) the volume flow rate of the liquid
(c) the mean velocity of flow of the liquid along the pipe

3

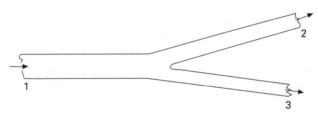

Water enters the Y-pipe at point 1 at a rate 1.8 l/s, and leaves through branches 2 and 3. The flow rate through branch 3 is 0.6 l/s. Find the mean velocity of the flow through branch 2, whose internal diameter is 30 mm.

29

Solutions

1 By the principle of continuity, the mass flow rate of water leaving the tube must be the same as the mass flow rate entering; since water is virtually incompressible, the volume flow rates must also be the same. Thus:

$$A_1 u_1 = A_2 u_2$$
$$u_1 = (25/65)^2 \times 4.8$$
$$= 0.71 \text{ m/s}$$

2 (a) The mass of liquid that has flowed during the 16 s period is $(29.7 - 1.4)$ kg, or 28.3 kg. Therefore the mass flow rate is $28.3/16 = 1.77$ kg/s.
   (b) The volume flow rate Q is equal to the mass flow rate divided by the density:

$$Q = 1.77/920$$
$$= 1.92 \times 10^{-3} \text{ m}^3/\text{s, or } 1.92 \text{ l/s}$$

   (c) The area of cross-section of the pipe is

$$\pi r^2 = \pi \times 0.035^2$$
$$= 3.85 \times 10^{-3} \text{ m}^2$$

Therefore the mean velocity of flow of the liquid is given by

$$u = (1.92 \times 10^{-3})/(3.85 \times 10^{-3})$$
$$= 0.50 \text{ m/s}$$

3 By the principle of continuity, the flow rate of water through branch 2 is just the difference between the rate with which water enters through branch 1, 1.8 l/s, and the rate with which it leaves through branch 3, 0.6 l/s: thus the flow rate Q_2 through branch 2 is 1.2 l/s.
   The mean velocity of flow in branch 2 is Q_2/A_2, or $1.2 \times 10^{-3}/\pi \times 0.015^2$, which comes to 5.33 m/s.

30

Work and energy

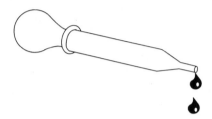

When a drop of liquid falls from a dropper, it accelerates downwards with acceleration $g = 9.81$ m/s² (neglecting the frictional effect of the air: at low speeds this resistance is small).

We could find the speed of the droplet after falling through a height h by using the well-known formula $v^2 = u^2 + 2as$ (s being equal to the height h), but a more generally useful method is to apply the principle of conservation of energy: with negligible frictional resistance, the sum of the kinetic and gravitational potential energies is constant.

So, the speed of the drop of liquid after falling a height $h = 0.6$ m is ...?

31

$$\boxed{3.43 \text{ m/s}}$$

Equating the loss in gravitational potential energy, mgh, to the gain in kinetic energy, $\frac{1}{2}mv^2$,

$$\frac{1}{2}mv^2 = mgh$$
$$v = \sqrt{2gh}$$
$$= \sqrt{2 \times 9.81 \times 0.6}$$
$$= 3.43 \text{ m/s}$$

A similar method can be used for a jet of liquid. Jets tend to break up into droplets eventually, but while the jet remains complete the air friction is quite small, so the mechanical energy (i.e. kinetic energy plus potential energy) is almost exactly conserved. An example of such a jet is introduced in the next frame.

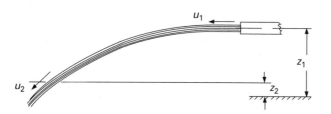

A jet of liquid emerges from a pipe with velocity u_1 as shown. Considering one particle of the liquid of mass m, as it falls from height z_1 to height z_2, its velocity changes from u_1 to u_2. The only force that affects the motion of the particle is that of gravity. (Because the jet is surrounded only by air, the pressure is everywhere atmospheric and so produces no net force. Incidentally, the symbol z is very commonly used in fluid mechanics to denote height above a reference level, as here.)

Neglecting the effect of air friction, the sum of the kinetic and potential energies of the particle remains constant, and so

$$\tfrac{1}{2}mu_1^2 + mgz_1 = \tfrac{1}{2}mu_2^2 + mgz_2$$

Dividing through by m,

$$\tfrac{1}{2}u_1^2 + gz_1 = \tfrac{1}{2}u_2^2 + gz_2 \tag{1}$$

Now let's try this with some realistic values. If $u_1 = 1.8$ m/s, $z_1 = 0.4$ m, and $z_2 = 0.2$ m, find the value of the final velocity u_2.

33

$\boxed{2.68 \text{ m/s}}$

Working: substituting the given values into the last equation of the previous frame, we have

$$\tfrac{1}{2}(1.8^2) + 9.81 \times 0.4 = \tfrac{1}{2}(u_2^2) + 9.81 \times 0.2$$
$$u_2^2 = 1.8^2 + 2 \times 9.81(0.4 - 0.2)$$
$$= 3.24 + 3.92 = 7.16$$
$$u_2 = 2.68 \text{ m/s}$$

This is straightforward, but it only gives a reasonably accurate result while the jet remains whole, when the frictional resistance is small compared with the weight. Once the jet breaks up into separate droplets the air friction becomes much larger, and a significant proportion of the mechanical energy (kinetic plus potential) will rapidly be lost to heat.

34

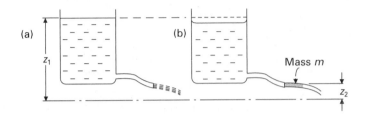

When the fluid is confined, in a tank for example, or in a tube, this difficulty does not arise and energy methods can be applied very successfully.

In diagram (a), a large tank is filled with liquid which is flowing steadily through a nozzle. After a short time interval (diagram (b)) a small mass m of liquid has flowed through the nozzle, and there is a corresponding space at the top of the tank, previously occupied by an equal mass m of liquid.

Comparing the two diagrams we can see that mass m has gone from the top of the tank and a corresponding mass m has appeared at the level of the nozzle, a distance $(z_1 - z_2)$ lower down. So by how much has the gravitational potential energy decreased?

35

$$\boxed{mg(z_1 - z_2)}$$

The gravitational potential energy is given by mgh, so when mass m effectively falls a distance $(z_1 - z_2)$ the gravitational potential energy decreases by $mg(z_1 - z_2)$.

If frictional losses are small enough to ignore, then the sum of the kinetic energy and the potential energy will be constant, so the potential energy lost must be balanced by a corresponding increase in kinetic energy of the liquid.

Now the liquid inside the tank is moving so slowly that its kinetic energy may be neglected (kinetic energy is proportional to velocity *squared*, so even a large mass has very little kinetic energy when it is moving slowly). The only change of kinetic energy occurs because the mass m of liquid which was initially moving extremely slowly at the top of the tank is changed in diagram (b) into a mass m of liquid moving relatively quickly with speed u_2.

So, in terms of these quantities, the increase of kinetic energy is ...?

$$\boxed{\tfrac{1}{2}mu_2^2}$$

The only change in kinetic energy comes from the mass m, which is initially hardly moving at all, and so has virtually zero kinetic energy, and is later moving with speed u_2, having kinetic energy $\tfrac{1}{2}mu_2^2$.

Equating this to the loss of potential energy, $\tfrac{1}{2}mu_2^2 = mg(z_1 - z_2)$.

Dividing through by m and rearranging, we get $gz_1 = \tfrac{1}{2}u_2^2 + gz_2$ (which is equation (1) of frame 32 again, with u_1 set equal to zero).

Therefore,

$$u_2 = \sqrt{2g(z_1 - z_2)}$$

Now try the question in the next frame.

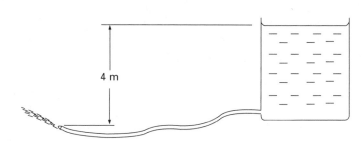

A garden hose is supplied from a large tank of water, the level of the surface of the water being 4 m above the nozzle at the end of the hose.

Neglecting any losses, estimate the speed of the water coming out of the nozzle.

38

$$\boxed{8.86 \text{ m/s}}$$

Using the result from Frame 36, $u = \sqrt{2g(z_1 - z_2)}$, we have

$$\text{velocity} = \sqrt{2 \times 9.81 \times 4} = 8.86 \text{ m/s}.$$

and of course this result is unchanged whether the nozzle points horizontally, upwards, downwards, or in any direction at all, so long as the outlet remains 4 m lower than the water surface. (In practice, the velocity could be significantly less if the hose was long and of narrow bore, owing to friction with the walls.)

Now try this one:

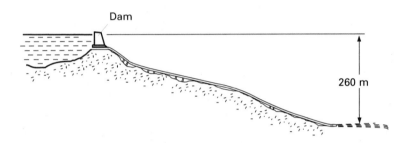

Dam

260 m

Water is carried from a reservoir in the mountains through a pipeline which terminates in a 20 mm diameter nozzle, which is 260 m lower than the surface of the water in the reservoir.

Neglecting losses, what is the velocity of the water leaving the nozzle?

39

$$\boxed{71.4 \text{ m/s}}$$

Just as before, $u = \sqrt{2g(z_1 - z_2)} = \sqrt{2 \times 9.81 \times 260} = 71.4 \text{ m/s}.$

Remembering that the nozzle diameter is 20 mm and the density of water is 1000 kg/m^3, find the mass flow rate.

$$\boxed{22.4 \text{ kg/s}}$$

Working:

$$\text{mass flow rate} = \text{density} \times \text{volume flow rate}$$
$$= (1000 \text{ kg/m}^3) \times (71.4 \times \pi \times 0.01^2)$$
$$= 22.4 \text{ kg/s}$$

Again, these results are the same whatever the direction of the jet. One of the great advantages of using an energy method is that the direction of the velocity does not come into it: when you want to find out how big the velocity is, but not its direction, an energy method is ideal. (As with the garden hose example in Frames 37 and 38, if the pipeline is long the velocity and mass flow will be less than these values owing to friction loss in the pipe.)

In all of these examples, the pressure was atmospheric both at the top position, where the liquid was effectively coming from, and at the bottom, where the final velocity was calculated; the pressure was the same at both places. If this had not been so, there would have been an additional force acting because of the pressure difference, and we would have had to take the work done by this force into account in calculating the value of the final velocity.

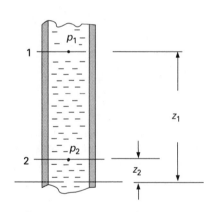

We already know about one case where there is a pressure difference: the one where all the velocities are zero. We covered this static situation in Programme 2 of this book. Here is an example:

The pipe shown is filled with a stationary fluid of uniform density ρ. What is the pressure difference $(p_2 - p_1)$, in terms of the heights z_2 and z_1?

$$\boxed{p_2 - p_1 = \rho g(z_1 - z_2)}$$

From Programme 2 we know that $p_2 - p_1 = \rho g h$, where h is the distance by which position 2 is lower than position 1. This distance is $h = z_1 - z_2$, so $p_2 - p_1 = \rho g(z_1 - z_2)$.

42

This equation for the static case can be rearranged, to give

$$\frac{p_1}{\rho} + gz_1 = \frac{p_2}{\rho} + gz_2 \tag{2}$$

which applies when the velocity is everywhere zero.

Compare this with equation (1), from frame 32:

$$\tfrac{1}{2}u_1^2 + gz_1 = \tfrac{1}{2}u_2^2 + gz_2 \tag{1}$$

which applies when the pressure does not vary.

Equations (1) and (2) both include the terms gz_1 and gz_2, and it looks as if a combination of the two equations might apply to the situation where *both* the pressure *and* the velocity vary. This is indeed the case, as we shall see in the next frame.

43

Bernoulli's equation

By this rather informal route we have come to one of the most useful equations in the whole of fluid dynamics, Bernoulli's equation, which may be written:

$$\frac{p_1}{\rho} + \tfrac{1}{2}u_1^2 + gz_1 = \frac{p_2}{\rho} + \tfrac{1}{2}u_2^2 + gz_2$$

We see that, when the pressures p_1 and p_2 are equal, we obtain our previous equation (1), and when the velocities u_1 and u_2 are equal we obtain our equation (2). Both equation (1) and equation (2) are just special cases of Bernoulli's equation.

Over the past few frames we have been assuming that flow is steady, that the density is constant (i.e. the fluid is incompressible), and that friction losses are negligible. Naturally enough, these conditions apply to Bernoulli's equation, too. Furthermore, the equation strictly relates conditions at two points 1 and 2 on a single streamline, but not on two different streamlines, even in the same flow.

It is impossible to satisfy all these conditions exactly in any real situation, but fortunately there are many cases where, even though conditions depart from the ideal, Bernoulli's equation still gives a very good answer. For example, viscous losses are often relatively small, and, even when the fluid concerned is a gas, pressure changes may not be large enough to cause significant variations in the density.

44

Before looking at further applications of Bernoulli's equation, we ought to see how it can be derived (you can skip this and go on to Frame 49, if you like: but you should refer back later, to see how we obtain the equation formally.)

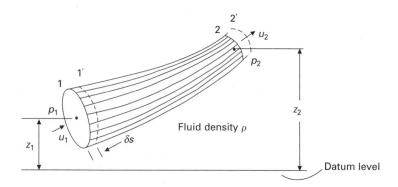

The diagram shows a streamtube between points 1 and 2 in a steadily flowing fluid of constant density ρ. The pressure, the velocity and the height are respectively p_1, u_1 and z_1 at 1, and p_2, u_2 and z_2 at 2.

During a brief time interval the fluid within the streamtube moves to a new position, shown dotted, between points $1'$ and $2'$. Because flow is steady, the conditions between points $1'$ and 2 are exactly the same as before, but in effect a small volume δV_1 has been removed at 1, and a small volume δV_2 has been added at 2. The mass removed at 1, $\rho \delta V_1$, must be equal to the mass added at 2, $\rho \delta V_2$, so, since the density ρ is constant,

$$\delta V_1 = \delta V_2 = \delta V$$

Thus a mass $\rho \delta V$ of fluid is removed at point 1, with velocity u_1 and height z_1, and an equal mass $\rho \delta V$ is added at point 2, with velocity u_2 and height z_2.

So, what is the gain in the kinetic energy of the fluid?

45

> The gain in kinetic energy is $\frac{1}{2}(\rho \delta V)(u_2^2 - u_1^2)$

The mass effectively added at point 2 is $(\rho \delta V)$ moving at speed u_2, which has kinetic energy $\frac{1}{2}(\rho \delta V)u_2^2$, and the mass removed at point 1 is also $(\rho \delta V)$, moving at speed u_1, and having kinetic energy $\frac{1}{2}(\rho \delta V)u_1^2$. The net gain in kinetic energy is therefore $\frac{1}{2}(\rho \delta V)(u_2^2 - u_1^2)$.

Similarly, what is the gain in the (gravitational) potential energy?

46

> The gain in potential energy is $(\rho\delta V)g(z_2 - z_1)$

The potential energy of the 'new' mass is 'mgh'= $(\rho\delta V)gz_2$, and that of the mass removed is $(\rho\delta V)gz_1$. The net gain is the difference between these.

Where has the overall change in the energy of the fluid in the streamtube come from? It cannot have come from work done on the walls of the streamtube, because, conditions being steady, the walls do not move. The only place where work can be done is on the two ends of the parcel of fluid.

If the area of the cross-section of the streamtube at 1 is A_1 and the fluid travels a distance δs in moving from 1 to 1', how much work is done by the pressure p_1 during the motion?

47

> $p_1 A_1 \delta s$

The force applied is (pressure $\times$ area) = $p_1 A_1$, so the work done in the motion δs is (force $\times$ distance) = $p_1 A_1 \delta s$.

Since $A_1 \delta s$ is equal to the volume δV, we can write this work as $p_1 \delta V$.

Similarly, at point 2 the work done by the pressure force is $-p_2 \delta V$, where we have to include a minus sign because the force and the motion are in opposite directions.

We can now equate the work done to the change in energy:

$$(p_1 - p_2)\delta V = \tfrac{1}{2}(\rho\delta V)(u_2^2 - u_1^2) + (\rho\delta V)g(z_2 - z_1)$$

Dividing through by δV and rearranging:

$$\frac{p_1}{\rho} + \tfrac{1}{2}u_1^2 + gz_1 = \frac{p_2}{\rho} + \tfrac{1}{2}u_2^2 + gz_2$$

This is Bernoulli's equation, just as it was introduced in Frame 43. Notice that in fluid mechanics we generally use the symbol u for velocity, rather than v, to avoid the risk of confusion with the symbol for volume.

The term gz on each side of the equation is the potential energy mgz of an element of fluid divided by its mass m, so the term represents the potential energy per unit mass of fluid. In just the same way, what do you think the term $\tfrac{1}{2}u^2$ on each side represents?

48

> The kinetic energy per unit mass of fluid

The kinetic energy of an element of fluid of mass m is $\frac{1}{2}mu^2$. Dividing by the mass, we get $\frac{1}{2}u^2$, which is thus the kinetic energy per unit mass.

Finally, the difference $(p_1/\rho - p_2/\rho)$ may be thought of as the work done by the pressure forces when the fluid moves a certain distance along the streamtube, divided by the mass of fluid that moves past a fixed point in that displacement.

The derivation of Bernoulli's equation may have seemed fairly lengthy, but fortunately the equation is quite easy to apply: we shall do an example in the next frame.

49

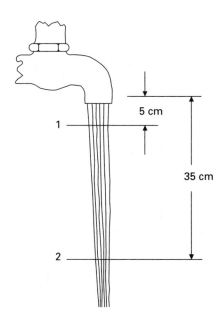

The diagram shows water flowing from a tap in a continuous stream. The stream is open to the air, so it is at atmospheric pressure throughout.

At position 1, 5 cm below the outlet, the velocity of the water is 1.3 m/s. Losses will be very small, so Bernoulli's equation can be used. What will be the velocity of the water at position 2, 35 cm below the outlet?

50

$$\boxed{2.75 \text{ m/s}}$$

Bernoulli's equation is $p_1/\rho + \frac{1}{2}u_1^2 + gz_1 = p_2/\rho + \frac{1}{2}u_2^2 + gz_2$, and with $p_1 = p_2$ (both being atmospheric) the equation becomes

$$\tfrac{1}{2}u_2^2 = \tfrac{1}{2}u_1^2 + g(z_1 - z_2) = \tfrac{1}{2}(1.3)^2 + 9.81(0.30)$$

Therefore $u_2^2 = 7.576$, so $u_2 = 2.75$ m/s.

Now, if the area of cross-section of the stream of water is 22 mm² at position 1, what is the area of cross-section at position 2? (Remember that water is not being created or destroyed between points 1 and 2.)

51

$$\boxed{10.4 \text{ mm}^2}$$

Earlier in this programme we worked through a number of examples on continuity, and we saw that for fluids of constant density (and all liquids are virtually incompressible, and so have constant density) the *volume* flow rate in a steady stream is the same at all points; so in this case

$$A_2 u_2 = A_1 u_1$$
$$A_2 = A_1(u_1/u_2) = 22(1.3/2.75) = 10.4 \text{ mm}^2$$

There will be many instances like this one, where we need to use the principle of continuity as well as Bernoulli's equation in order to find a solution.

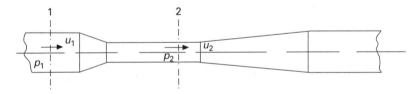

Here is another: a fluid of constant density $\rho = 950$ kg/m³ flows steadily through the tapered tube shown. The diameters of the tube at points 1 and 2 are $d_1 = 100$ mm and $d_2 = 70$ mm. The gauge pressure p_1 at inlet is 200 kN/m², and the velocity u_1 of the fluid at inlet is 6 m/s. We wish to find the gauge pressure p_2 at section 2. We shall use the Bernoulli equation to do this; but first we need to know the velocity u_2 at point 2. Using the principle of continuity, the velocity at point 2 is ...?

$$\boxed{12.2 \text{ m/s}}$$

The volume flow rate is the same at points 1 and 2, so

$$A_2 u_2 = A_1 u_1$$
$$u_2 = u_1 (A_1/A_2) = u_1 (d_1/d_2)^2$$
$$= 6 (100/70)^2 = 12.2 \text{ m/s}$$

Now use Bernoulli's equation to find the gauge pressure p_2 at point 2. (Make sure the units of all terms in the equation are the same!)

$$\boxed{146.4 \text{ kN/m}^2}$$

Here is the working: this time the tube is horizontal, so the heights z_1 and z_2 will be equal, wherever they are measured from, and Bernoulli's equation reduces to

$$(p_1/\rho) + \tfrac{1}{2}u_1^2 = (p_2/\rho) + \tfrac{1}{2}u_2^2$$
$$p_1 - p_2 = \tfrac{1}{2}\rho(u_2^2 - u_1^2)$$
$$= \tfrac{1}{2} \times 950(12.2^2 - 6^2) = 53.6 \times 10^3 \text{ N/m}^2$$

The inlet pressure is 200 kN/m^2 gauge, or 200×10^3 N/m^2 gauge, so the pressure at 2 is

$$p_2 = 200 \times 10^3 - 53.6 \times 10^3$$
$$= 146.4 \times 10^3 \text{ N/m}^2 = 146.4 \text{ kN/m}^2 \text{ gauge}$$

We notice that the pressure is *lower* at point 2, where the fluid is moving more quickly, than it was at the inlet. This reduction of pressure where the fluid is moving quickly sometimes comes in useful: one such instance is described in the next frame.

54

One device which uses the reduction of pressure where the fluid velocity is high is the *injector*, fitted for example to fire hoses to add foam concentrate to water.

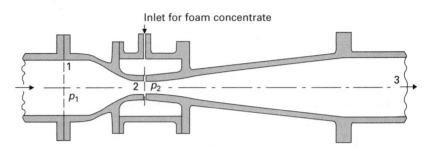

Inlet for foam concentrate

The foam concentrate is held in a container at atmospheric pressure.

Water is pumped in at 1. At the nozzle 2 the velocity is greatly increased, and the pressure is correspondingly decreased – it needs to be less than atmospheric, so that the foam concentrate will flow into the stream of water. The mixture of water and concentrate flows out at 3.

The diameters at 1 and 2, d_1 and d_2, are 42 mm and 10 mm respectively. If the flow rate Q of the water is 3.5 l/s and the flow of concentrate is negligibly small, what are the velocities at points 1 and 2?

55

$$\boxed{u_1 = 2.53 \text{ m/s}; u_2 = 44.3 \text{ m/s}}$$

Working: the areas of the cross-sections at 1 and 2 are

$$A_1 = \pi \times 42^2/4 = 1385 \text{ mm}^2 = 1.385 \times 10^{-3} \text{ m}^2$$
$$A_2 = \pi \times 10^2/4 = 78.5 \text{ mm}^2 = 0.0785 \times 10^{-3} \text{ m}^2$$

The flow rate Q is 3.5 l/s, or 3.5 $\times 10^{-3}$ m^3/s, so the velocities are

$$u_1 = \frac{Q}{A_1} = \frac{3.5 \times 10^{-3}}{1.385 \times 10^{-3}} = 2.53 \text{ m/s}$$

and

$$u_2 = \frac{Q}{A_2} = \frac{3.5 \times 10^{-3}}{0.0785 \times 10^{-3}} = 44.6 \text{ m/s}$$

The gauge pressure at point 2 is to be –0.2 bar (i.e. 0.2 bar, or 20 kN/m^2, less than atmospheric). Using Bernoulli's equation, find the gauge pressure p_1 needed at the inlet to the injector, point 1.

$$\boxed{p_1 = 9.58 \text{ bar (gauge)}}$$

When the answer we want is a pressure, it is often more convenient to write the Bernoulli equation in the form

$$p + \tfrac{1}{2}\rho u^2 + \rho g z = \text{constant along a streamline}$$

where all the terms of the equation are now pressures. We must still remember the conditions under which the equation is satisfied: no losses, incompressible fluid, and steady flow. If you like, you can use the word 'liss' to help you to remember these four conditions:

no **L**osses in

    Incompressible,

        Steady flow, with conditions measured along

a single **S**treamline

('*Liss*' can be found in the dictionary, by the way, though its meaning has nothing to do with Bernoulli's equation!)

For the example about the fire-hose injector, no change in height occurs, so $z_1 = z_2$. The equation reduces to

$$p_1 + \tfrac{1}{2}\rho u_1^2 = p_2 + \tfrac{1}{2}\rho u_2^2$$
$$\begin{aligned}
p_1 &= p_2 + \tfrac{1}{2}\rho(u_2^2 - u_1^2) \\
&= -20 \times 10^3 + \tfrac{1}{2} \times 1000\,(44.3^2 - 2.53^2) \\
&= -20 \times 10^3 + 978 \times 10^3 \\
&= 958 \times 10^3 \text{ N/m}^2 \\
&= 9.58 \text{ bar}
\end{aligned}$$

Thus, neglecting any losses between points 1 and 2 (and the losses should be quite small in this contracting part of the injector), the supply pressure should be nearly 10 bar above atmospheric, and then the pressure at the throat, where the velocity is greatest and the pressure is least, will be 0.2 bar below atmospheric.

In the next frame we look at another example.

57

A very common device which makes use of the reduction of pressure at a restriction is the carburettor – the device used in many petrol engines to produce the fuel–air mixture. The schematic diagrams below relate to a down-draught type of carburettor (so called because the air passes through the carburettor more or less vertically downwards).

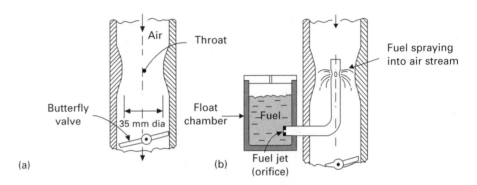

(a)   (b)

Diagram (a) shows the principal air passage, containing a fixed restrictor whose throat diameter is 35 mm. (Also shown is the butterfly valve, which is used to control the amount of fuel–air mixture entering the engine.)

At a certain setting, the engine is taking in 17 l of air per second through the carburettor. We wish to find the pressure at the throat; but first we need to find the velocity. Assuming the density remains virtually constant, what will be the velocity of the air at the throat?

58

$$\boxed{17.7 \text{ m/s}}$$

Working: the area of the throat is $\pi \times 35^2/4 = 962 \text{ mm}^2$. We assume that, even though the pressure has changed, the volume of air passing the throat is still 17 l/s, so the velocity here will be

$$u = \frac{17 \times 10^{-3}}{962 \times 10^{-6}} = 17.7 \text{ m/s}$$

Now use Bernoulli's equation, in the form

$$p_1 + \tfrac{1}{2}\rho u_1^2 + \rho g z_1 = p_2 + \tfrac{1}{2}\rho u_2^2 + \rho g z_2$$

to find the pressure at the throat. Take point 1 to be 0.12 m above the throat (in the atmosphere, where the velocity is very small – virtually zero – and the pressure is the ambient atmospheric pressure) and take the density of the air to be constant at 1.2 kg/m³.

> The pressure at the throat is 186.6 N/m^2 below atmospheric

In Bernoulli's equation, $p_1 + \frac{1}{2}\rho u_1^2 + \rho g z_1 = p_2 + \frac{1}{2}\rho u_2^2 + \rho g z_2$, we shall take point 1 at 0.12 m above the throat, and point 2 at the throat itself.

Using gauge pressures, so that atmospheric pressure is zero, and taking the level of the throat itself as the datum from which the heights z are measured, this gives

$$0 + 0 + 1.2 \times 9.81 \times 0.12 = p_2 + \frac{1}{2} \times 1.2 \times 17.7^2 + 0$$
$$1.41 = p_2 + 188.0$$
$$p_2 = -186.6 \text{ N/m}^2$$

Being a gauge pressure, this represents a pressure 186.6 N/m^2 below atmospheric pressure.

You will have noticed that the $\rho g z$ term is rather insignificant. When Bernoulli's equation is applied to gases, their density is so small that, unless we are dealing with stratospheric heights (in which case the density of the gas will alter too much for Bernoulli's equation to be applied at all – the fluid is supposed to be incompressible), this term can be neglected.

Diagram (b) in Frame 57 shows how the petrol fuel is supplied from the adjoining float chamber into the air stream at the throat by virtue of the pressure difference between the throat and the float chamber. Atmospheric pressure acts on the surface of the fuel in the chamber. With the pressure at the throat about 187 N/m^2 below atmospheric, and taking the density of the liquid fuel as 720 kg/m^3, what is the maximum distance h the petrol can be lifted to the air stream at the throat?

60

> 26 mm

The pressure difference is 187 N/m^2, and if the density of the petrol is ρ this difference must be greater than $\rho g h$.

$$187 > \rho g h$$

and so

$$h < 187/\rho g$$
$$h < 187/(720 \times 9.81)$$
$$h < 0.026 \text{ m}$$

61

Revision exercise: Bernoulli's equation

In all three of these exercises, friction losses may be neglected.

1

The velocity u of the water leaving the jet of an ornamental fountain is required to be 23 m/s. What gauge pressure is needed at point X in the pipe? (The pipe is large diameter, so the velocity at X is negligible.)

2 Water flows through the tapered pipe shown. The gauge pressure p_1 at point 1 is 1.5×10^5 N/m^2, and the velocity u_1 is 2.7 m/s.

Find (a) the velocity at point 2, and (b) the gauge pressure at that point.

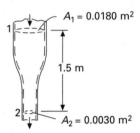

3

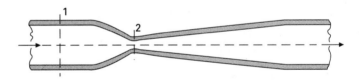

A liquid of density 1050 kg/m^3 flows through the shaped tube shown above. At point 1, upstream of the restriction, the velocity of the flow is 1.4 m/s, and at point 2 the velocity is 36.1 m/s.

The gauge pressure at point 1 is 6.5×10^5 N/m^2. What is the gauge pressure at point 2?

Worked solutions

62

1 We use Bernoulli's equation:

$$p_1 + \tfrac{1}{2}\rho u_1^2 + \rho g z_1 = p_2 + \tfrac{1}{2}\rho u_2^2 + \rho g z_2$$

In this case the z terms will be the same on both sides of the equation, because point X is at the same level as the jet outlet. The equation becomes

$$p_1 + \tfrac{1}{2}\rho u_1^2 = p_2 + \tfrac{1}{2}\rho u_2^2$$

Furthermore, the velocity u_1 at point X is small, and so the term $\tfrac{1}{2}\rho u_1^2$ can be neglected. Finally, the jet is open to the atmosphere, so pressure p_2 is atmospheric, i.e. the gauge pressure is zero. Thus

$$\begin{aligned}
p_1 &= \tfrac{1}{2}\rho u_2^2 \\
&= \tfrac{1}{2} \times 1000 \times 23^2 \ \text{N/m}^2 \\
&= 265 \ \text{kN/m}^2
\end{aligned}$$

2 First we use continuity to find the velocity u_2:

$$u_2 \times 0.0030 = 2.7 \times 0.0180$$
$$u_2 = 16.2 \ \text{m/s}$$

and then we can substitute directly into Bernoulli's equation:

$$1.5 \times 10^5 + \tfrac{1}{2} \times 1000 \times 2.7^2 + 1000 \times 9.81 \times 1.5 = p_2 + \tfrac{1}{2} \times 1000 \times 16.2^2 + 0$$

from which we find that $p_2 = 37.1 \ \text{kN/m}^2$

3 Points 1 and 2 are at the same level, so we do not need to consider the z terms in Bernoulli's equation. Thus

$$p_1 + \tfrac{1}{2}\rho u_1^2 = p_2 + \tfrac{1}{2}\rho u_2^2$$
$$6.5 \times 10^5 + \tfrac{1}{2} \times 1050 \times 1.4^2 = p_2 + \tfrac{1}{2} \times 1050 \times 36.1^2$$
$$p_2 = -33 \times 10^3 \ \text{N/m}^2$$

So the gauge pressure at point 2 is *negative*. This means that the pressure at that point is less than atmospheric pressure.

63

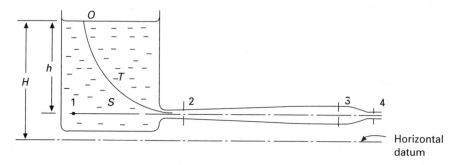

The system shown here is very like the one in Frame 34, except that the outlet tube has three different diameters, terminating in a small diameter d_4 where the liquid emerges to atmosphere. The tank is large, so that the height h changes only very slowly. As the liquid in the tank is practically stationary, the gauge pressure p_1 at point 1 is ρgh.

If losses in the system are negligible, find the outlet velocity u_4; you can use Bernoulli's equation between points 1 and 4 on streamline S, or between O and 4 on streamline T (or even the result from Frame 36).

64

$$\boxed{u_4 = \sqrt{2gh}}$$

Using Bernoulli's equation between 1 and 4, at the outlet 4 the velocity is u_4 and the pressure is atmospheric, i.e. the gauge pressure is zero. Since streamline S is horizontal, $z_1 = z_4$, so

$$p_1/\rho + \tfrac{1}{2}u_1^2 = p_4/\rho + \tfrac{1}{2}u_4^2.$$
$$(\rho gh)/\rho + 0 = 0 + \tfrac{1}{2}u_4^2$$
$$u_4 = \sqrt{2gh}$$

We could have taken streamline T instead and used Bernoulli's equation between points O and 4. In this case the pressure is atmospheric at both points, but the heights z_O and z_4 differ by a distance h. Thus

$$\tfrac{1}{2}u_O^2 + gz_O = \tfrac{1}{2}u_4^2 + gz_4$$
$$0 + gh = \tfrac{1}{2}u_4^2 + 0$$
$$u_4 = \sqrt{2gh}$$

The result is just as before – as of course it must be. Now, if the ratio of diameter d_3 to diameter d_4 is $d_3/d_4 = 1.3$, what is the ratio of the velocities u_3/u_4?

$$\boxed{u_3/u_4 = 0.592}$$

If $d_3/d_4 = 1.3$, then the ratio of the areas is $A_3/A_4 = (d_3/d_4)^2 = 1.69$. By continuity, the ratio of velocities must be the reciprocal of this:

$$(u_3/u_4) = (1/1.69) = 0.592$$

Likewise, if $d_2/d_4 = 1.1$, the ratio of velocities is $(u_2/u_4) = (1/1.1)^2 = 0.826$.

We have already seen that Bernoulli's equation can be written in the form

$$p + \tfrac{1}{2}\rho u^2 + \rho gz = \text{constant along a streamline}$$

Applying Bernoulli in this form along the horizontal streamline S, if the pressures in the tube at points 2, 3 and 4 are p_2, p_3 and p_4, which of these is the largest pressure? Which is the smallest?

$$\boxed{p_3 \text{ is the largest pressure; } p_4 \text{ is the smallest}}$$

Once again, we can see from Bernoulli's equation that, for a horizontal streamline (i.e. with z constant), as the velocity increases the pressure must decrease, and vice versa. Consequently the largest pressure in the tube arises where the velocity is least – in the largest-diameter part of the tube – and the smallest pressure is where the velocity is greatest, in the narrowest part.

The pressures can be measured via openings made in the wall of the tube. The openings, or tappings, must be normal to the flow and free from burrs: any projecting edges that tended to scoop the fluid into the opening would give a misleadingly large reading of pressure.

The pressure is sometimes called the *static pressure* – which may strike you as a rather illogical choice of name, since the fluid is clearly moving. The word 'static' is included to make clear that, since the tapping is normal to the flow and free from sharp edges etc., the pressure in the tapping is the same as the pressure exerted on the inner wall of the tube, and its value is not falsely increased or reduced by the motion of the fluid.

A diagram illustrating this is shown in the next frame.

67

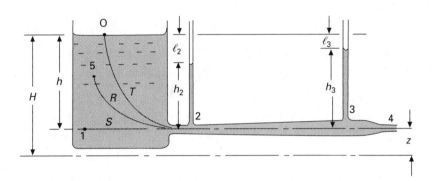

Our system is shown again, but now fitted with vertical gauge glasses connected to static-pressure tappings into the horizontal tube at 2 and 3. Such tappings are often called simply *static tappings*; as we learned in Programme 1, the vertical glass tubes are sometimes known as *piezometers*.

Considering the vertical tube at 2: the liquid in the tube (of density ρ) has risen to a height h_2. What is the gauge pressure at the bottom of this tube?

68

> The gauge pressure is $\rho g h_2$

The pressure increase due to the liquid column is given by $\rho g h_2$. The gauge pressure is zero at the top of the column, i.e. atmospheric pressure acts at this point. Therefore the gauge pressure at the bottom of the liquid column is $\rho g h_2$.

If the gauge pressure at the bottom of the liquid column is p_2, then $p_2 = \rho g h_2$, so $h_2 = (p_2/\rho g)$.

In the same way, the height h_3 is ...?

$$h_3 = (p_3/\rho g)$$

The height of the column of liquid at 3 is related to the gauge pressure at the base of the column, in other words to the static pressure in the horizontal tube, in just the same way as at position 2.

The form of the terms $(p/\rho g)$ suggests that we might divide the Bernoulli equation through by the (constant) density ρ and so obtain yet a third form for the equation:

$$\frac{p}{\rho g} + \frac{u^2}{2g} + z = \text{constant along a streamline}$$

Each term in this equation is a length. As we have just seen, $p/\rho g$ is the height to which the liquid rises in a vertical sight-glass. The third term, z, is the height above the horizontal datum of the point we are considering on the streamline. Now let's see what the other terms represent.

We will consider a general streamline R, starting from point 5 in the tank, where the height is z_5, the depth is $(H - z_5)$, so the gauge pressure is $\rho g(H - z_5)$. Everywhere in the tank the velocity is virtually zero, and so $u_5 = 0$.

Substituting these values into Bernoulli's equation in the form

$$\frac{p}{\rho g} + \frac{u^2}{2g} + z = C \text{ (constant)}$$

what is the value of the constant C on the right-hand side?

$$C \text{ is equal to the height } H$$

This value is the same wherever the point 5 is chosen to be, and so for any streamline that originates in the tank the constant on the right-hand side of the equation is simply H. This quantity is of course a length, and it is called the *total head*.

The three components on the left-hand side of the equation are called the *pressure head*, the *velocity head*, and the *elevation* respectively.

On the diagram, the elevation z is obvious; the pressure head is shown by the heights h_2, h_3 etc. of the liquid in the gauge glasses. So what do the lengths ℓ_2, ℓ_3 of the empty parts of the sight-glasses represent?

71

The velocity head

The three quantities on the left-hand side of the equation, the pressure head, the velocity head and the elevation, sum to the total head, H. The diagram in Frame 67 showed how each of these quantities is represented physically: moving upwards from the horizontal datum level, the elevation z comes first, then the pressure head $h = p/\rho g$. The remaining length ℓ must therefore be the velocity head.

The faster the fluid moves, the greater the velocity head at each point, so the further the level in the sight-glasses falls below the total-head level.

The kind of physical arrangement shown, with vertical gauge glasses, is rarely seen in practice (partly because it makes a very good fountain if the pressure rises too far), but the concept of pressure head, velocity head and elevation is a very useful one.

72

In our diagrams so far, the elevation z was constant along the tube. But often the tube will not be horizontal – it may be a pipeline that follows the surface of the ground, for example. Provided there are no losses, the total head H will still be constant even when z varies.

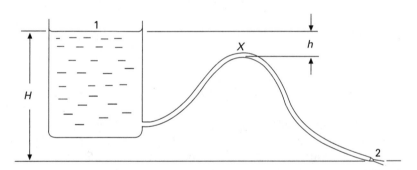

The diagram above shows a tank or reservoir supplying water along a pipe to a nozzle, where the water emerges to atmosphere. The total head measured above the level of the nozzle is H. What will be the speed u of the water emerging from the nozzle, if there are no losses?

$$u = \sqrt{2gH}$$

Working: applying Bernoulli's equation between the nozzle (point 2), where the pressure is atmospheric, and a point 1 at the surface of the water in the reservoir, we have

$$\frac{p_1}{\rho g} + \frac{u_1^2}{2g} + z_1 = \frac{p_2}{\rho g} + \frac{u_2^2}{2g} + z_2$$

$$0 + 0 + H = 0 + \frac{u_2^2}{2g} + 0$$

$$u_2 = \sqrt{2gH}$$

just as before.

We will suppose the diameter of the tube is twice the diameter of the jet. The area of the tube is then four times the area of the jet, so the velocity of the water in the tube will be one quarter the velocity at the jet, i.e. $\frac{1}{4}\sqrt{2gH}$.

In this case, what is the velocity head in the tube?

74

$$H/16$$

The velocity head is given by $u^2/2g$, so in this case it is

$$\frac{\left(\frac{1}{4}\sqrt{2gH}\right)^2}{2g} = \frac{H}{16}$$

Since the area of cross-section of the tube is proportional to the square of the diameter d, the velocity for a given flow rate is proportional to $1/d^2$, and the velocity head to $1/d^4$.

At the highest point of the tube, X, the tube is a distance h below the total head line. Remembering that the velocity head is $H/16$, what is the pressure head at point X, in terms of h and H?

75

$$\boxed{h - H/16}$$

Subtracting the elevation of the tube at X from the total head H, we see that the distance h is equal to the sum of the pressure head and the velocity head. So the pressure head at X is the distance h minus the velocity head:

$$\text{Pressure head} = (h - H/16)$$

If the distance h is less than the velocity head ($H/16$ in this case), then the pressure head at the point X is negative; in other words, the pressure at this point is less than atmospheric. Any part of the tube where the pressure is less than atmospheric is called a *siphon*, just like a tube used to take the water out of a fish tank, wine from a jar, or even fuel from a fuel tank. In all of these cases the liquid in part of the tube is at less than atmospheric pressure.

Finally in this section of the programme, we shall consider a system in which both the elevation and the diameter of the tube vary.

76

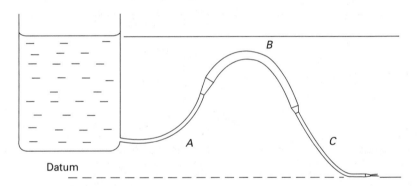

The system shown has three sections of pipe, A, B and C, all of different diameters. In which of the three sections will the velocity head be the greatest?

Section *C*

Section *C* of the pipe has the smallest diameter of the three, so the velocity in this section is the greatest, and the velocity head $u^2/2g$ is likewise greatest in this section.

Vertical gauge glasses, or piezometers, could be fitted to this system in the same way as to the system in Frame 67. In each vertical tube the liquid rises to a height equal to the pressure head, and the difference between the top of the liquid column and the total head line is the velocity head.

A line can be drawn following the top of the liquid columns in the piezometer tubes, as shown on the diagram below. At any point of the pipe the vertical distance between this line and the centre-line of the pipe is the pressure head, and similarly the distance between the line and the total head line is the velocity head. This line is called the *hydraulic grade line*.

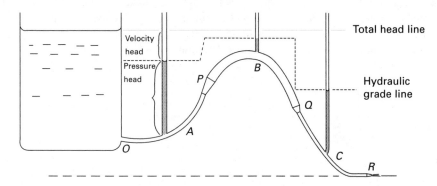

The velocity head is largest in section *C* of the pipe, which has the smallest diameter, and is least in section *B*, where the diameter is greatest.

From the diagram above, can you see at which point in the tube the pressure head is least?

78

At point Q the hydraulic grade line is closest to the centre-line of the pipe, and so the pressure head, which is represented by the distance between the pipe and the grade line, is least at this point.

The hydraulic grade line is particularly useful because it enables us to see immediately the size of the pressure head at every point along the pipe. Remember though that, because the hydraulic grade line is $(u^2/2g)$ below the total head line, its position depends on the flow rate. A new line has to be drawn if the flow rate alters.

So far we have assumed in every case that losses due to viscous friction or other causes were negligible, and that the total energy per unit mass remained virtually constant along a streamline.

In fact, every real system does suffer losses, so the total energy will gradually decrease as we move downstream. Likewise, the total head gradually decreases; the total-head line is not actually horizontal but gradually declines, as shown in the diagram below. (There are also losses of energy, or of head, at changes of diameter – hence the downward steps in the line.)

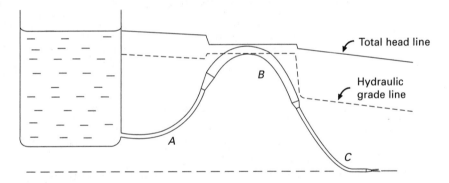

The hydraulic grade line is still everywhere a distance below the total head line equal to the velocity head $u^2/2g$.

Referring to the diagram above, what can be said about the pressure in section B of the pipe?

79

| In part of section B the pressure is below atmospheric |

When losses are taken into account, we see that part of section B of the pipe rises above the hydraulic grade line. This part of the pipe is a siphon, in which the pressure is below atmospheric.

Major pipelines often include sections which are siphons, because it is cheaper to go over hills than to tunnel through them, but these siphons do introduce complications. Whenever the pressure goes below atmospheric, dissolved air will tend to come out of solution, and pockets of air, or of vapour, may form and be trapped at the top of the inverted U. This is often called an *air lock* or a *vapour lock*, and it results in higher pressure being required at the source. Any pumps have to work harder, so energy is wasted; in extreme cases the liquid may not flow at all unless the vapour is removed.

If you were the designer of the pipeline shown in Frame 78, could you suggest ways in which the pressure in section B of the pipe might be increased? (Try not to look at the next frame before having a good think about it!)

80

There are several things the designer could consider.

One possibility would be to use a larger diameter pipe for section B. In this larger pipe the velocity head would be reduced, so the pressure head would be greater; but if the pipe of section B was already quite large, this might not be a very fruitful approach.

Another method would be to increase the diameter of pipe used for section A. In this larger pipe the friction loss would be reduced, and so the pressure in section B would be greater.

Yet a third possibility would be to cut the flow rate through the pipe, so reducing the friction losses and the velocity head everywhere: but if a fixed flow rate is specified, this may not be practicable.

In fact, none of these methods is very attractive. The first and the second involve additional capital cost, and the third reduces performance; which to choose must depend on the circumstances. If a sufficient increase of pressure cannot be achieved, we may have to tunnel through the hill after all.

Now we come to the last part of this programme, so turn over to frame 81.

81

Moving frames of reference

Sometimes we may wish to apply Bernoulli's equation to flow around objects which are moving: for example, to investigate the pressure at the intake to an aero-engine in actual flying conditions.

We can only use Bernoulli's equation if flow is steady – if conditions at any point do not alter with time. If we consider a point that is fixed relative to the ground, then conditions at this point will alter continuously as the aircraft passes, so the state is not steady, and Bernoulli's equation cannot be applied.

However, if we observe the airflow around the engine from a position on the aircraft, then (provided the aircraft is flying at constant speed) conditions *will* be steady. As with all the equations of dynamics, Bernoulli's equation is true in any frame of reference that is moving without acceleration, so if the aircraft flies in a straight line with constant speed Bernoulli can be applied.

Here is an example: the speed U of an aircraft through the air is 135 m/s, so to an observer on the aircraft the air appears to be approaching with this speed. Just in front of the engine intake the air has accelerated to a speed of 178 m/s, again as observed from the aircraft.

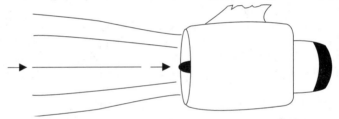

If the ambient air pressure and density at this altitude are 45 kN/m^2 (absolute) and 0.58 kg/m^3 respectively, use the Bernoulli equation to find the air pressure just before the intake.

82

$$\boxed{41.1 \text{ kN/m}^2}$$

Since the velocities are horizontal the z terms can be omitted, and Bernoulli's equation becomes

$$p_1 + \tfrac{1}{2}\rho u_1^2 = p_2 + \tfrac{1}{2}\rho u_2^2$$

Entering the values:

$$45 \times 10^3 + \tfrac{1}{2} \times 0.58 \times 135^2 = p_2 + \tfrac{1}{2} \times 0.58 \times 178^2$$
$$p_2 = 41.1 \times 10^3 \text{ N/m}^2 \text{ (abs.)}$$

Now try the example in the next frame.

83

To avoid having to stop to take on water, long-distance steam locomotives used to pick up water from long troughs between the rails into which a suitably shaped scoop was lowered. The diagram below illustrates the arrangement.

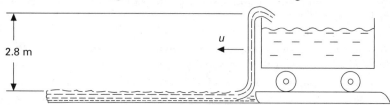

If the scoop supplies water into a tube discharging into the top of the tank, 2.8 m above the level of the water in the trough, what is the minimum train speed u at which water will flow into the tank? (Neglect losses.)

84

$$\boxed{7.4 \text{ m/s}}$$

If we view the situation from a fixed position on the ground and watch the locomotive rush past, the situation changes continuously and conditions are clearly not steady. However, if we imagine ourselves observing things from a vantage point on the train, the water appears to be approaching us steadily at a speed u and, if u is large enough, flowing steadily into the tank.

Initially the speed of the water is u and the pressure is atmospheric. At the point of discharge from the tube, the pressure is again atmospheric; the water has gained 2.8 m height, and at the minimum speed for flow to occur the velocity of the water emerging from the tube will be close to zero.

Using Bernoulli's equation:

$$\frac{p_1}{\rho} + \tfrac{1}{2}u_1^2 + gz_1 = \frac{p_2}{\rho} + \tfrac{1}{2}u_2^2 + gz_2$$

we have

$$0 + \tfrac{1}{2}u^2 + 0 = 0 + 0 + g \times 2.8$$
$$u^2 = 2 \times 9.81 \times 2.8 = 54.9$$
$$u = 7.4 \text{ m/s}$$

Bernoulli's equation is just as easy to use when the observer is moving as when the observer is stationary on the Earth's surface. We use the Earth as a reference only because we are used to thinking of it as fixed, but of course it isn't really, and any other frame of reference that has no acceleration is just as good.

This brings us to the end of this programme; all that remains to do is to check the revision summary in the next frame and then work through the short test exercise that follows. You should have no difficulty with it.

85

Revision summary

1 *Streamline*: a line which at every point has the same direction as the fluid velocity.
2 *Streamtube*: an imaginary tubular surface, the walls of the imaginary tube being formed of streamlines.
3 *Discharge*: the volume flow rate of fluid.
4 *Control surface*: an imaginary surface drawn around some part of the system, through which fluid can enter at some points and leave at other points.
5 *Continuity Principle*: the principle of conservation of matter applied to fluids. In steady conditions, the amount of matter in a defined space such as a control surface must be constant, so the total mass flow inwards must be equal to the total mass flow outwards.
6 *Bernoulli's equation:*

$$\frac{p}{\rho} + \frac{u^2}{2} + gz = \text{constant along a streamline}$$

for steady flow without losses of an incompressible fluid (or one whose density does not vary). In this form the terms of the equation represent energy per unit mass.
7 *Bernoulli in pressure form*: since the density ρ is constant, we can multiply by it and get

$$p + \tfrac{1}{2}\rho u^2 + \rho gz = \text{constant along a streamline}$$

8 *Bernoulli in head form*: again, we can divide the original form by g and get

$$\frac{p}{\rho g} + \frac{u^2}{2g} + z = \text{constant along a streamline}$$

9 *Moving frames of reference*: like all the equations of dynamics, Bernoulli's equation is equally valid when all velocities etc. are measured in relation to a frame of reference which is moving without acceleration.

Test exercise

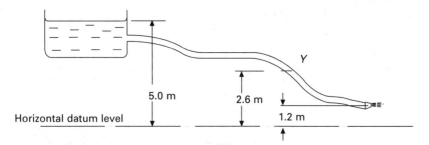

1 Water from the tank flows through the tube, whose internal diameter is 12 mm, and emerges through a nozzle of diameter 8 mm. Neglecting all friction losses, find the velocity of the water leaving the jet, and the values of the pressure head and the velocity head at point Y in the tube.

2 In a certain car, the air intake to the ventilation system is at the front of the car facing forwards. When the car is travelling at 30 m/s, the air velocity just inside the air intake is 1.2 m/s, relative to the car. Given that the density of the air is 1.20 kg/m^3, estimate the gauge pressure just inside the air intake.

3

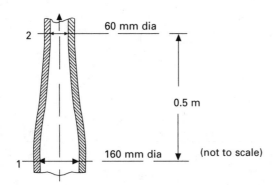

A liquid of density 880 kg/m^3 flows upwards through the vertical tapered pipe shown. The velocity at point 1 is 1.35 m/s, and the gauge pressure at this point is 500 kN/m^2. Find (a) the velocity at the outlet 2 from the tapered pipe, and (b) the gauge pressure at the outlet, neglecting all losses.

87

Further problems

1 Water flows through the tapered pipe shown below. The entry velocity u_1 is 0.4 m/s. Find the exit velocity u_2.

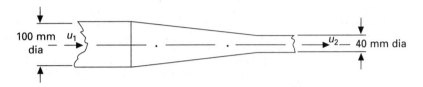

2 A river is flowing at 1.1 m/s. Between the piers of a bridge the speed increases to 1.8 m/s. Estimate the height of the water under the bridge relative to the upstream level (say whether it is lower or higher!).

3 Sheets of materials like leather and some fabrics are often cut using a fine jet of water, which minimises both dust and the risk of fire. In a certain cutter the water is supplied to the jet at a pressure of 4000 bar. What is the velocity of the jet?

4 A liquid of density 1260 kg/m³ flows down an inclined pipe as shown below. Neglecting losses, estimate the static pressure at section 1, given that $u_1 = 20$ m/s, $u_2 = 30$ m/s and $p_2 = 500$ kN/m², where u_1 and u_2 are the velocities at sections 1 and 2 and p_2 is the static pressure at section 2.

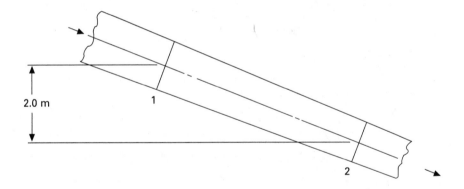

Programme 5

FLOW MEASUREMENT:
PITOT TUBE, VENTURI METER
AND ORIFICE METER

1

Introduction: the pitot tube

In the previous programme we saw that the relationship between the pressure p, the velocity u and the elevation z of a flowing fluid is given by Bernoulli's equation:

$$\frac{p}{\rho} + \tfrac{1}{2}u^2 + gz = \text{constant}$$

The equation applies only along a single streamline, and does not relate the situation on one streamline to that on another, even in the same flow.

There are three other conditions that must be satisfied if Bernoulli's equation is to hold. Can you recall what these three conditions are?

2

> Flow must be steady, the density must be constant and there must be no losses

Did you remember all three of these? If you had any trouble, perhaps the word 'liss', which we introduced in Frame 56 of the previous programme would have helped you to remember. The four conditions are:

No Losses; Incompressible flow (i.e. with constant density); Steady flow, along a single Streamline.

Now suppose a fluid of density ρ is flowing steadily with velocity u. If a blunt-ended object is placed in the flow, the fluid will flow around it as shown in the diagram below by the streamlines.

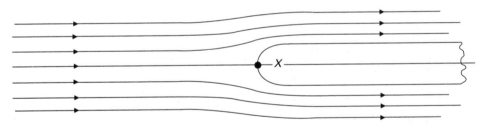

Some of the fluid flows to one side and some to the other. One particular streamline forms the division between particles of fluid that pass to the left and those that pass to the right; particles close to this line come almost to a standstill near point X before moving to one side or the other. Point X is therefore called a *stagnation point*.

If the pressure well upstream is p_1, what is the pressure at point X? (Assume losses are negligible, so that Bernoulli's equation can be used.)

$$\boxed{p_1 + \tfrac{1}{2}\rho u^2}$$

Applying Bernoulli's equation $p_1 + \tfrac{1}{2}\rho u_1^2 = p_2 + \tfrac{1}{2}\rho u_2^2$, with point 1 well upstream and point 2 at the stagnation point X:

$$p_1 + \tfrac{1}{2}\rho u^2 = p_2 + 0$$

and so immediately

$$p_2 = p_1 + \tfrac{1}{2}\rho u^2$$

(Points 1 and 2 being on the same level, the z terms were omitted.)

The increase in pressure $\tfrac{1}{2}\rho u^2$ when the fluid is brought to rest is called the *dynamic pressure*, and the pressure $(p_1 + \tfrac{1}{2}\rho u^2)$ at point X, where the velocity is zero, is called the *stagnation pressure* or *total pressure*.

The blunt end of the object does not have to be solid. It could be a tube filled with stationary fluid, as in the diagram below of a pipe in which a liquid of density ρ is flowing steadily with velocity u.

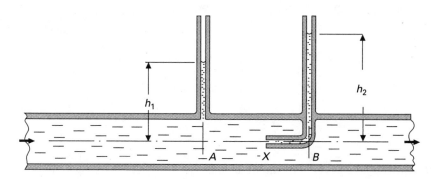

The piezometer (vertical glass tube) fitted at A indicates that the static pressure p_1 at the centre-line of the pipe is $\rho g h_1$. Piezometer B shows that the pressure p_2 at the entry to the tube X is $\rho g h_2$.

We already know that the pressure at X is $p_2 = p_1 + \tfrac{1}{2}\rho u^2$, so

$$\rho g h_2 = \rho g h_1 + \tfrac{1}{2}\rho u^2$$
$$g(h_2 - h_1) = \tfrac{1}{2}u^2$$
$$u = \sqrt{2g(h_2 - h_1)}$$

With this simple arrangement the velocity of flow of the fluid is readily found: let's try an example. Water is flowing along the pipe shown above. The water rises in tube A to a height $h_1 = 320$ mm, and in tube B to $h_2 = 730$ mm. Find the speed u of the water in the pipe.

4

$$2.84 \text{ m/s}$$

The working is:

$$u = \sqrt{2g(h_2 - h_1)} = \sqrt{2 \times 9.81 \times (0.73 - 0.32)}$$
$$= \sqrt{2 \times 9.81 \times 0.41} = 2.84 \text{ m/s}$$

The small tube facing into the oncoming flow is called a *pitot tube*, after its originator the Frenchman Henri Pitot.

When the fluid is a gas and not a liquid, a piezometer cannot be used. Often we use a manometer: an arrangement using a U-tube manometer is shown in the diagram below. (Manometers, and pressure measurement in general, were covered in Programme 1, Frames 33–59, so turn back and check if you are in any doubt.)

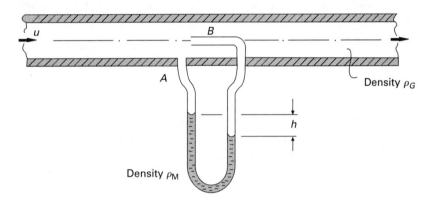

If the density of the gas flowing along the pipe is ρ_G and its velocity is u, the dynamic pressure is ...?

5

$$\tfrac{1}{2}\rho_G u^2$$

The dynamic pressure is $\tfrac{1}{2}\rho u^2$, just as before, but in this case the density is denoted by ρ_G. The dynamic pressure is the difference between the stagnation pressure (sensed by tube B) and the static pressure (tube A).

This pressure difference is indicated by the manometer, in which the liquid has density ρ_M.

Taking the following values, $\rho_M = 1000 \text{ kg/m}^3$ and $h = 44 \text{ mm}$, what pressure difference between A and B does the manometer indicate?

6

$$432 \text{ N/m}^2$$

The pressure difference is given by

$$\rho_M gh = 1000 \times 9.81 \times 0.044$$
$$= 432 \text{ N/m}^2$$

(The more exact answer here is $(\rho_M - \rho_G)gh$, but the density ρ_M of the liquid is so much larger than that of any gas that ρ_G can be ignored.)

If $\rho_G = 1.05 \text{ kg/m}^3$, we can now equate this measured pressure difference to the dynamic pressure $\frac{1}{2}\rho_G u^2$. So what is the velocity of flow of the gas along the tube?

7

$$28.7 \text{ m/s}$$

We have

$$\frac{1}{2}\rho_G u^2 = 432$$

$$u = \sqrt{\frac{2 \times 432}{1.05}} = 28.7 \text{ m/s}$$

Now here is an example where a pitot tube is used in an inclined pipe.

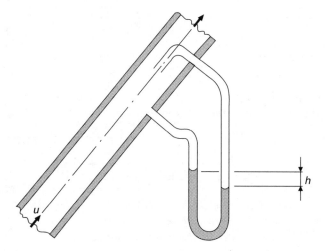

CO_2 gas is flowing along the pipe as shown. The manometer contains water and the difference in levels is $h = 51$ mm. If the density ρ_G of the CO_2 in the pipe is 1.9 kg/m^3, what is the velocity of the flow?

8

$$\boxed{23 \text{ m/s}}$$

Equating the dynamic pressure $\frac{1}{2}\rho_G u^2$ to the pressure $\rho_M g h$ indicated by the manometer, we have

$$\tfrac{1}{2} \times 1.9 \times u^2 = 1000 \times 9.81 \times 0.051$$

$$u^2 = 527$$

$$u = 23.0 \text{ m/s}$$

The diagram below shows a manometer fitted to an inclined pipe which contains a liquid, rather than a gas. The density of the liquid in the pipe is ρ and that of the (denser) liquid in the manometer tube is ρ_M.

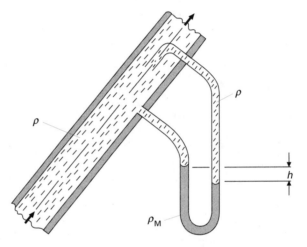

Initially, the liquid in the pipe is stationary. In this situation, on which side of the manometer is the level higher, the left, the right, or neither?

9

$$\boxed{\text{Neither} - \text{the levels are the same}}$$

When the liquid is stationary, it must all be in equilibrium, and the manometer will then show zero pressure difference. When the manometer does show a pressure difference, this must be due *only* to the dynamic pressure.

Here is an example: the liquid flowing in the pipe is water, of density $\rho = 1000 \text{ kg/m}^3$, and the second liquid in the manometer is mercury, of density $\rho_M = 13.6 \times 10^3 \text{ kg/m}^3$. The difference in the two mercury levels is 72 mm. We wish to find the speed of flow of the water; but first, what is the pressure difference indicated by the manometer? (Remember how to deal with two-fluid manometers? We dealt with them in Programme 1, Frames 40–52.)

10

$$\boxed{8900 \text{ N/m}^2}$$

In a two-fluid manometer, the pressure difference is equal to $\rho'gh$, where ρ' is the difference between the densities of the two fluids. In this case $\rho' = (13.6 - 1.0) \times 10^3 = 12.6 \times 10^3 \text{ kg/m}^3$, and so the pressure difference is

$$\rho'gh = (12.6 \times 10^3) \times 9.81 \times 0.072 = 8900 \text{ N/m}^2$$

If you had any difficulty at all with this, turn back to Programme 1, Frames 40–52, and check over the material on two-fluid manometers before going on.

This pressure difference is equal to the dynamic pressure, $\frac{1}{2}\rho_1 u^2$, so it is a straightforward matter to calculate the flow velocity.

11

$$\boxed{4.21 \text{ m/s}}$$

Equating the dynamic pressure $\frac{1}{2}\rho u^2$ to 8900 N/m^2, we get

$$\frac{1}{2} \times 1000 \times u^2 = 8900$$
$$u^2 = 17.8$$
$$u = 4.21 \text{ m/s}$$

Thus when the water flows at 4.21 m/s the level difference at the manometer is 72 mm. Since the dynamic pressure is proportional to u^2, a velocity one tenth as large would give one hundredth of the level difference, i.e. only 0.72 mm, which is too small to measure accurately. The pitot tube is one of several devices which use dynamic pressure changes to indicate flow velocity: all of them suffer from the same drawback of being very insensitive to low flow velocities.

The range of operation of a pitot tube can be extended to lower velocities and to fluids of smaller density by using a more sensitive manometer, for example one employing two fluids of similar density.

An example of this is given in the next frame.

12

In the system shown in the diagram below, the flowing liquid is again water, but this time the second fluid in the manometer is paraffin. Because the density of paraffin – 830 kg/m³ – is less than that of water, the U-tube is inverted.

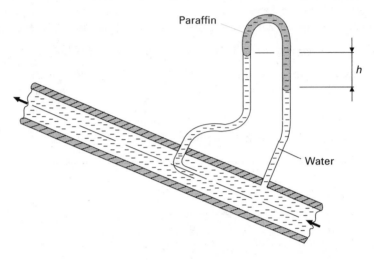

When the flow velocity is 0.6 m/s, what will be the value of the height difference h?

13

$$\boxed{108 \text{ mm}}$$

In the situation shown in the frame above, the dynamic pressure is

$$\tfrac{1}{2}\rho_{\text{water}}u^2 = \tfrac{1}{2} \times 1000 \times 0.6^2 = 180 \text{ N/m}^2$$

The pressure difference indicated by the manometer is

$$(\rho_{\text{water}} - \rho_{\text{paraffin}})gh = (1000 - 830) \times 9.81 \times h$$

Equating these:

$$170 \times 9.81 \times h = 180$$
$$h = 0.108 \text{ m, or } 108 \text{ mm}$$

This height difference is sufficient for the manometer to be read quite accurately, so the manometer can be used to determine quite low speeds of flow with reasonable confidence.

14

We quite often wish to measure the velocity of a free stream, say of air emerging from a fan or blower. With a small pitot tube it is possible to explore in detail the way the velocity varies from place to place in the stream.

But a pitot tube only gives the total or stagnation pressure: we also need to measure the static pressure.

A combination instrument, the so-called pitot-static tube, incorporates both the forward-facing opening (to sense the stagnation pressure) and several side holes (which sense the static pressure). A typical design of pitot-static tube is shown in the diagram below.

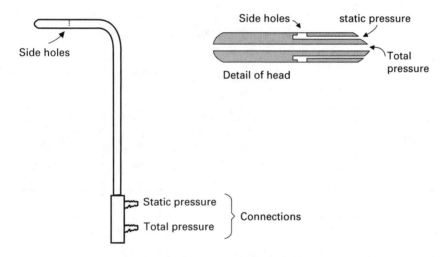

A manometer connected between the two outlets provides an immediate indication of the dynamic pressure, which is of course the difference between the stagnation pressure and the static pressure. (In fact, the design of the pitot-static tube is not quite as simple as it looks. The pressure at the static pressure holes is affected both by the pattern of flow around the open front end of the tube and by the presence of the stem; the geometry has to be carefully arranged so that these two effects cancel each other.)

The next frame gives a worked example of the application of a pitot-static tube, and is followed by one for you to try yourself.

15

Example

A pitot-static tube is used to measure the speed of a stream of air, whose density is $1.2 \ \text{kg/m}^3$. The dynamic pressure (that is, the difference between the total and static pressures) is sensed by a differential manometer instrument which indicates a pressure difference of $4350 \ \text{N/m}^2$. We wish to find the velocity of the air.

The dynamic pressure is

$$\tfrac{1}{2}\rho u^2 = \tfrac{1}{2} \times 1.2 \times u^2$$
$$= 4350 \ \text{N/m}^2$$

Therefore

$$u^2 = \frac{2 \times 4350}{1.2} = 7250$$

and

$$u = 85 \ \text{m/s}$$

Now, here is one for you to try: the speed of a stream of warm air is to be investigated using a pitot-static tube. The density of the air is $1.15 \ \text{kg/m}^3$.

A manometer containing paraffin (density $830 \ \text{kg/m}^3$) is connected to the pitot-static tube. If the difference in the levels is 278 mm, what is the speed of the air?

16

$$\boxed{58 \ \text{m/s}}$$

Working: the pressure difference indicated by the manometer is

$$\rho_{\text{paraffin}} g h = 830 \times 9.81 \times 0.278 = 2264 \ \text{N/m}^2$$

and this is equal to the dynamic pressure, $\tfrac{1}{2}\rho_{\text{air}} u^2$. Writing this as an equation:

$$\tfrac{1}{2} \times 1.15 \times u^2 = 2264$$
$$u^2 = 3937$$
$$u = 62.7 \ \text{m/s}$$

A pitot-static tube is a very useful instrument for sensing the velocity of a free stream of fluid, but when we wish to measure the discharge, or volume flow rate, of fluid in a pipe the pitot tube has the drawback that it indicates the velocity at only one point in a flow that will certainly not be exactly uniform. Also, if solid particles are present in the flow they tend to build up on the tube and possibly block it.

In these circumstances a different kind of instrument is generally used. One such instrument is described in the next frame.

The venturi meter

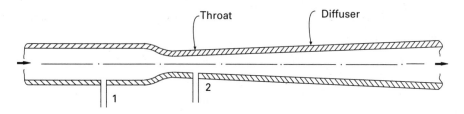

17

The venturi meter consists of a rapid convergence in a pipe, followed by a short throat of constant cross-section and then a diverging 'diffuser' section whose final diameter is the same as that of the pipe in which the meter is mounted. At the throat 2 the velocity is higher, so the pressure is lower, than the upstream values at 1. Measuring the pressure difference allows the velocity of the flow to be calculated, and so the discharge.

We have already done an example on a shaped pipe of this kind (Frame 51 of the previous programme), but just to remind you here is another.

The diameters at points 1 and 2 are $d_1 = 80$ mm, $d_2 = 40$ mm. An incompressible fluid of density 900 kg/m³ is flowing through the venturi, and the velocity at entry 1 is 3.5 m/s. What is the velocity at the throat 2? (Assume the velocities are uniform over the cross-section.)

$$\boxed{14 \text{ m/s}}$$

The ratio of the diameters is two, so the ratio of the areas is four. Since the volume flow rate is the same at both places, the velocity at the throat 2 must be four times that at the entry 1, i.e. $4 \times 3.5 = 14$ m/s.

Now, with this flow, use Bernoulli's equation to find the pressure difference between points 1 and 2, assuming no losses due to friction etc.

19

$$\boxed{82.7 \text{ kN/m}^2}$$

We can write Bernoulli's equation without the z terms, because the venturi is horizontal:

$$p_1 + \tfrac{1}{2}\rho u_1^2 = p_2 + \tfrac{1}{2}\rho u_2^2$$
$$p_1 - p_2 = \tfrac{1}{2}\rho(u_2^2 - u_1^2)$$
$$= \tfrac{1}{2} \times 900 \, (14^2 - 3.5^2)$$
$$= 82.7 \times 10^3 \text{ N/m}^2$$

This is all quite straightforward, but usually we want to do the calculation the other way round, i.e. to deduce the velocity having first measured the pressure difference. If the areas at points 1 and 2 are A_1 and A_2, then $A_1 u_1 = A_2 u_2$, since the volume flow rate is the same at both places. Therefore, assuming no losses,

$$p_1 - p_2 = \tfrac{1}{2}\rho(u_2^2 - u_1^2) = \tfrac{1}{2}\rho \left[u_2^2 - \left(\frac{A_2}{A_1} u_2 \right)^2 \right]$$

$$p_1 - p_2 = \tfrac{1}{2}\rho u_2^2 \left[1 - \left(\frac{A_2}{A_1} \right)^2 \right]$$

Here is an example: for the same venturi and fluid as above, if the pressure difference is 27 kN/m², we wish to find the velocity u_2 at the throat.

Substituting in the equation above,

$$27 \times 10^3 = \tfrac{1}{2} \times 900 \times u_2^2 \left(1 - \left(\tfrac{1}{4} \right)^2 \right) = \tfrac{1}{2} \times 900 \times u_2^2 \times \frac{15}{16}$$

$$u_2^2 = \frac{27 \times 10^3 \times 16}{450 \times 15} = 64$$

$$u_2 = 8.0 \text{ m/s}$$

Now one for you to try: for the same venturi once again, but now passing a liquid of density of 950 kg/m³, find the velocity u_2 at the throat (assuming no losses) when the pressure difference is 64 kN/m².

$$u_2 = 12 \text{ m/s}$$

Once again we can use the expression we derived from the Bernoulli and continuity equations on the previous page:

$$p_1 - p_2 = \tfrac{1}{2}\rho u_2^2 \left[1 - \left(\frac{A_1}{A_2} \right)^2 \right]$$

$$64 \times 10^3 = \tfrac{1}{2} \times 950 \times u_2^2 \times \left(1 - \frac{1}{16} \right)$$

$$u_2^2 = \frac{2 \times 64 \times 10^3 \times 16}{950 \times 15} = 143.7$$

$$u_2 = 12 \text{ m/s}$$

Knowing that the diameter d_2 at the throat is 40 mm, and assuming the velocity is uniform over the whole cross-section, we can now find the volume flow rate, which is ...?

$$15.1 \text{ l/s}$$

Here is the working: the volume flow rate is

$$Q = A_2 u_2$$
$$= (\pi d_2^2/4) u_2$$
$$= \pi \times [(40 \times 10^{-3})^2/4] \times 12$$
$$= 15.1 \times 10^{-3} \text{ m}^3/\text{s}$$
$$= 15.1 \text{ l/s}$$

Venturi meters are sometimes mounted in pipes which are vertical or inclined, rather than horizontal. In the next frame we see what difference this makes to the use of the meter, so *turn over now*.

22

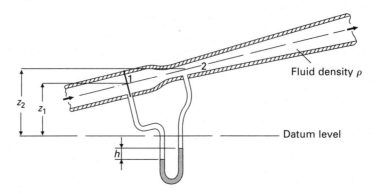

Fluid density ρ

z_2 z_1

Datum level

h

The static tappings at the throat 2 and the upstream section 1 are connected to a manometer. The fluid in the pipe has density ρ, and the manometer fluid has density ρ_M.

When there is no flow and the fluid is everywhere stationary, the situation is just as it was with the pitot tube in Frame 8: all is in equilibrium, so the difference between the levels of the fluid in the two legs of the manometer is …?

23

> Zero: there is no difference

When the fluid is everywhere in equilibrium, the pressure must be the same at all points on a given horizontal plane, so the levels of the fluid in the two legs of the manometer must be the same.

The difference in the levels when the fluid *is* flowing can only be due to the motion of the fluid, in other words to the difference between the *dynamic* pressures at points 1 and 2.

The pressure difference indicated by the manometer is $(\rho_M - \rho)gh$. This must be equal to the change of dynamic pressure $\frac{1}{2}\rho(u_2^2 - u_1^2)$ as the fluid flows from point 1 to point 2.

This result is quite straightforward, but it needs to be justified; we will do this in the next frame.

24

Applying Bernoulli's equation between points 1 and 2:

$$p_1 + \tfrac{1}{2}\rho u_1^2 + \rho g z_1 = p_2 + \tfrac{1}{2}\rho u_2^2 + \rho g z_2$$

Rearranging:

$$(p_1 + \rho g z_1) - (p_2 + \rho g z_2) = \tfrac{1}{2}\rho(u_2^2 - u_1^2)$$

The right-hand side of this is the change of dynamic pressure between points 1 and 2.

In leg 1 of the manometer U-tube, the increase in the hydrostatic pressure between point 1 and the datum level is $\rho g z_1$, so the pressure at the datum level is $(p_1 + \rho g z_1)$. Likewise the pressure at the datum level in the other leg of the manometer is $(p_2 + \rho g z_2)$. Thus the left-hand side of the equation represents the difference between the pressures in the two legs of the manometer: this is, of course, the pressure indicated by the manometer, which is $(\rho_m - \rho)gh$.

So, the pressure difference indicated by the manometer is equal to the difference in the dynamic pressures at points 1 and 2, and is not affected at all by the angle at which the venturi meter is mounted. It can be horizontal, vertical or inclined at any angle: provided the flow rate remains the same, the manometer reading will be unchanged.

Move on now to the next frame, and an example on an inclined venturi.

25

Referring to the diagram in Frame 22 on the opposite page, we will suppose that the fluid flowing through the venturi meter is water, and that mercury is used in the manometer (the relative density of mercury is 13.6).

If the levels of the mercury differ by 470 mm, what pressure difference is indicated by the manometer?

26

$$\boxed{58.1 \ \text{kN/m}^2}$$

The pressure difference indicated by the manometer is given by $(\rho_m - \rho)gh$, which in this case is equal to

$$(13.6 - 1) \times 1000 \times 9.81 \times 0.47 = 58.1 \times 10^3 \ \text{N/m}^2$$
$$= 58.1 \ \text{kN/m}^2$$

The diameters for our venturi meter are as follows:

upstream diameter $d_1 = 100$ mm

throat diameter $d_2 = 60$ mm

so the ratio of the areas of cross-section at the throat and upstream is $(A_2/A_1) = \ldots?$

27

$$\boxed{0.36}$$

$$(A_2/A_1) = (d_2/d_1)^2 = (60/100)^2 = 0.36$$

Now find the velocity of the water at the throat, u_2. You can use the equation we obtained in Frame 19,

$$p_1 - p_2 = \tfrac{1}{2}\rho u_2^2 \left[1 - \left(\frac{A_2}{A_1} \right)^2 \right]$$

28

$$\boxed{11.6 \ \text{m/s}}$$

Working: using the equation quoted above,

$$58.1 \times 10^3 = \tfrac{1}{2} \times 1000 \times u_2^2 (1 - 0.36^2) = \tfrac{1}{2} \times 1000 \times u_2^2 \times 0.87$$
$$u_2^2 = 133.5$$
$$u_2 = 11.6 \ \text{m/s}$$

Finally, calculate the volume flow rate, assuming the velocity u_2 is the mean velocity over the whole cross-section at the throat.

$$\boxed{32.8 \text{ l/s}}$$

If the mean velocity of flow is 11.6 m/s, then the volume flow rate is

$$Q = A_2 u_2 = (\pi d_2^2 / 4) u_2 = (\pi \times 0.06^2 / 4) \times 11.6 = 32.8 \times 10^{-3} \text{ m}^3/\text{s}$$

which is more readily visualised when written as 32.8 l/s.

It is of course possible to derive a formula which will give the volume flow rate Q directly in terms of the difference between the levels in the manometer, but such formulae have drawbacks. They are quite lengthy, it is difficult to remember them correctly, and they do not provide any information on the intermediate steps in the calculation – the magnitude of the mean velocity, for instance. Unless you are doing a large number of such calculations, it is much safer to go back to the fundamental Bernoulli and continuity equations.

We have been assuming all the time that Bernoulli's equation is exactly satisfied – in particular, that there are no friction losses, and that velocities are uniform over the whole of each cross-section.

In reality, some energy is always dissipated by friction, and because of this the pressure drop between the upstream tapping 1 and the throat 2 is greater than that predicted by ideal theory.

Conversely, for a given measured pressure drop, the actual flow rate is less than the value we calculate from the continuity and Bernoulli equations.

Fortunately, the ratio of the actual discharge to the 'ideal' discharge calculated on the basis of frictionless flow varies very little over a wide range of conditions. We call this ratio the *coefficient of discharge*, denoted by the symbol C_d. Thus

$$\text{Actual discharge} = C_d \times \text{ideal discharge}$$

For the example we have just done, if the coefficient of discharge for the venturi is $C_d = 0.96$, what will be the value of the volume flow rate?

31

$$\boxed{31.5 \; \text{l/s}}$$

Here is the working: the discharge, or volume flow rate, calculated on the assumption that conditions are ideal (no friction losses, uniform velocity over the whole cross-section etc.) is 32.8 l/s.

If the coefficient of discharge is $C_d = 0.96$, then the actual discharge will be $(0.96 \times 32.8) = 31.5$ l/s.

Before we go on to the next topic, the next frame gives three straightforward examples for you to try.

Revision exercise: pitot tube, pitot-static tube and venturi meter

1 A pitot-static tube used in a stream of air of density 1.2 kg/m³ is connected to a U-tube manometer containing water. The difference in the levels of the water in the manometer is 75 mm. What is the speed of the air?

2 The velocity of flow of a liquid of density $\rho = 920$ kg/m³ is sensed by a pitot tube connected to a manometer containing mercury (density 13.6×10^3 kg/m³). When the liquid is flowing at a speed of 3.75 m/s, what is the difference in the levels of the mercury in the two legs of the tube?

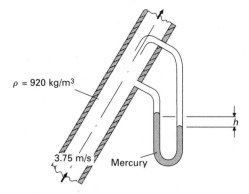

3 A venturi meter is fitted in a pipe carrying a liquid of density 1400 kg/m³. The manometer shown contains mercury. If the difference in the levels of the mercury is $h = 180$ mm, then assuming no losses (a) find the velocity of the liquid at the throat section; (b) find the discharge. Finally, (c) if the coefficient of discharge is $C_d = 0.97$ find the actual discharge.

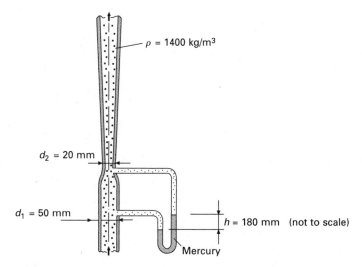

The solutions are given in the next frame – but don't turn over until you have answered all three questions.

33

Solutions

1 The pressure indicated by the manometer is $\rho gh = 1000 \times 9.81 \times 0.075$ $= 736 \text{ N/m}^2$. This is equal to the dynamic pressure $\frac{1}{2}\rho_{air}u^2$, so, equating,

$$\tfrac{1}{2} \times 1.2 \times u^2 = 736$$
$$u^2 = 2 \times 736/1.2 = 1226$$
$$u = 35 \text{ m/s}$$

2 When the liquid flows at 3.75 m/s, the dynamic pressure is

$$\tfrac{1}{2}\rho u^2 = \tfrac{1}{2} \times 920 \times 3.75^2 = 6469 \text{ N/m}^2$$

The pressure indicated by the manometer is $(\rho_m - \rho)gh$. Equating these:

$$(13.6 - 1) \times 1000 \times 9.81 \times h = 6469$$
$$h = 0.052 \text{ m}$$
$$= 52 \text{ mm}$$

3 The difference in the mercury levels is 180 mm, so the pressure indicated by the manometer is

$$(\rho_m - \rho)gh = (13.6 - 1) \times 1000 \times 9.81 \times 0.18 = 22.25 \times 10^3 \text{ N/m}^2$$

and this is equal to the dynamic pressure difference $\frac{1}{2}\rho(u_2^2 - u_1^2)$.
From continuity, $A_1 u_1 = A_2 u_2$, so $u_1 = u_2 \times (20/50)^2 = u_2 \times 0.16$. Therefore

$$\tfrac{1}{2}\rho[u_2^2 - (u_2 \times 0.16)^2] = 22.25 \times 10^3$$
$$\tfrac{1}{2} \times 1400 \times u_2^2 \times (1 - 0.16^2) = 22.25 \times 10^3$$
$$u_2^2 = 32.62$$
$$u_2 = 5.71 \text{ m/s} \tag{a}$$

The discharge is

$$A_2 u_2 = (\pi \times 0.01^2) \times 5.71 = 1.79 \times 10^{-3} \text{ m}^3/\text{s}$$
$$= 1.79 \text{ l/s} \tag{b}$$

Finally, if the coefficient of discharge is $C_d = 0.97$, the actual discharge is

$$0.97 \times 1.79 = 1.74 \text{ l/s} \tag{c}$$

This should be all clear now, so carry on to the next frame.

Flow through a sharp-edged orifice

34

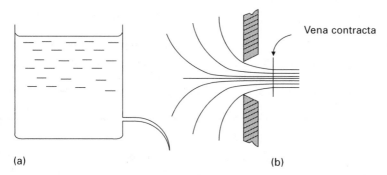

Vena contracta

(a)   (b)

Diagram (a) shows liquid issuing from a sharp-edged hole in the side of a tank. In diagram (b) we see a close-up view of the flow through the hole or orifice.

Inside the tank liquid approaches the orifice from all directions, as shown by the streamlines. The direction of motion of the liquid cannot change instantaneously, so, after it has emerged from the orifice, the jet continues to converge for some distance. In this converging part, the pressure is not uniform across the jet, and the velocity will not be uniform either.

After travelling a short distance (about half the diameter of the orifice) the jet does become parallel. The point where it first becomes parallel is called the *vena contracta* (literally 'contracted vein', in Latin). At this point both the pressure and the velocity are uniform across the jet; the pressure is atmospheric, because the jet is in the open air.

You may remember the result for the velocity of a jet whose source is a tank of liquid when the orifice is a depth h below the surface. Try to recall the expression before you look at the next frame.

35

$$u = \sqrt{2gh}$$

We have answered this kind of question several times before, in the previous programme, and even if you couldn't recall the result a moment ago perhaps it comes back to you now you see it. If not, it would be a good idea to look back at Programme 4 and check over the section dealing with this, particularly Frames 63 and 64.

When you have satisfied yourself about this, move on to the next frame.

36

In the real world, nothing is ever perfect. Friction losses occur at the edge of the orifice and within the jet itself, so the actual velocity at the vena contracta will be slightly less than predicted by Bernoulli's equation. The ratio (actual velocity/ideal velocity) is called the *coefficient of velocity*, denoted by the symbol C_v.

Now try this example: a sharp-edged orifice is fitted in the side of a large tank of water, at a depth 2.6 m below the surface. Find the velocity of the water jet at the vena contracta, assuming that Bernoulli's equation is exactly satisfied; also find the actual velocity if the coefficient of velocity is $C_v = 0.98$.

37

> Velocity assuming no friction losses: 7.14 m/s
>
> Actual velocity: 7.00 m/s

Assuming ideal conditions (no friction losses etc.), the velocity at the vena contracta is

$$u = \sqrt{2gh} = \sqrt{2 \times 9.81 \times 2.6} = 7.14 \text{ m/s}$$

In reality, the velocity will be less than this in the ratio given by $C_v = 0.98$, so its true value will be $0.98 \times 7.14 = 7.00$ m/s.

The discharge may be found by multiplying together the velocity at the vena contracta and the area of the jet at that point. The area of the jet at the vena contracta is obviously less than that of the orifice: the ratio (area at vena contracta)/(area of orifice) is called the *coefficient of contraction*, denoted by the symbol C_c. The value of C_c depends very much on the shape of the edges of the orifice; if the edge is razor-sharp, then for a circular orifice the value of C_c is found to be between 0.61 and 0.66.

So, for a sharp-edged circular orifice whose diameter is 10 mm and coefficient of contraction C_c is 0.62, what is the area of cross-section of the jet at the vena contracta?

$$\boxed{48.7 \text{ mm}^2}$$

Here is the working: the area of the circular orifice is $\pi \times 5^2 = 78.5 \text{ mm}^2$; so the area at the vena contracta is $0.62 \times 78.5 = 48.7 \text{ mm}^2$.

The discharge, or volume flow rate, Q in the jet of liquid is then given by $Q = A \times u$, where A and u are the area and the velocity of the jet at the vena contracta. Substituting for A and u:

$$Q = [C_c \times (\text{area of orifice})] \times [C_v \times \sqrt{2gh}]$$
$$= (C_c \times C_v) \times (\text{area of orifice}) \times \sqrt{2gh}$$

The area of the orifice is easy to determine by measurement, and the ideal velocity $\sqrt{2gh}$ depends only on the depth h of liquid and is readily calculated. The combined coefficient $(C_c \times C_v)$ is called the *coefficient of discharge* C_d for the orifice (defined in a similar way to the coefficient of discharge for the venturi, Frame 30). Thus

$$Q = C_d \times (\text{area of orifice}) \times \sqrt{2gh}$$

Often it is sufficient to know the value of the coefficient of discharge C_d; we do not need the values of the coefficients of velocity and contraction if we are interested only in the discharge through the orifice. For a sharp-edged circular orifice the value of C_d is usually between 0.60 and 0.65.

Now try this example: a sharp-edged circular orifice of diameter 20 mm is fitted in the base of a tank of liquid (our work so far applies in just the same way whatever the direction in which the orifice discharges). The coefficient of discharge of the orifice is $C_d = 0.61$. When the depth of the liquid in the tank is 1.7 m, what is the discharge?

$$\boxed{1.11 \text{ l/s}}$$

The ideal velocity for this case is $\sqrt{2gh} = \sqrt{2 \times 9.81 \times 1.7} = 5.78$ m/s; the area of the orifice is $\pi \times 10^2 = 314 \text{ mm}^2$, so the discharge is

$$Q = 0.61 \times (314 \times 10^{-6}) \times 5.78 = 1.11 \times 10^{-3} \text{ m}^3/\text{s} = 1.11 \text{ l/s}$$

40

So, knowing the coefficient of discharge for a particular orifice, we are now able to calculate the discharge – the volume flow rate – through the orifice when it is supplied by a given head of liquid.

We ought to pause here, briefly, to consider how the values of the coefficients C_v, C_c and C_d may be found experimentally.

The true velocity of the jet of liquid emerging from an orifice set in the vertical side of a tank can be calculated from observations of the trajectory of the jet. The coefficient of velocity C_v is then determined by dividing this true velocity by the ideal value $\sqrt{2gh}$.

The true discharge may be found by catching the liquid in a container for a known time interval and weighing it to find out how much liquid has passed in that time. The volume of this liquid is then divided by the 'ideal discharge' (the product of the area of the orifice and the ideal velocity $\sqrt{2gh}$), to obtain the coefficient of discharge C_d.

The coefficient of contraction C_c can be found then from the relationship $C_d = C_v \times C_c$. Alternatively, one can attempt to measure the size of the jet at the vena contracta directly, usually by means of pins set in a ring around the jet. The pins are advanced until they almost touch the jet of liquid, then the ring is removed and the diameter of the circle between the pins is measured – but it is not easy to get a very accurate result by this method.

41

The values found for these coefficients depend mainly on the shape of the orifice. The contraction after the orifice can be virtually eliminated by shaping it as shown in the diagram below, so that the flow is already parallel before emerging from the orifice. C_c is then close to 1.0, but the coefficient of velocity C_v is much less than unity because of the effects of friction, both within the jet and more particularly along the walls.

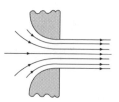

Consistent manufacture of orifices of this kind is not easy. Their shapes tend to vary slightly, and so the values both of C_c and, especially, of C_v will usually be found to vary slightly from one orifice to another. A sharp edge is relatively easy to make in a consistent way – this is why the sharp-edged orifice is much the most commonly used shape.

42

It is easy to observe liquid discharging through an orifice into the atmosphere – to see the vena contracta, and generally to watch how the jet of liquid behaves. We call this a *free jet*.

When liquid is discharged into more of the same liquid, or a gas into more of the same gas – called a *submerged jet* – it is impossible to observe the behaviour in this way. We may expect that the motion of the fluid just before and after the orifice will be similar to that of the free jet, and careful measurement shows that this is indeed so. There is a vena contracta, there are friction losses in the jet etc., and the coefficients of velocity, discharge and contraction have roughly the same values as for a free jet from an orifice of the same shape.

To find the velocity of the fluid leaving the submerged orifice, assuming that friction losses may be neglected, we use Bernoulli's equation. This is tackled in the next frame.

43

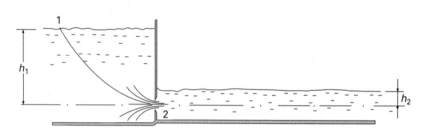

In the diagram a tank of liquid is discharging through a sharp-edged orifice directly into a reservoir of the same liquid.

At the vena contracta, where the streamlines are straight and parallel, the gauge pressure is that of the surrounding fluid, $\rho g h_2$. Applying Bernoulli's equation between points 1 and 2,

$$p_1 + \tfrac{1}{2}\rho u_1^2 + \rho g z_1 = p_2 + \tfrac{1}{2}\rho u_2^2 + \rho g z_2$$
$$0 + 0 + \rho g h_1 = \rho g h_2 + \tfrac{1}{2}\rho u_2^2 + 0$$
$$u_2 = \sqrt{2g(h_1 - h_2)}$$

So the 'ideal' velocity at the vena contracta, assuming no losses due to friction, depends on the *difference* of head across the orifice.

Referring to the diagram above, if the depths of the liquid above the orifice are $h_1 = 7.5$ m and $h_2 = 2.0$ m, what is the value of the velocity u_2 at the vena contracta, assuming no losses?

44

$$\boxed{10.4 \text{ m/s}}$$

Here is the working:

$$h_1 - h_2 = 7.5 - 2.0 = 5.5 \text{ m}$$
$$u_2 = \sqrt{2 \times 9.81 \times 5.5} = 10.4 \text{ m/s}$$

Now, if the diameter of the orifice is 24 mm and the coefficient of discharge is $C_d = 0.64$, find the discharge.

45

$$\boxed{3 \text{ l/s}}$$

The area of the orifice is $\pi \times 12^2 = 452 \text{ mm}^2$, so the discharge is

$$Q = 0.64 \times (452 \times 10^{-3}) \times 10.4 = 3.01 \times 10^{-3} \text{ m}^3/\text{s}$$
$$= 3 \text{ l/s approx}$$

The equation $u_2 = \sqrt{2g(h_1 - h_2)}$ is all very well when it is a liquid that is flowing through the orifice, but when the fluid flowing is a gas it is meaningless to speak in terms of heads h_1 and h_2, and a different form of the expression is needed. We deal with this in the next frame.

46

Air is passing from a large tank through the orifice shown in the diagram below, the pressures being p_1 on one side of the orifice and p_2 on the other.

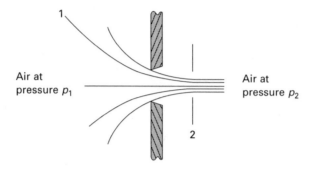

We can use Bernoulli's equation, provided the density of the air does not change significantly as it passes through the orifice (Bernoulli applies only to incompressible flow, remember – in other words, to flow where the density of the fluid remains constant). Since we are dealing with a gas, the $\rho g z$ terms in the equation will be negligible compared with the pressure and velocity terms. Thus

$$p_1 + \tfrac{1}{2}\rho u_1^2 = p_2 + \tfrac{1}{2}\rho u_2^2$$

The air originates in a large-volume tank, so the velocity u_1 at point 1 is small, and u_1^2 is negligible. Solving for u_2, we get

$$u_2 = \sqrt{\frac{2(p_1 - p_2)}{\rho}}$$

Now try this example: air of density 1.2 kg/m^3 is flowing through the nozzle shown in the diagram above. The pressure drop in passing through the orifice is 580 N/m^2. Assuming no losses, find the velocity of the air at the vena contracta.

$$\boxed{31.1 \text{ m/s}}$$

The velocity may be found directly by substituting in the equation given in the previous frame:

$$u_2 = \sqrt{\frac{2(p_1 - p_2)}{\rho}} = \sqrt{2 \times 580/1.2} = 31.1 \text{ m/s}$$

Our next topic – the final section of this programme – is orifice plates fitted in pipes, so turn over now.

48

Orifice meter

An orifice plate is often used in preference to a venturi as a pipe flow meter, because an orifice plate is more compact and less expensive (although, as we shall see later, they do have some disadvantages too).

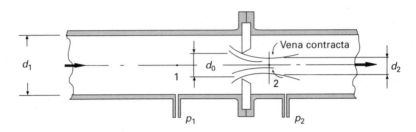

An orifice plate is shown, fitted in a horizontal pipe. Assuming for the moment that friction losses can be neglected, we can apply Bernoulli's equation:

$$p_1 + \tfrac{1}{2}\rho u_1^2 = p_2 + \tfrac{1}{2}\rho u_2^2$$

Rearranging:

$$p_1 - p_2 = \tfrac{1}{2}\rho(u_2^2 - u_1^2)$$

We can now eliminate u_1, using the continuity equation $A_1 u_1 = A_2 u_2$, where A_1 is the area of cross-section of the pipe upstream of the orifice, and A_2 is the area of the flow at the vena contracta. We get

$$p_1 - p_2 = \tfrac{1}{2}\rho u_2^2\left[1 - \left(\frac{A_2}{A_1}\right)^2\right]$$

so

$$u_2 = \sqrt{\frac{2(p_1 - p_2)}{\rho\left[1 - (A_2/A_1)^2\right]}}$$

The true value of the velocity at the vena contracta will be less than this ideal value; the ratio is given by the coefficient of velocity, C_v. The discharge is then $Q = A_2 u_2$, so

$$Q = A_2 C_v\sqrt{\frac{2(p_1 - p_2)}{\rho\left[1 - (A_2/A_1)^2\right]}}$$

This expression gives the true value of the discharge, allowing for the effect of friction losses, but it is not much use as it stands because the area A_2 at the vena contracta cannot be directly measured. Provided the value of the coefficient of contraction C_c is known (and measured values have been tabulated for certain standard shapes of orifice), we can replace the area A_2 by its equivalent $C_c A_o$, where A_o is the area of the orifice.

Continued in frame 49

49

This gives

$$Q = C_c A_o C_v \sqrt{\frac{2(p_1 - p_2)}{\rho\left[1 - (C_c A_o/A_1)^2\right]}}$$

which is a rather cumbersome expression – certainly not one we should expect to commit to memory.

To simplify the expression, what is usually done is to replace the effect of all the occurrences of coefficients C_c and C_v in the equation by a single constant multiplier, again called a coefficient of discharge and denoted by C_d:

$$Q = C_d A_o \sqrt{\frac{2(p_1 - p_2)}{\rho\left[1 - (A_o/A_1)^2\right]}}$$

This expression is still quite involved, but because of the way all the coefficients are taken care of by the one multiplier C_d there is no advantage in going back to first principles each time. (Note that this C_d is not the same as the C_d defined in Frame 38; it is not equal to the product of C_v and C_c.) This form of equation is used very widely in industrial practice for calculating the discharge through orifice plates. Usually the only variable on the right-hand side of the equation is the pressure difference $(p_1 - p_2)$, all the other terms being constants, so the equation is quite easy to use.

50

Example: a sharp-edged orifice plate is fitted at a joint in a pipe, as shown below. The coefficient of discharge for the orifice is $C_d = 0.61$.

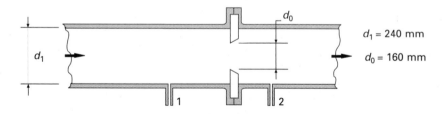

A liquid of density $\rho = 880$ kg/m^3 is passing along the pipe. We wish to find the volume flow rate when the pressure difference is $(p_1 - p_2) = 14$ kN/m^2. Substituting in the equation for Q:

$$Q = 0.61 \times (\pi \times 0.16^2/4)\sqrt{\frac{2 \times 14\,000}{880(1 - (160/240)^4)}} = 0.076 \text{ m}^3/\text{s} = 76 \text{ l/s}$$

Notice that $(A_o/A_1)^2 = (d_o/d_1)^4$: don't forget the fourth power!

Turn over now to the next frame, where there is an example for you to do.

51

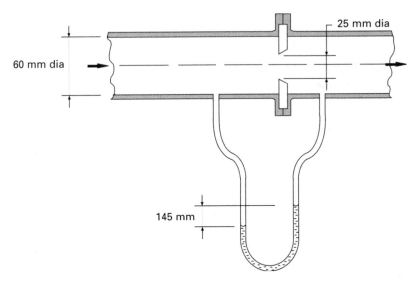

60 mm dia

25 mm dia

145 mm

A gas of density ρ = 4.8 kg/m³ is flowing along the pipe shown. The manometer fluid is paraffin (density 830 kg/m³) and the difference in the levels of the paraffin in the legs of the manometer is 145 mm. If the coefficient of discharge is C_d = 0.603, find (a) the volume flow, and (b) the mass flow rate of the gas.

52

(a) 6.67×10^{-3} m³/s; (b) 32.0×10^{-3} kg/s

Working: the pressure difference is $\rho gh = 830 \times 9.81 \times 0.145 = 1180$ N/m²

$$\left[1 - \left(\frac{A_o}{A_1}\right)^2\right] = \left[1 - \left(\frac{25}{60}\right)^4\right] = (1 - 0.030) = 0.970$$

and

$$A_o = \pi \times 25^2/4 = 491 \text{ mm}^2$$

so

$$Q = C_d A_o \sqrt{\frac{2(p_1 - p_2)}{\rho\left[1 - (A_o/A_1)^2\right]}}$$

$$= 0.603 \times (491 \times 10^{-6})\sqrt{\frac{2 \times 1180}{4.8\,(0.970)}}$$

$$= 6.67 \times 10^{-3} \text{ m}^3/\text{s}$$

The mass flow rate is $\rho Q = 4.8 \times 6.67 \times 10^{-3} = 32.0 \times 10^{-3}$ kg/s.
Carry on now to the next frame.

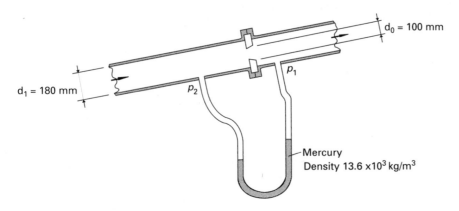

Orifice flow meters are often used in pipes which are not horizontal. In these cases we can reason in exactly the same way as with the venturi meter: when no flow is taking place, all of the fluid is in equilibrium and the manometer levels are the same, indicating no pressure difference. It is only when flow is occurring that the manometer levels differ – the indicated pressure difference is then equal to the difference in the dynamic pressure between points 1 and 2. This pressure difference shown on the manometer is not affected in the slightest by the angle at which the pipe is mounted. (If you want to refer back, Frames 22–24 of this programme are the relevant ones.)

Example: for the installation shown in the diagram above, the pressure difference across the orifice plate, for which the coefficient of discharge is $C_d = 0.610$, is sensed by a mercury manometer. Ethyl alcohol, of density 790 kg/m^3, is flowing along the pipe, and also fills the manometer tubes above the mercury. When the mercury levels differ by 220 mm, what is the volume flow rate of the ethyl alcohol, expressed in l/min ?

$$\boxed{2340 \text{ l/min}}$$

For this example, the pressure difference is

$$(\rho_M - \rho)gh = (13.6 - 0.79) \times 1000 \times 9.81 \times 0.22$$
$$= 27.6 \times 10^3 \text{ N/m}^2$$

Therefore the flow rate is

$$Q = 0.610 \times (\pi \times 0.05^2)\sqrt{\frac{2 \times 27.6 \times 10^3}{790 \left[1 - (100/180)^4\right]}}$$
$$= 0.039 \text{ m}^3/\text{s} = 39 \text{ l/s} = 2340 \text{ l/min}$$

55

One of the disadvantages of orifice flow meters is that the fall of pressure in the fluid as it accelerates through the orifice is not matched by a similar increase of pressure as the fluid slows down again.

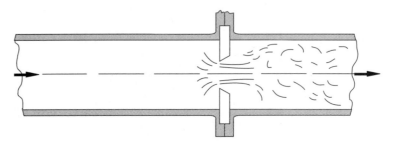

The high-speed fluid leaving the orifice mixes with the surrounding slower-moving fluid in disorderly eddies, and most of the kinetic energy is dissipated by viscous action. Bernoulli's equation certainly does not apply in this region!

56

Usually the pressure hardly rises at all after the vena contracta, and a substantial amount of energy may be required to maintain the flow. To find just how much energy is needed, consider a slug of fluid in a pipe with an orifice plate:

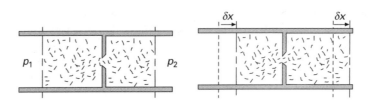

The fluid moves a distance δx in time δt. If the cross-sectional area of the pipe is A, the volume traversed in time δt is $A\delta x$, so the discharge is $Q = A \, dx/dt$.

The net force on the slug of fluid is $(p_1 A - p_2 A) = (p_1 - p_2)A$, so the work done in moving distance δx is $(p_1 - p_2)A \, \delta x$.

The power is the work done per unit time: $(p_1 - p_2)A \, \delta x/\delta t = (p_1 - p_2)Q$. We see that the power required to keep the fluid flowing through the orifice is given by the product of the pressure drop and the discharge.

In our previous example, in Frame 54, we found that, for a discharge of $0.039 \text{ m}^3/\text{s}$, the pressure drop through the orifice was $27.6 \times 10^3 \text{ N/m}^2$. So what power is needed in this case?

$$\boxed{1.08 \text{ kW}}$$

The power needed is given by the product

$$(p_1 - p_2)\, Q = (27.6 \times 10^3) \times 0.039 = 1.08 \times 10^3 \text{ W or } 1.08 \text{ kW}$$

We see then that a pipe system containing several orifice flow meters may require pumps to supply considerable amounts of energy to keep the flow going. Venturi meters cause much less pressure drop, so are preferable in this respect.

A second important drawback of orifice meters is that the value of the coefficient of discharge can vary significantly if the form of the edge of the orifice alters; this can easily happen if the fluid is abrasive or corrosive. A venturi meter is much less susceptible to this, because the throat diameter is likely to alter only very slightly over the life of the venturi.

On the other hand, an orifice meter is much less expensive than a venturi.

Comparing the orifice and venturi meters:

Orifice meter	*Venturi meter*
Relatively inexpensive	Quite expensive
Large pressure drop	Small pressure drop
C_d may change with time	C_d virtually constant

Despite their drawbacks, orifice flow meters are very widely used.

58

The purpose of the diffuser in a venturi meter is to ensure gradual and orderly deceleration after the throat, so that the pressure rises again to somewhere near its original value. The angle of the diffuser cone is generally 6° to 8°. With a wider angle than this there is some risk that the flow will separate (diagram (a) below), become disorderly, and give increased pressure loss; with a narrower angle the diffuser becomes needlessly long and the pressure loss increases due to friction with the walls.

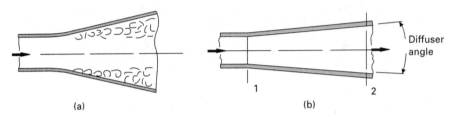

(a)   (b)

Consider the diffuser shown in diagram (b) above. Assuming for the moment that there are no losses, Bernoulli's equation will be obeyed, so

$$p_1 + \tfrac{1}{2}\rho u_1^2 = p_2 + \tfrac{1}{2}\rho u_2^2$$
$$p_2 - p_1 = \tfrac{1}{2}\rho(u_1^2 - u_2^2)$$

In practice the increase of pressure $(p_2 - p_1)$ is always less than Bernoulli suggests. The ratio of the actual increase in pressure to the ideal increase, i.e. to the reduction in the dynamic pressure, is called the *diffuser efficiency:*

$$\text{diffuser efficiency } \eta = \frac{\text{increase in pressure across the diffuser}}{\text{decrease in dynamic pressure}}$$

Diffuser efficiencies of 80% or better can be achieved when the inner surface of the conical walls is smooth and the cone angle is in the range 6° to 8°.

The next frame has a worked example on this.

Taking once again the situation described in Frame 53, where ethyl alcohol of density 790 kg/m^3 is flowing along a pipe of diameter $d_1 = 180$ mm, we will now investigate what happens if a venturi is used instead of an orifice flow meter.

We will select a venturi that gives roughly the same pressure difference as the orifice plate. This requires the throat area of the venturi to be the same as the area A_2 of the vena contracta of the orifice. The orifice diameter is 100 mm and the coefficient of contraction (though not stated in the original frame) is approximately $C_c = 0.60$, and so the area of the vena contracta is $0.60 \times \pi \times 100^2/4$ mm^2. If the throat diameter of the venturi is d_2, we have

$$\pi d_2^2/4 = 0.60 \times \pi \times 100^2/4$$
$$d_2 = 100\sqrt{0.60} = 77.5 \text{ mm}$$

With this geometry, the change of dynamic pressure from the throat 2 to the exit 3 of the diffuser will be

$$\tfrac{1}{2}\rho(u_2^2 - u_3^2) = \tfrac{1}{2} \times 790 \times \left[\left(\frac{Q}{A_2}\right)^2 - \left(\frac{Q}{A_3}\right)^2\right]$$
$$= \tfrac{1}{2} \times 790 \times 0.039^2 \left(\frac{1}{[\pi \times 77.5^2/4]^2} - \frac{1}{[\pi \times 180^2/4]^2}\right)$$
$$= 26.1 \times 10^3 \text{ N/m}^2$$

We will suppose that the efficiency of the diffuser part of the venturi is 0.8, or 80%. Then the pressure recovery in the diffuser is 80% of the change in dynamic pressure, so the pressure 'lost' across the venturi is 20% of the change in dynamic pressure.

With the flow rate $Q = 0.039$ m^3/s, find the power then required to cause the fluid to pass through the venturi.

60

$$\boxed{204 \text{ W}}$$

The pressure loss across the venturi is 20% of the change in dynamic pressure, that is 0.2×26.1 kN/m^2 or 5.22 kN/m^2.

The power required for the flow is then

$$\text{(pressure drop)} \times \text{discharge} = (5.22 \times 10^3) \times 0.039 = 204 \text{ W}$$

which is a considerable improvement on the 1.08 kW needed for the orifice.

This concludes Programme 5: the next frame is a revision summary.

61

Revision summary

1 *Stagnation point*: a point at which particles of fluid come almost to a standstill. When fluid flows round a body, there is always a stagnation point at the leading edge.

2 *Dynamic pressure*: the increase of pressure that occurs when moving fluid is brought to a standstill: equal to $\frac{1}{2}\rho u^2$.

3 *Stagnation pressure* or *total pressure*: the pressure at a stagnation point: equal to $(p + \frac{1}{2}\rho u^2)$, where p is the upstream static pressure.

4 *Pitot tube*: a small tube facing into the oncoming flow of fluid, used to sense the total pressure.

5 *Pitot-static tube*: a pitot tube with the addition of extra holes and a second tube so that the static pressure can be sensed as well as the dynamic.

6 *Diffuser*: a gradually diverging section of pipe, in which the flow velocity gradually decreases as the area increases. The intention is that flow should remain approximately uniform across the width of the tube and not separate from the walls.

7 *Diffuser efficiency*: defined as (increase in pressure across the diffuser)/(decrease in dynamic pressure). Efficiencies of 80% or more can be achieved in well-designed and made diffusers.

8 *Venturi meter*: a rapid convergence in a pipe, followed by a short throat and then a diverging diffuser section. Pressure tappings are provided upstream of the convergence and at the throat.

9 *Vena contracta*: the point where the flow in a jet issuing from an orifice first becomes parallel. At the vena contracta both the pressure and the velocity are uniform across the jet; the pressure is the same as that of the surrounding fluid.

10 *Free jet* and *submerged jet*: a jet of liquid issuing from an orifice into gaseous surroundings, such as the atmosphere, is called a free jet. When the jet of fluid (whether a liquid or a gas) is discharged into more of the same fluid, this is called a submerged jet.

11 *Orifice meter*: a section of pipe fitted with an orifice through which the flow passes, and provided with pressure tappings both upstream of and downstream of the orifice.

12 *Coefficient of velocity, C_v*: the ratio (actual velocity/ideal velocity), the ideal velocity being calculated on the assumption that no viscous losses occur.

13 *Coefficient of contraction, C_c*: used in relation to a jet of fluid emerging from an orifice or a nozzle, this is the ratio (area of flow at the vena contracta/area of the orifice or nozzle).

14 *Coefficient of discharge, C_d*: the ratio (actual discharge/ideal discharge). For a venturi, the ideal discharge is calculated assuming no viscous losses. For an orifice plate, it is calculated assuming no viscous losses and also that the area of the flow at the vena contracta is the same as the orifice area, in other words that $C_c = 1.0$.

When you have read and absorbed the content of this programme, try the test exercise in the next frame.

Test exercise

1 The flow rate of water along a pipe is continuously measured by a simple pitot tube and a static tapping in the pipe wall. The two tubes are connected to the two arms of an inverted manometer containing oil of density 840 kg/m³ as shown in the left-hand diagram below, and the difference in the levels in the manometer is 64 mm. Estimate the speed of flow of the water.

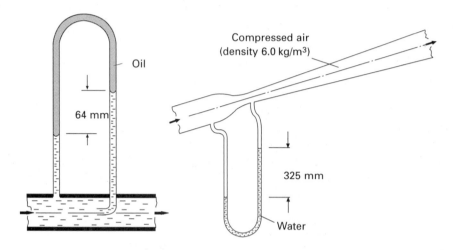

2 In the inclined venturi shown on the right above, the upstream pipework diameter is 75 mm and the throat diameter is 30 mm. Compressed air of density 6.0 kg/m³ is flowing along the pipe. Assuming the density does not vary appreciably, estimate (a) the speed of the air at the throat, and (b) the mass flow rate of the air. The coefficient of discharge is 0.98.

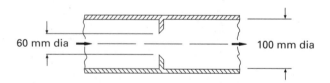

3 Liquid of density 950 kg/m³ is to flow at a discharge rate of 700 l/min along the pipe shown, and the orifice plate is to be used to monitor the flow rate. The coefficient of contraction C_c is 0.64, and the coefficient of velocity C_v is approximately 1.0. Estimate (a) the pressure drop across the orifice plate, and (b) the pumping power needed.

63

Further problems

1 A pitot-static tube in a wind tunnel records a pressure difference of 30 mm water. If the air density is 1.20 kg/m³, what is the air velocity in the wind tunnel?

2 The pipe shown below carries oil of density 790 kg/m³. A pitot tube is fitted in the pipe as shown, and a manometer is used to compare the pressure sensed by the pitot tube to the static pressure in the pipe. The U-tube manometer contains water, with the oil above.

For the situation shown in the figure, what is the velocity of the oil at the centre of the pipe?

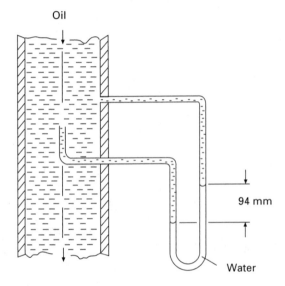

Oil

94 mm

Water

3 A venturi flowmeter is mounted in an inclined pipe carrying benzene of density 890 kg/m^3, as shown in the diagram below. A manometer containing mercury with benzene above is used to indicate the pressure difference between conditions upstream and at the venturi throat. The upstream pipe diameter is 100 mm, and the diameter at the throat is 40 mm; other dimensions are as shown. Estimate the volume flow rate of the benzene.

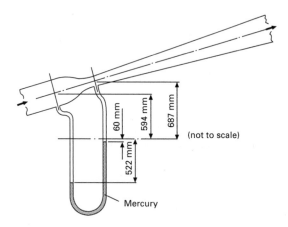

4 In a certain chemical plant a sharp-edged orifice is used to measure the flow rate of ethyl alcohol along a pipe, as shown in the diagram below. The pressure difference across the orifice is indicated by a U-tube manometer with ethyl alcohol over mercury. Calculate this pressure difference. The density of ethyl alcohol is 790 kg/m^3.

The coefficient of discharge of the orifice is 0.64. Estimate the volume flow rate of ethyl alcohol along the pipe.

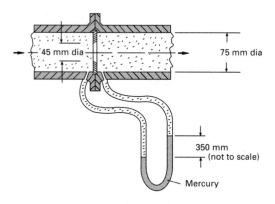

Programme 6

FORCES AND
MOMENTUM OF MOVING FLUIDS

1

We know that moving fluids can exert forces. The lift forces that support an aircraft are exerted by the air flowing across the wings; a rocket works by burning fuel and expelling the hot products of combustion at high speed; in some countries the force of a jet of water is used to disperse rioters.

We will begin by considering a rocket which is being tested while attached to a fixed support.

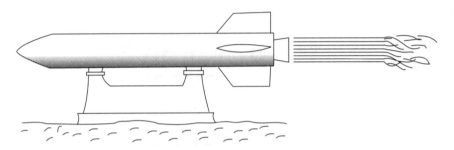

As the fuel burns, large volumes of hot gases are generated and expelled. The gaseous matter is being continuously accelerated to the right (see the diagram above), so it must be subject to a continuous force to the right.

In which direction is the force that the gases exert on the rocket?

2

To the left

This is fairly obvious, since we can see from the diagram that the rocket would move to the left if it were not fastened down: it clearly must experience a force to the left.

This is an example of the operation of Newton's Third Law, which tells us that every force has an equal and opposite reaction: the rocket pushes the gases to the right, and the gases push the rocket to the left.

3

Now, let's imagine we are the engineers who have designed the rocket. Before testing the rocket on the test rig, we shall already have a pretty good idea of the rate at which the fuel will burn; knowing this, we can estimate by calculation how large the thrust on the rocket will be.

We shall need to use Newton's Second Law, but if we try to use this law in the form $F = ma$, we get into difficulties because it is not clear what mass of moving fluid we should use.

The way out of this is to go back to Newton's Second Law more nearly in its original form: 'The rate of change of _____ of a body is equal to the resultant force acting on the body, and takes place in the direction of the force'.

You probably know this form of Newton's Second Law, but we have left a word out. Can you fill in the missing word?

4

Momentum

Here is the complete statement: the rate of change of momentum of a body is equal to the resultant force acting on the body, and takes place in the direction of the force.

Of course fluid is not a 'body' in the normal sense of the word, but a quantity of fluid obeys Newton's Laws just as a solid body does.

Now, let's see if we can work out what the rate of change of momentum is in this case. The rocket itself, and the unburnt fuel within it, remain stationary and therefore have no momentum. But as the fuel burns it turns into gases, which are expelled with high velocity and certainly do have momentum. First of all, we need to know the mass flow rate in the rocket exhaust – we shall represent this by the symbol $\dot{m}$ (short for dm/dt, just as $\dot{x}$ is sometimes written instead of dx/dt). The SI units of the mass flow rate will be kg/s.

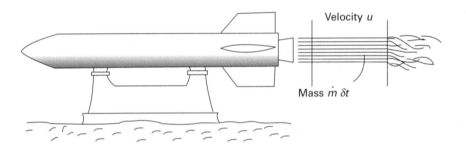

In a short time interval δt the mass ejected is $\dot{m}\,\delta t$, and its velocity is u to the right. What is the momentum of this mass of gas?

5

$\dot{m}u\,\delta t$, to the right

The momentum is the product of the mass $\dot{m}\,\delta t$ and the velocity u. Remember that momentum is a vector quantity, so we should *always* state the direction as well as the magnitude.

So, the gases ejected in time δt have momentum $\dot{m}u\,\delta t$ to the right.

Can you now see at what *rate* the gases gain momentum to the right?

6

$$\boxed{\dot{m}u}$$

The rate of gaining momentum is equal to the momentum gained in a short time, divided by the time:

$$\text{Rate of gaining momentum to the right} = (\dot{m}u\,\delta t)/\delta t$$

$$= \dot{m}u$$

According to Newton's Second Law, the gases must therefore be subject to a force $\dot{m}u$ to the right: and, by Newton's Third Law, the rocket experiences a force $\dot{m}u$ to the left. This force is the thrust.

Now try this numerical example: a fixed rocket expels exhaust products at a rate 3.7 kg/s with velocity 550 m/s. What is the thrust on the rocket?

7

$$\boxed{2.04 \text{ kN}}$$

Working: the thrust on the rocket is given by

$$\text{Thrust} = \dot{m}u = 3.7 \times 550$$

$$= 2035 \text{ N}$$

Before going on we should check that the units are correct, rather than just assuming that the answer comes out in newtons automatically. On the left-hand side we have $\dot{m}u$, whose units are (kg/s) $\times$ (m/s), or (kg m/s^2). This doesn't look much like newtons, on the face of it. But if we think about the equation $F = ma$, we know that the equation tells us the force acting when a mass m has acceleration a. If m is measured in kg units and a is measured in m/s^2, then the right-hand side of the equation is in kg m/s^2 units; to be consistent, the left-hand side must have the same units. For measuring forces, a unit like kg m/s^2 would seem very clumsy, so we give this a name of its own, the newton. Thus kg m/s^2 and newtons are just different ways of writing the same unit, so the units in our calculation above are correct.

Turn on now to the next frame, in which we look at a different example of a force exerted by moving fluid.

8

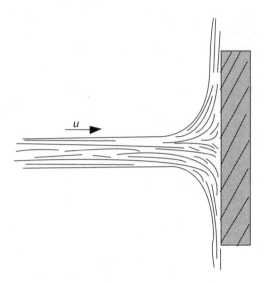

The diagram above shows a jet of water striking a stationary flat surface – a rioter's back, for example, or a steel plate.

The water jet approaches the surface with speed u to the right. Once again the mass flow rate is $\dot{m}$. As it reaches the surface, the water moves off in all directions over the surface, without bouncing back (try running water on to the back of a dinner plate if you don't believe it!)

We know from experience that the water exerts a force to the right on the surface.

In which direction is the force that the surface exerts on the water?

9

> To the left

Newton's Third Law tells us that, if the water pushes the surface to the right, the surface pushes the water to the left.

Now let us consider how the momentum of the water changes. At first the water is moving to the right, all with velocity u, so its momentum is to the right. After reaching the plate, the water is deflected equally in all directions along the surface. The momentum of the particles that move upwards is balanced by that of the particles that move downwards, and the same applies to the sideways directions; overall the momentum of the water leaving the surface sums to zero.

The situation is like that of the rocket, but in the opposite order: the water *arrives* with speed u to the right and mass flow rate $\dot{m}$, and *leaves* with no overall momentum at all.

What is the rate of change of momentum in this case?

10

> $\dot{m}u$ to the left

The argument here is similar to that for the rocket. The momentum of the water arriving in the jet in time δt is $\dot{m}u\,\delta t$, and this is all destroyed by the plate. Thus the rate of change of momentum is from (initially) $\dot{m}u$ to the right to (finally) zero, i.e. the change is $\dot{m}u$ to the left.

Therefore the water must experience a force $\dot{m}u$ to the left, and it exerts a force on the surface $\dot{m}u$ to the right.

Here are some numerical values: if the velocity of the water jet is 35 m/s and the mass flow rate is 7.2 kg/s, what is the force exerted on the surface by the water?

11

> 252 N to the right

Working:

$$\text{the force on the plate} = \dot{m}u$$
$$= 7.2 \times 35$$
$$= 252 \text{ N to the right}$$

This calculation should be quite straightforward. Note that we are always taking care to state the direction of the force, as well as its magnitude.

We should always do this with quantities like force, velocity, acceleration and momentum because they are not scalars but ...?

12

> Vectors

...and vector quantities have direction as well as magnitude. Vectors are not properly specified unless both the direction and the magnitude are given.

With the rocket, the fluid started off with zero momentum, and in the example of the water jet hitting the plate the fluid ended up with zero momentum. Now we turn to a case where the fluid has momentum both as it arrives and as it leaves.

13

The diagram below shows a jet engine on an aircraft flying at speed 210 m/s. The air velocities shown are as observed from the aircraft.

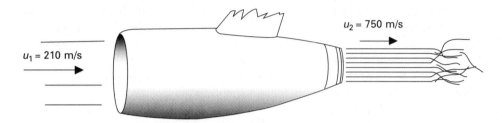

The mass flow rate of air through the engine is $\dot{m} = 52$ kg/s. We wish to find the thrust of the engine.

As before, the thrust is equal to the rate of change of momentum of the fluid – in this case, of the air passing through the engine. (In fact, the mass flow rate of the exhaust is slightly larger than that of the intake air, because the mass of the fuel used has to be added, but the proportion of fuel is small, usually no more than 1/40 of the mass of the air. In this example we will keep things as simple as possible by ignoring the increased mass flow of the jet exhaust.)

Assuming that the mass flow rate is 52 kg/s for both the intake and the jet exhaust, can you calculate the thrust of the engine?

14

$$\boxed{28.1 \text{ kN}}$$

Working: the force exerted by the engine on the air is equal to the rate of change of momentum.

The momentum of the air entering the engine is to the right, and that of the jet exhaust is also to the right. Because the directions of these two momentum quantities are the same, the rate of change is simply the difference between their magnitudes.

$$\text{Rate of change of momentum} = \dot{m}u_2 - \dot{m}u_1$$
$$= 52(750 - 210)$$
$$= 28\,080 \text{ N to the right}$$

The thrust on the engine is equal and opposite to this, i.e. 28.1 kN to the left.

The next frame introduces another example.

15

A jet of water strikes a fixed vane, which deflects the water through an angle θ.

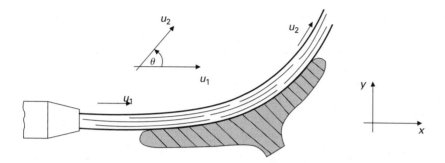

To find the force exerted on the vane, we shall use the momentum method once again; but because the entry and exit velocities are not in the same direction we cannot readily see in which direction the force on the vane will act.

A straightforward approach is to find the x and y components of the force. (We have chosen the x direction to be the same as that of the incoming velocity u_1.)

Being a vector quantity, a velocity can be resolved into components in just the same way as with a force. What are the x and y components of the exit velocity u_2?

16

$$\boxed{u_2 \cos \theta; \;\; u_2 \sin \theta}$$

This should be quite familiar.

Taking the y direction first, the water enters with no momentum component at all in this direction, and it leaves at a momentum rate of $\dot{m}u_2 \sin \theta$ in the y direction.

So what force component must be exerted on the water in the y direction?

17

$$\boxed{\dot{m}u_2 \sin \theta}$$

The reasoning is as follows: the momentum of the water in the y direction changes from zero initially to a rate of $\dot{m}u_2 \sin \theta$ at the exit. To produce this rate of change of momentum, a force $\dot{m}u_2 \sin \theta$ must be exerted on the water in the y direction.

Now let us look at the x direction: the momentum changes from a rate of $\dot{m}u_1$ initially to $\dot{m}u_2 \cos \theta$ at exit, so the rate of change of momentum of the water in the x direction is

$$(\dot{m}u_2 \cos \theta - \dot{m}u_1)$$

or

$$\dot{m}(u_2 \cos \theta - u_1)$$

Is this likely to be positive or negative?

18

$$\boxed{\text{Negative}}$$

The exit velocity u_2 is likely to be slightly less than the entry velocity u_1, because of friction, and $\cos \theta$ is certainly less than 1, so $(u_2 \cos \theta - u_1)$ is bound to be negative. In terms of the force on the water, this result confirms what experience probably tells us, that the x component of the force on the water is to the left in the diagram on the previous page, tending to slow the water down.

To fix this in our minds, we shall do a numerical example: the mass flow rate is $\dot{m} = 20$ kg/s and the velocities are $u_1 = 25$ m/s and $u_2 = 24$ m/s. If the angle of the vane is $\theta = 40°$, find the x and y components of the force exerted by the vane on the water.

> x component: -132 N; y component: 309 N

This is just a matter of substituting the numerical values into the expressions we derived earlier. These numbers are the forces exerted by the vane on the water in the x and y directions, and (as expected) the force on the water in the x direction is negative, i.e. the x component of the force exerted by the vane on the water is to the left.

The force components exerted by the water on the vane are equal and opposite to these, i.e. to the right and downwards.

Remembering that we can add these components together by the usual vector method of drawing a parallelogram or a triangle, can you find the magnitude and direction of the resultant force exerted by the water on the vane?

20

> 336 N at $66.9°$ to the x direction

Working: drawing a parallelogram of the forces on the vane:

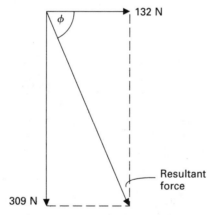

The two force components are perpendicular to each other, so our parallelogram is a rectangle. We can use Pythagoras' theorem to find the resultant force:

$$\text{Resultant force} = \sqrt{132^2 + 309^2}$$
$$= 336 \text{ N}$$

and angle ϕ is given by

$$\tan \phi = 309/132$$
$$\phi = 66.9°$$

21

When we wish to calculate the force on the vane, or the thrust of the jet engine, we only need to know the entry and exit velocities of the fluid together with the mass flow rate. In fact, we could draw a box round the vane or the jet engine and ignore what is inside – provided we know the entry and exit flows, we can calculate the force without needing to know anything at all about what is inside the box.

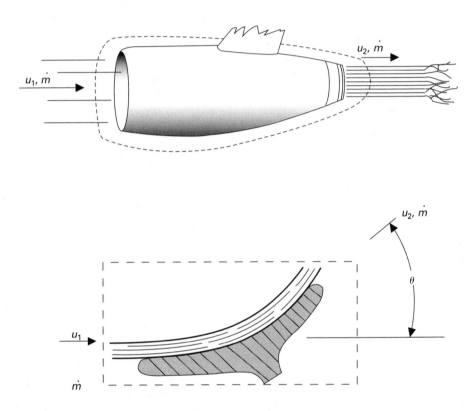

This idea was introduced back in Programme 4, when we were discussing *continuity* (in Frame 21 of that programme, to be exact), and indeed this kind of imaginary surface enclosing an object or system is often useful in fluid mechanics and other areas of engineering.

Can you recall what we call such an imaginary box?

22

| A control surface |

Referring to the upper diagram opposite: in Frame 14 we calculated the force to the right on the air passing through the jet engine as

$$(\dot{m}u_2 - \dot{m}u_1)$$

The quantity $\dot{m}u_1$ can be thought of as the rate at which momentum flows *into* the control surface; likewise, $\dot{m}u_2$ is the rate at which momentum flows *out of* the control surface.

Thus, the force on the air in this case is equal to (the rate of momentum outflow, $\dot{m}u_2$) – (the rate of momentum inflow, $\dot{m}u_1$).

This straightforward way of dealing with momentum examples works in every case. In the next frame we see how it applies to the water jet and the 40° vane.

23

This time we refer to the lower diagram in Frame 21. Once again, the force on the fluid is equal to (the rate of momentum outflow) – (the rate of momentum inflow), but we must remember that the quantities in brackets are *vectors*.

Unless they are in the same direction, as they were for the jet engine, we cannot simply subtract the magnitudes. We must resolve the momentum outflow and the momentum inflow into their x and y components, as we did in Frames 15–20. In the x direction, for example

Force on fluid in the x direction = (momentum outflow in the x direction) –

(momentum inflow in the x direction)

$$= \dot{m}u_2 \cos\theta - \dot{m}u_1$$

We could write a similar equation for the y direction, or indeed for any direction we care to choose.

Now turn over to the next frame, where we shall do another example.

24

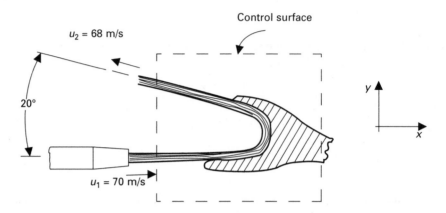

In the diagram above, a control surface has been drawn around another vane, but this time the water jet is turned through a much larger angle, namely 160°. The volume flow rate of the water is 14 l/s. We wish to find the x and y components of the force on the vane.

First of all, calculate the mass flow rate.

25

$$\boxed{14 \text{ kg/s}}$$

Working:

$$\text{mass flow rate} = \text{density} \times \text{volume flow rate}$$
$$= 1000 \times (14 \times 10^{-3})$$
$$= 14 \text{ kg/s}$$

(It is worth remembering that the mass of 1 litre of freshwater is 1 kg.)

Now, taking the y direction first, the rate of momentum outflow in this direction is $\dot{m}u_2 \sin 20°$, and the rate of momentum inflow is zero, because the water jet enters in the x direction.

So what is the magnitude of the force on the water in the y direction?

26

326 N

Working: the force on the water in the y direction is equal to (the momentum outflow rate in the y direction) – (the momentum inflow rate in the y direction). Thus:

$$\text{force on water in } y \text{ direction} = 14 \times 68 \sin 20° - 0$$
$$= 326 \text{ N}$$

Now for the x direction: the water arrives moving to the right, and leaves moving to the left. It has gained momentum to the left. In which direction must the x component of force on the water act, to the left or to the right?

27

To the left

The water gains momentum to the left, so the x force on the water must act to the left.

Next we need to calculate the magnitude of this x component of force. We must be careful about signs: the x direction is positive to the right, so in the x direction the rate of momentum outflow is $-\dot{m}u_2 \cos 20°$ (negative because its direction is to the left), and the rate of momentum inflow is $\dot{m}u_1$ (positive, because it is to the right).

Then the force on the water in the positive x direction must be equal to (momentum outflow rate in the x direction) – (momentum inflow rate in the x direction), which is

$$(-\dot{m}u_2 \cos 20°) - (\dot{m}u_1)$$

The magnitude of this is

$$\dot{m}(u_2 \cos 20° + u_1)$$

The sign is negative; this is as it should be, because the force on the water must act towards the left.

28

As to the size of the force needed, we can think of it like this: the vane has to exert a force on the water to the left sufficient *both* to destroy all its initial momentum, *and* to produce the final momentum to the left.

To destroy the initial momentum requires a force $\dot{m}u_1$ to the left; to produce the final momentum the vane must exert a further force $\dot{m}u_2 \cos 20°$, also to the left. So the total force exerted on the water in the x direction is

$$(\dot{m}u_1 + \dot{m}u_2 \cos 20°) \text{ to the left}$$

just as we worked out more formally in the last frame.

Now, put in the numerical values (given in Frames 24 and 25) and calculate the size of the x component.

29

$$\boxed{1.88 \text{ kN}}$$

There should have been no difficulty about this.

Vanes like these can be used in a water turbine: the vanes are arranged around the outside of a disc-shaped rotor, and a jet of water is used to propel the vanes, so turning the rotor.

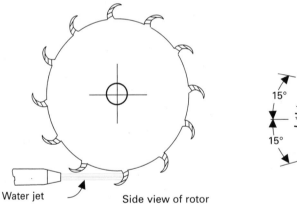

Water jet   Side view of rotor

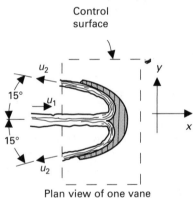

Plan view of one vane

In practice the vanes are invariably double-sided so as to divide the jet, sending half the water to one side of the rotor and half to the other. What is then the y component of the force on the vane?

30

> Zero

Since the flow pattern is symmetrical, the y component of the force is zero, and the rotor bearings do not have to carry any thrust in this direction.

A turbine of this kind is called a *Pelton wheel*; the vanes on a Pelton wheel are usually called buckets.

Let us calculate the force on a bucket when the rotor is stationary. In this example the velocities are $u_1 = 90$ m/s and $u_2 = 85$ m/s, and the diameter of the inlet jet is 5 cm.

First we must find the mass flow rate $\dot{m}$ of the water jet entering the control volume. What do you get?

> $\dot{m} = 167$ kg/s

This is given by

$$\dot{m} = \text{density} \times \text{volume flow rate}$$
$$= \rho \times (u_1 \times \pi d^2/4)$$
$$= 167 \text{ kg/s}$$

When conditions are steady, the mass of water inside the control volume must be constant, so the total mass flow rate coming out must be equal to the mass flow rate going in, i.e. to 167 kg/s. Since roughly half the water goes to one side and half to the other, the mass flow rate in each of the side streams will be approximately 83.5 kg/s.

Now we can calculate the force on the bucket. The rate of momentum inflow to the control volume is $\dot{m}u_1$ to the right. The numerical value in this case is

$$\dot{m}u_1 = 167 \times 90 \text{ N}$$
$$= 15.0 \text{ kN to the right}$$

What is the total rate of momentum outflow from the control volume?

32

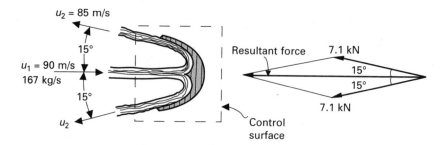

| 13.7 kN to the left |

Working: the rate of momentum outflow in the upper stream in the diagram is (85×83.5) N, or 7.1 kN, in the direction shown. The rate of momentum outflow in the lower stream has the same magnitude, but is in the other direction shown.

As the vector diagram above shows, the resultant of these two momentum flows, expressed in kN, is $2 \times 7.1 \cos 15°$ to the left.

Calculating this, we get 13.7 kN to the left.

Finally, what is the total force exerted on the bucket by the water?

33

| 28.7 kN to the right |

Working: as in the previous example, the water enters with momentum to the right, and departs with overall momentum to the left. It must be subject to a force to the left sufficient both to kill its initial momentum to the right, and to produce its final momentum to the left.

This total force is $(15.0 + 13.7)$ kN, or 28.7 kN (to three significant figures). The force on the water is to the left, and the corresponding force on the bucket is to the right.

Now it is time for you to try some revision examples, to make sure that you have followed everything we have done so far in this programme. The solutions are over the page, but try not to look at them until you have attempted the revision questions.

34

Revision exercise

1 A stationary jet engine takes in air at a rate 27 kg/s (see the left-hand diagram below). Fuel is added in the ratio 1:45, i.e. the mass flow rate of fuel is 1/45 of the mass flow rate of air. The exit velocity of the hot gases from the engine is 470 m/s. Assuming the momentum of the air entering the engine is negligibly small, estimate the thrust of the engine.

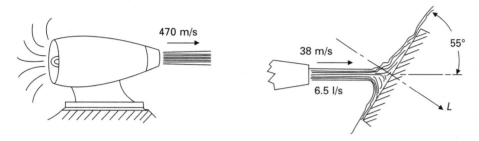

2 A jet of water, carrying a volume flow rate of 6.5 l/s of water and travelling at 38 m/s, strikes a flat plate inclined at 55° to the direction of the jet. The situation is shown in the right-hand diagram above. After impact, the water moves off in all directions over the surface of the plate. Calculate the force exerted by the water on the plate in the direction L, normal to the surface.

3

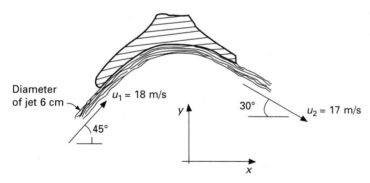

Find the x and y components of the force exerted on the fixed vane by the water jet shown.

35

Solutions

1 The rate of momentum outflow from the control volume is

$$\dot{m}u_2 = .27 \times (1 + 1/45) \times 470 \text{ N}$$
$$= 13.0 \text{ kN}$$

The rate of momentum inflow is negligible, so the rate of change of momentum of the air and fuel is 13.0 kN, and this is the value of the thrust of the engine.

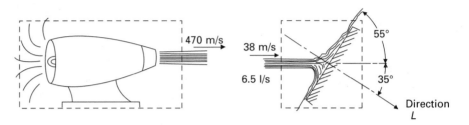

2 Since the mass of 1 litre of water is 1 kg, the mass flow rate is 6.5 kg/s. Considering the direction L perpendicular to the plate, the rate of momentum inflow is

$$\dot{m}u_1 \sin 55° = 6.5 \times 38 \times \sin 55°$$
$$= 202 \text{ N}$$

All the water moves away over the surface of the plate, so its velocity is perpendicular to direction L. The momentum outflow in direction L is thus zero. Therefore the force on the plate is equal to 202 N.

3 First we must find the mass flow rate:

$$\dot{m} = 1000 \times (\pi \times 0.03^2) \times 18$$
$$= 50.9 \text{ kg/s}$$

In the x direction, the force on the water is

$$F_x = \text{momentum outflow} - \text{momentum inflow in } x \text{ direction}$$
$$= \dot{m}u_2 \cos 30° - \dot{m}u_1 \cos 45°$$
$$= 50.9(17 \cos 30° - 18 \cos 45°)$$
$$= 101.5 \text{ N}$$

Similarly, $F_y = 50.9(-17 \sin 30° - 18 \sin 45°) = -1081$ N. Thus the force on the vane is:

$$x \text{ component: } 101.5 \text{ N to the left}$$
$$y \text{ component: } 1081 \text{ N upwards}$$

36

Going back to the Pelton Wheel bucket for a while: in Frames 29–33 we calculated the force acting on the bucket when the rotor is stationary.

But with the rotor stationary the turbine produces no useful output. Usually the rotor is turning, and all the buckets are moving with speed v.

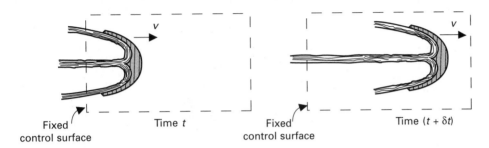

Fixed control surface   Time t Fixed control surface   Time $(t + \delta t)$

The two diagrams above show one bucket at two moments a short time interval apart. The control surface shown is fixed, i.e. it is stationary with respect to the Earth.

There is clearly more water inside the control volume in the second diagram than in the first. Would you say that conditions in the control volume are steady, or unsteady?

37

Unsteady

We spent a few frames at the beginning of Programme 4 on the subject of steady and unsteady flow. When conditions are steady, the parameters of the flow at any point do not vary with time, so diagrams of the flow at two different instants should look exactly the same.

The diagrams in the previous frame are *not* the same – there is a greater mass of water inside the control surface in the second diagram than in the first – so it is clear that conditions are not steady.

We can overcome this by having the control volume move along with the bucket, at the same speed v as the bucket is moving. Provided speed v is constant, so that the control volume is not accelerating, Newton's laws still apply. This is just what we did with the jet engine example in Frames 13–14.

38

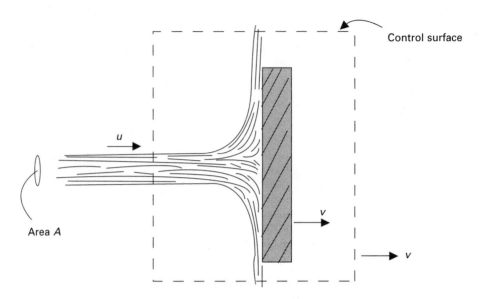

Control surface

u

v

v

Area *A*

Before getting into detail on the Pelton bucket, we will consider a simpler example, that of a jet of water striking a flat plate (as in Frame 8), but now with the plate moving. The speed of the water in the jet is *u*, to the right, and the plate is moving with speed *v*, also to the right (*u* is greater than *v*). The area of cross-section of the jet is *A*.

In order for conditions to be steady, our control surface must move along with the plate, at speed *v* to the right. All velocities are then measured relative to the plate and its surrounding control surface.

What is the velocity of the incoming water jet relative to the plate and the control surface?

39

$(u - v)$, to the right

Because the velocities of the jet and the plate are in the same direction, the velocity of the jet relative to the plate is just the difference between the magnitudes of the two velocities.

So, as viewed from the plate and the control surface, the water jet is entering the control surface at speed $(u - v)$. In terms of *u*, *v* and *A*, what is the *volume* flow rate at which water in the jet is entering the control surface?

40

$$A(u - v)$$

Relative to the plate and the surrounding control surface, the water jet is approaching at speed $(u - v)$, so the volume flow rate is $A(u - v)$.

Now we will take some numerical values. Let the speed u of the water in the jet be 21 m/s and its area A of cross-section be 8×10^{-5} m^2. If the plate is moving with speed v of 12 m/s, find the *mass* flow rate $\dot{m}$ at which water is entering the control surface. The density of the water is 1000 kg/m^3.

41

$$0.72 \text{ kg/s}$$

Working: the volume flow rate is $A(u - v)$, and the mass flow rate $\dot{m}$ is the volume flow rate multiplied by the density, that is

$$8 \times 10^{-5} \times (21 - 12) \times 1000 \text{ kg/s, or } 0.72 \text{ kg/s}$$

We saw in our earlier example where a jet of water is striking a flat plate (Frames 8–12) that, because the water spreads out in all directions in the plane of the plate, the overall momentum of the water leaving the plate is zero. The water exerts a force on the plate which is equal to the rate at which momentum flows into the control surface in the jet. Remembering that all velocities are taken as viewed from the control surface (moving at 12 m/s), you can now calculate the rate of momentum inflow. What do you get?

42

$$6.5 \text{ N to the right}$$

The rate of momentum inflow to the control volume is given by $\dot{m}(u - v)$ – we use $(u - v)$, not just u, because all velocities have to be measured *relative to the control surface*. The calculation is as follows:

$$\dot{m}(u - v) = 0.72 \times (21 - 12)$$
$$= 6.5 \text{ N}$$

and this is the force exerted by the water on the plate.

In the next few frames we will look again at the case of the Pelton bucket.

43

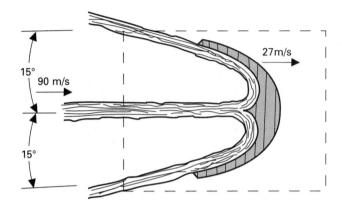

Here we have the same jet of water as in our earlier Pelton bucket example, moving at 90 m/s and with a mass flow rate of 167 kg/s as observed from a fixed reference such as the Earth; but now the bucket is moving in the same direction as the jet, at 27 m/s.

At what velocity must the control volume move so that conditions within it will be steady?

44

> 27 m/s to the right

For steady conditions the control surface must move along with the bucket, at 27 m/s to the right.

Relative to the bucket and the control volume, the velocity of the incoming water jet will be (90 − 27) m/s, or 63 m/s, to the right.

In Frames 29–33, when the bucket was stationary, the mass flow rate into the control volume was 167 kg/s; but now the bucket and the control volume are moving, and the velocity of the incoming water jet relative to the control volume is reduced from 90 m/s to 63 m/s.

The rate of mass flow into the control volume will now be less than 167 m/s. Can you estimate the new, reduced value of the mass flow rate of water into the control volume?

$$\boxed{117 \text{ kg/s}}$$

Working: the diameter of the jet is unchanged, of course; the mass flow rate is proportional to the observed velocity of the jet. (To illustrate this by an extreme case: if we viewed the jet from a vehicle travelling at the same speed as the water, no mass would pass us at all, and we would observe the mass flow rate to be zero.)

At 90 m/s the mass flow rate was 167 kg/s, so at 63 m/s we shall have

$$\text{mass flow rate} = 167 \times (63/90) \text{ kg/s}$$
$$= 117 \text{ kg/s}$$

Now we have all the figures we need to calculate the rate of momentum inflow to the control volume. What do you get?

$$\boxed{7.37 \text{ kN to the right}}$$

This is just the product of the mass flow rate (117 kg/s) and the inflow velocity (63 m/s to the right).

Now we must consider the rate of momentum outflow. The outward water flows will be moving a little more slowly (relative to the bucket) than the incoming one, because of friction. We will estimate the speed as 60 m/s relative to the bucket, at 15° as before.

Since conditions in the control volume are steady, the total mass flow rate of water leaving in the two outgoing flows must be equal to the incoming mass flow, 117 kg/s.

All this is shown in the diagram at the top of the next page.

47

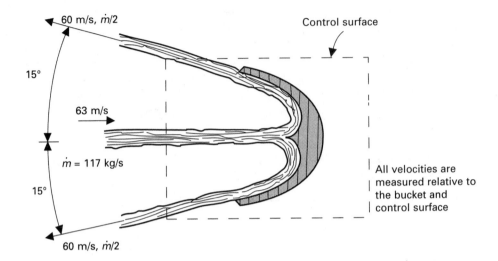

As before, the momentum components in the y direction are equal and opposite; they add up to zero, so we need to give our attention only to the momentum in the x direction.

Can you now calculate the rate of momentum outflow? Refer back to Frame 32 if necessary – the method is just the same.

48

> 6.78 kN to the left

Working:

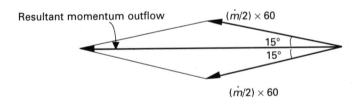

As the diagram shows, the resultant momentum outflow is $2 \times (\dot{m}/2) \times 60 \cos 15°$, which, when we put in the value $\dot{m} = 117$ kg/s, comes to 6.78 kN.

As we have already seen, the total force exerted on the water is equal to the rate of momentum outflow from the control surface, minus the rate of momentum inflow. What is the total force on the water in this case?

49

> 14.2 kN to the left

Working: the force on the water is (6.78 kN + 7.36 kN), or 14.2 kN, to the left. (The value given is to three significant figures.)

The second term in the brackets is the force needed to destroy the momentum of the water in the jet; the first term is the force necessary to produce the final momentum of the water leaving the bucket in the two outflows. If we think about in this way it should be clear that the two amounts should be added together, not subtracted.

Should you prefer to look at the situation mathematically, rather than physically, you could substitute directly into the formula of Frame 17: the rate of change of momentum of the water in the x direction is

$$\dot{m}(u_2 \cos\theta - u_1)$$

Here $\theta = 165°$; $\cos 165°$ is negative, so the terms in the bracket have the same sign, as they should. The rate of change of momentum is

$$117(60 \cos 165° - 63) = -14.2 \text{ kN to the right}$$

i.e. 14.2 kN to the left, just as before.

The force exerted on the bucket is equal and opposite to that on the water, and so it is 14.2 kN to the right.

50

In the examples we have looked at so far in this programme, the incoming and outgoing flows have all been open to the air. The pressure is then the same all round the plate, or the vane, or the Pelton bucket: that is, atmospheric pressure. The force exerted on the plate, or vane, or Pelton bucket, comes only from the momentum change of the fluid, and not from any variation in external pressure.

But there are many situations where fluid is flowing in closed pipes or conduits, and then the pressure is usually not atmospheric. In the next frame we consider a case of this kind.

51

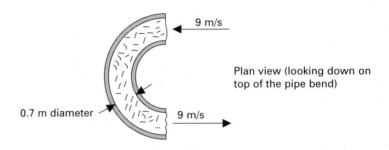

Plan view (looking down on top of the pipe bend)

9 m/s

0.7 m diameter

9 m/s

Water is flowing through the 180° pipe bend at speed 9 m/s, and the gauge pressure is 120 kN/m². We wish to calculate the force exerted on the pipe bend by the water. We will use a control surface ...

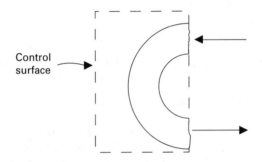

Control surface

... and, as before, the resultant of all the forces acting on the contents of the control surface is equal to (rate of momentum outflow) – (rate of momentum inflow); but this time we must take into account the extra force that arises because the fluid in the pipe is not at atmospheric pressure.

First we will calculate the rate of change of momentum of the water: we will begin by finding the mass flow rate $\dot{m}$:

$$\dot{m} = \rho A u = 1000 \times (\pi \times 0.35^2) \times 9 = 3464 \text{ kg/s}$$

The water enters the pipe bend moving at 9 m/s to the left, and leaves moving at 9 m/s to the right.

Now work out the rate of change of momentum of the water as it flows through the pipe bend: that is, (the rate of momentum outflow) – (the rate of momentum inflow).

52

62.4 kN to the right

Working: the rate of momentum outflow is $\dot{m}u$ to the right; the rate of momentum inflow is $\dot{m}u$ to the left. The rate of change of momentum of the water is the difference between these vector quantities, which is $2\dot{m}u$ to the right. Substituting the values into this expression, we get 62.4 kN to the right.

The water must therefore be subject to a resultant force 62.4 kN to the right. This can be provided only by the pipe bend, which will itself be subject to an equal force to the left, and must be anchored by a fixing that is capable of resisting at least this force.

But the water is at a pressure higher than atmospheric, and so, at each of the joints between our pipe elbow and the rest of the pipe, the water outside the control surface exerts a force pA on the water inside, where p is the gauge pressure and A the area of cross-section of the pipe. This is a further force to the left, and must also be withstood by the pipe bend.

What is the magnitude of the force pA?

53

46.2 kN

Working:

$$pA = 120 \times \pi \times 0.35^2$$
$$= 46.2 \text{ kN}$$

There are two such joints, and so two forces. (If you are in any doubt about these forces due to the pressure of the water, go back to Programme 2 and look at Frames 67–71 where we dealt with the force acting on a pipe elbow. Of course, in Programme 2 the fluid was stationary, whereas here it is moving; but the pressure force is still there.)

In the next frame we show all the forces acting on the control surface.

54

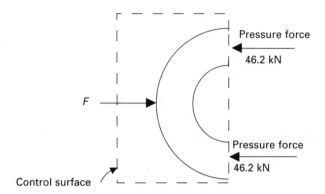

The forces acting on the water are shown on the diagram: the force F holding the pipe bend, and the two pressure forces where the control surface intersects the fluid in the pipe. (This is a plan view; the weight force, which acts perpendicular to the paper, is not shown.)

The resultant of these forces is equal to the rate of change of momentum of the water as it flows through the pipe; that is, the resultant of the forces is 62.4 kN to the right. Writing this as an equation, summing forces to the right (expressed in kN) we get

$$F - 2(46.2) = 62.4$$

and so the value of the force F is …?

55

155 kN

This should be very straightforward:

$$F = 92.4 + 62.4$$
$$= 155 \text{ kN, to three significant figures}$$

The first of the two figures in the equation above, 92.4 kN, is the part of the force F that has to be exerted on the pipe bend because of the pressure in the pipe; the second, 62.4 kN, is the part of the force F needed to produce the continuous change of momentum of the water.

The force exerted on the pipe bend by the water is equal and opposite to the total force F: 155 kN to the left.

In the next frame we look at a similar example, but this time of a 90° elbow.

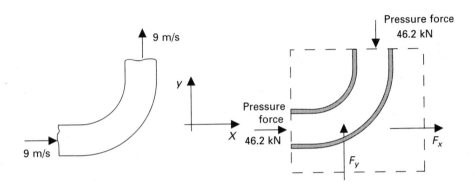

To save on arithmetic, we will take the same conditions in the 90° pipe elbow as in the 180° bend we discussed in the last few frames: water is flowing at 9 m/s and the gauge pressure is 120 kN/m². The diameter is 0.7 m. We shall need x and y directions: let us define them as shown.

The magnitude of the pressure forces at entry and exit is 46.2 kN, as before; the mass flow rate is 3464 kg/s, the rate of momentum inflow is 31.2 kN (in the x direction), and the rate of momentum outflow is 31.2 kN (in the y direction). To produce this momentum change, and also overcome the pressure forces at entry and exit, the pipe elbow must exert force components on the water in the x and y directions. We do not know yet whether these will be in the positive or the negative directions, so we have assumed the positive directions; the calculations will soon show whether our assumptions are wrong.

We will take the y direction first. There is a momentum outflow of 31.2 kN in this direction, but the inflow is perpendicular to the y direction and its component is therefore zero. Thus the rate of change of momentum in the y direction is 31.2 kN.

You should now be able to work out the value of the force F_y exerted by the pipe elbow on the water in the y direction. What do you get?

57

$$\boxed{77.4 \text{ kN}}$$

Working: taking the upward y direction as positive, we have

$$\text{resultant force} = \text{rate of change of momentum}$$
$$F_y - 46.2 = 31.2$$
$$F_y = 77.4 \text{ kN}$$

Now find the value of the force component F_x.

58

$$-77.4 \text{ kN}$$

Working: in the x direction the rate of momentum inflow is 31.2 kN. Because the outflow vector is perpendicular to the x direction, the outflow momentum component is zero. Thus

$$F_x + 46.2 = 0 - 31.2$$
$$F_x = -77.4 \text{ kN}$$

The minus sign here tells us that the force that has to be exerted on the water in the x direction is actually to the left.

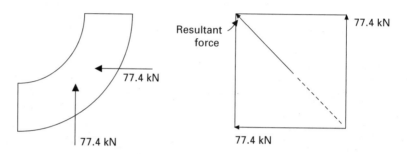

We can think of the x component as being composed of 46.2 kN to the left, needed to match the pressure force at the entry to the pipe elbow, plus 31.2 kN to the left to destroy the momentum of the water entering in the x direction.

Likewise, the y component consists of 46.2 kN to balance the pressure force on the delivery end of the elbow, plus 31.2 kN to produce the momentum of the water leaving.

Now, if we take the two 77.4 kN forces and add them together as vectors, what is the resultant force that has to act on the water?

59

$$109.5 \text{ kN at } 45° \text{ to the } y \text{ direction}$$

Because they are vectors, we add the two forces together using the parallelogram rule (in this case the parallelogram is a square). The resultant is $77.4 \times \sqrt{2}$, or 109.5 kN.

In the next frame we look at a tapering pipe or nozzle.

60

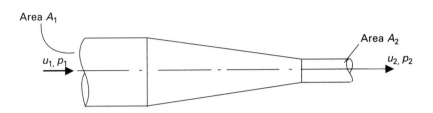

Area A_1

u_1, p_1

Area A_2

u_2, p_2

Fluid flows along the horizontal pipe shown. As the fluid passes through the tapering part, the area is decreasing and so the flow speed must increase. What happens to the pressure in this part of the pipe: does it increase or decrease?

61

The pressure decreases

Remember Bernoulli's equation? Just in case your memory is shaky, here it is:

$$p_1 + \tfrac{1}{2}\rho u_1^2 + \rho g z_1 = p_2 + \tfrac{1}{2}\rho u_2^2 + \rho g z_2$$

The z terms are the same on the two sides of the equation, because the tapering pipe is horizontal. The speed of the flow is *greater* at the outlet than at the inlet; so, to balance the two sides of the equation, the pressure must be *less* at the outlet than at the inlet.

The fluid enters with velocity u_1 to the right and gauge pressure p_1, and leaves with velocity u_2 and gauge pressure p_2. The volume flow rate is Q, and the density is ρ.

In terms of ρ, Q and the velocities u_1 and u_2, what is the rate of change of momentum of the fluid?

62

$$\boxed{\rho Q(u_2 - u_1) \text{ to the right}}$$

Working: the mass flow rate is ρQ, so the rate of momentum outflow is $\rho Q u_2$ to the right, and the rate of momentum inflow is $\rho Q u_1$, also to the right. The difference between these is $\rho Q(u_2 - u_1)$.

This change of momentum must be associated with a resultant force to the right on the fluid. What is the force exerted on the fluid by the pressure at the entry to the nozzle, point 1?

63

$$\boxed{p_1 A_1 \text{ to the right}}$$

This is just the gauge pressure multiplied by the area of cross-section. We use the gauge pressure because the whole of the control surface is surrounded by air at atmospheric pressure, apart from where it crosses the flow passage.

Likewise, the fluid beyond the control surface boundary at the outlet exerts a force $p_2 A_2$ to the left.

The pressure forces on the inner tapering surfaces almost always result in a force to the right on the nozzle, and an equal and opposite force to the left on the water. This force on the water to the left is denoted by F.

All these forces are shown in the diagram below.

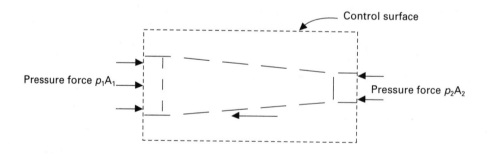

64

Three forces act on the water in the nozzle: the two pressure forces, and the force F. The resultant of these forces is equal to the rate of change of momentum of the fluid. Writing this as an equation:

$$p_1 A_1 - p_2 A_2 - F = \rho Q (u_2 - u_1)$$

in which we have taken the rightward direction as positive.

Incidentally, the water exerts a force F to the right on the nozzle. The nozzle is in equilibrium, so this force must be balanced by an equal and opposite force F to the left, usually supplied by the surrounding pipework.

We can solve the above equation for F once we know all the other quantities. To illustrate this, here is an example with numerical values.

For a certain tapered pipe, the inlet area A_1 is 2.0×10^{-3} m^2 and the outlet area A_2 is 0.8×10^{-3} m^2. Water of density 1000 kg/m^3 flows through the pipe at a rate 20 l/s, and the gauge pressure p_2 at outlet is 5 kN/m^2. We wish to estimate the force F needed to hold the pipe in place (the thrust exerted on the pipe by the water is equal and opposite to this).

We know the pressure at the outlet, but not at the inlet. To find this pressure we shall have to use Bernoulli's equation, assuming no friction losses in the pipe; and before we can use Bernoulli's equation we need to calculate the velocities of the water at entry and exit, u_1 and u_2.

Go ahead and work these out now.

65

$$u_1 = 10 \text{ m/s}; \qquad u_2 = 25 \text{ m/s}$$

Working: the volume flow rate is 20 l/s, or 20×10^{-3} m^3/s. Dividing this by the inlet area A_1, we obtain the inlet velocity $u_1 = 10$ m/s. Similarly, the outlet velocity is $u_2 = 25$ m/s.

Now use Bernoulli's equation to work out the upstream pressure p_1. Remember that we can omit the z terms because the flow is horizontal, so the equation becomes

$$p_1 + \tfrac{1}{2}\rho u_1^2 = p_2 + \tfrac{1}{2}\rho u_2^2$$

66

$$268 \text{ kN/m}^2$$

Working:

$$
\begin{aligned}
p_1 &= p_2 + \tfrac{1}{2}\rho(u_2^2 - u_1^2) \\
&= 5 \times 10^3 + \tfrac{1}{2} \times 1000(25^2 - 10^2) \\
&= 10^3(5 + 262.5) \text{ N/m}^2 \\
&= 267.5 \text{ kN/m}^2
\end{aligned}
$$

In using Bernoulli's equation we are assuming that friction losses are small, which is probably not unreasonable in a short length of pipe whose diameter is decreasing, not increasing.

Having used Bernoulli's equation to find out the upstream pressure, now substitute the figures into the momentum equation

$$p_1 A_1 - p_2 A_2 - F = \rho Q(u_2 - u_1)$$

and find the value of the force F.

67

$$F = 231 \text{ N}$$

Working: evaluating the terms of the equation:

$$
\begin{aligned}
p_1 A_1 &= (267.5 \times 10^3) \times (2 \times 10^{-3}) = 535 \text{ N} \\
p_2 A_2 &= (5 \times 10^3) \times (0.8 \times 10^{-3}) = 4 \text{ N} \\
\rho Q(u_2 - u_1) &= 1000 \times (20 \times 10^{-3})(25 - 10) = 300 \text{ N}
\end{aligned}
$$

and hence

$$
\begin{aligned}
535 - 4 - F &= 300 \\
F &= 231 \text{ N}
\end{aligned}
$$

We assumed that the force F needed to hold the pipe in place acts to the left, and on that basis we found that F has a positive value. This confirms that our assumption was correct.

This brings us to the end of this programme. The revision summary follows: read this carefully to make sure you have fully understood the contents of the programme, then go on to the test exercise as a final check.

68

Revision summary

1 Newton's three laws of motion apply to fluids just as much as to solid particles or bodies.

2 When applying Newton's second law to fluids, we generally use a control surface – an imaginary surface through which fluid flows.

3 When conditions are steady, the resultant external force acting on the contents of the control surface is equal to the rate of momentum outflow from the control surface minus the rate of momentum inflow.

4 The rates of momentum outflow and inflow are given in each case by the product $\dot{m}u$, where $\dot{m}$ is the mass flow rate and u the velocity. These are vector quantities, having direction as well as magnitude; when adding or subtracting vectors, we must either use a vector diagram or work in terms of x and y components.

5 The resultant external force includes any weight forces, any external viscous forces and any external pressure forces.

69

Test exercise

1 Water at gauge pressure 65 kN/m² flows through the pipe bend shown below left at speed 5.8 m/s. Find the force exerted by the water on the pipe bend.

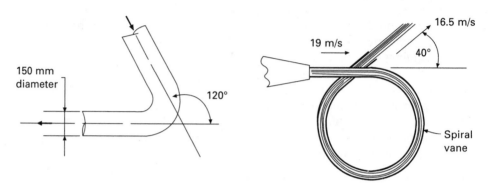

2 A jet of water 10 mm diameter is deflected by a spiral vane through 320°, as shown in the diagram above right. The speed of the water in the jet is 19 m/s, and it leaves the vane at 16.5 m/s. The pressure is atmospheric throughout. Find the resultant force on the vane, giving both magnitude and direction.

3 A liquid of density 1150 kg/m³ flows through the tapered horizontal pipe shown below. At entry to the pipe the gauge pressure is 200 kN/m², and the flow velocity at entry is 3.8 m/s. Neglecting any friction losses, find the force exerted on the tapered pipe by the liquid.

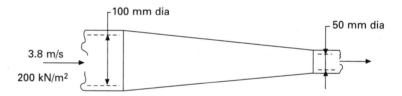

Further problems

1 A jet of water of velocity 20 m/s is deflected by a stationary curved vane, as shown below. Find the magnitude and direction of the reaction force acting on the vane if the mass flow rate of water in the jet is 0.5 kg/s.

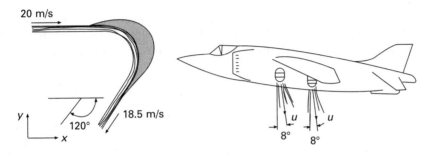

2 The mass of a certain single-engined vertical take-off aircraft, including fuel, armaments etc., is 9.3 tonne. If the total mass flow of exhaust gases from the engine is 360 kg/s in the direction shown in the diagram above, find the mean velocity u at which the gases must leave the nozzles when the aircraft is taking off.

3

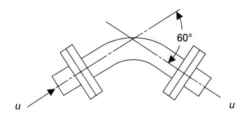

Liquid of density ρ flows with velocity u through the 60° pipe bend, whose area of cross-section A is uniform. The gauge pressure of the liquid is p, and the pipe bend lies in a horizontal plane. Find the force exerted by the liquid on the bend.

4

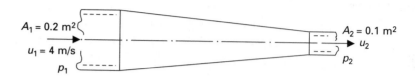

Water flows through the tapered pipe as shown. Given that the gauge pressures at inlet and outlet are $p_1 = 72$ kN/m^2 and $p_2 = 48$ kN/m^2, find the force exerted on the tapered pipe by the water (give both magnitude and direction).

5

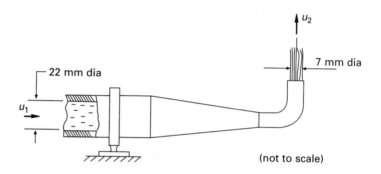

Water is supplied to the jet of a fountain as shown in the diagram. The gauge pressure of the water supply is 360 kN/m^2. Estimate (a) the velocity u_2 of the water leaving the jet, and (b) the vertical and horizontal components of the force exerted on the pipe due to the pressure and motion of the water. State the directions of the forces.

Programme 7

DIMENSIONS AND
DIMENSIONAL CONSISTENCY

Introduction

The ideas of this programme and the next apply not only to fluid mechanics, but also much more widely in the fields of engineering and physics. While many of the examples used will be of topics in fluid mechanics, some will be drawn from other areas of mechanics.

Fluid mechanics courses usually include a section on dimensional analysis and similarity because these ideas have been applied more extensively in the study of fluid mechanics than in any other area – but, as you will see, the application of some of the principles set out in these two programmes can be enormously helpful in any field of engineering and science.

1

Consistency of equations and conversion of units

Suppose we wish to compare the heights of two children. We find by measurement that the height of one is 132 cm and the height of the other is 95 cm.
　So the difference in their heights is . . .?

2

$$\boxed{37 \text{ cm}}$$

The difference is simply $132 - 95 = 37$ cm.
　A different pair of children are also measured, this time in inches. One is 50 in tall, the other 41 in.
　Between these two children the difference in height is . . .?

3

$$\boxed{9 \text{ in}}$$

In Frame 2 the heights are expressed in inch units instead of centimetre units, but the difference between the heights is calculated in exactly the same way, by subtraction: $50 - 41 = 9$ in.
　However, if we wished to compare the heights of the taller children of each pair, one 132 cm tall and the other 50 in tall, then we would not be able to carry out a subtraction immediately because the units of length, or height, are not the same. Before subtracting we would have to convert one length to the same units as the other.
　Knowing that 1 in = 2.54 cm, can you now find the difference in their heights?

4

$$\boxed{5 \text{ cm, or 2 in}}$$

We can work in either centimetres or inches, of course. Since 1 in = 2.54 cm, we can readily convert the height 50 inches to centimetre units:

$$50 \text{ in} = 50 \times 2.54 \text{ cm} = 127 \text{ cm}$$

so the difference in height between the two children is

$$132 - 127 = 5 \text{ cm}$$

Alternatively, we can convert 132 cm to inches:

$$132 \text{ cm} = \frac{132}{2.54} \text{ in} = 51.96 \text{ in}$$

and the difference in height is $51.96 - 50 = 1.96$ in.

It is not possible to measure human heights to the accuracy of hundredths of an inch, so it is sensible to round off this result to 2 in.

5

The conversion between centimetres and inches is quite straightforward, involving only multiplying or dividing by the factor 2.54. Because the centimetre is a smaller unit than the inch we can see that the number of centimetres in a given length must be greater than the number of inches, and so when converting from inches to centimetres we must *multiply* by 2.54. When converting the other way we must *divide* by 2.54, of course.

When converting the units of more complicated quantities, it is quite easy to make mistakes, so it pays to be systematic about it. Here is a method: we write

$$50 \text{ (inch)} = 50(2.54 \text{ cm}) = 127 \text{ cm}$$

where we have replaced the unit (inch) by its exact equivalent (2.54 cm).

Try this method in the following case: given that 1 ft = 0.3048 m, convert 42 ft to metre units.

6

$$\boxed{12.80 \text{ m}}$$

Working:

$$42 \text{ (ft)} = 42(0.3048 \text{ m}) = 12.80 \text{ m}$$

The unit (ft) is replaced by (0.3048 m), which is exactly the same thing.

Areas are measured in units of (length)^2, e.g. m^2, ft^2, km^2. Conversion of units can be done in exactly the same way as before, replacing the original unit by its exact equivalent, but because the units are of (length)^2 the conversion factor will inevitably be squared also. For example,

$$1 \text{ yard} = 3 \text{ ft}$$

so we can replace the unit (yard) by (3 ft) wherever it occurs. Thus

$$4840 \text{ yard}^2 = 4840(3 \text{ ft})^2$$
$$= 4840 \times 9 \text{ ft}^2$$
$$= 43\,560 \text{ ft}^2$$

Now try this example: the size of a room is measured in feet, and the floor area is calculated to be 152 ft^2. The carpet to be fitted is sold by the m^2: what is the area of carpet required, in m^2?

7

$$\boxed{14.12 \text{ m}^2}$$

In this case the conversion can be written

$$152 \text{ ft}^2 = 152(0.3048 \text{ m})^2 = 14.12 \text{ m}^2$$

The same method can be used to convert the units of a volume. Try converting a volume of 38 m^3 to ft^3 units; remember that 1 ft = 0.3048 m, so 1 m = (1/0.3048) ft.

8

$$\boxed{1342 \text{ ft}^3}$$

In just the same way as before:

$$38 \text{ m}^3 = 38\left(\frac{1}{0.3048} \text{ ft}\right)^3 = 1342 \text{ ft}^3$$

Now let's look at the conversion of units which involve time as well as distance, such as the units of velocity. Suppose we wish to convert a speed of 90 km/h to m/s units. We know that 1 km = 1000 m and 1 h = 3600 s, so the conversion can be written as

$$90\left(\frac{\text{km}}{\text{h}}\right) = 90\left(\frac{1000 \text{ m}}{3600 \text{ s}}\right) = 25\left(\frac{\text{m}}{\text{s}}\right)$$

It is probably best to write the units as fractions as has been done here, rather than using the slash (/), to make it quite clear what is happening. The unit km has been replaced by its equivalent 1000 m, and likewise the unit h has been replaced by 3600 s.

If you prefer to use the negative index form, such as km h^{-1} and m s^{-1}, the result is just the same:

$$90 \text{ km h}^{-1} = 90(1000 \text{ m})(3600 \text{ s})^{-1} = 90 \times 1000 \times 3600^{-1} \text{ m s}^{-1} = 25 \text{ m s}^{-1}$$

Now try this example: the surface speed of drive belts is sometimes expressed in m/s, and sometimes in ft/min. If a certain belt is running at a surface speed of 2400 ft/min, what is its surface speed in m/s?

9

$$\boxed{12.2 \text{ m/s}}$$

Working:

$$2400\left(\frac{\text{ft}}{\text{min}}\right) = 2400\left(\frac{0.3048 \text{ m}}{60 \text{ s}}\right) = 12.2\left(\frac{\text{m}}{\text{s}}\right)$$

or in the negative index form

$$2400 \text{ ft min}^{-1} = 2400(0.3048 \text{ m})(60 \text{ s})^{-1}$$
$$= 2400 \times 0.3048 \times 60^{-1} \text{ m s}^{-1}$$
$$= 12.2 \text{ m s}^{-1}$$

Here is another example: the discharge, or volume flow rate, of a certain pump is 0.27 m^3/s. Given that 1 m^3 = 221 gallon, express this discharge in gallon/min units.

3580 gallon/min

Writing in the negative index form

$$0.27 \text{ m}^3\text{s}^{-1} = 0.27(221 \text{ gallon})\left(\frac{1}{60} \text{ min}\right)^{-1}$$

$$= 0.27 \times 221 \times 60 \text{ gallon min}^{-1}$$

$$= 3580 \text{ gallon min}^{-1}$$

This method of converting quantities from one unit system to another is completely general and quite easy to use. We shall have more opportunities to use the method in the rest of this programme. Here is another example:

Two cars A and B are travelling in the same direction along a straight road. The speed of car A is 72 km/h. Car B, preparing to overtake, is moving 4 m/s faster than car A. What is the speed of car B, in m/s?

11

24 m/s

To find the speed of car B we add the speed difference, 4 m/s, to the speed of car A, 72 km/h; but before we can add the values to obtain the speed of car B in m/s, we must convert the speed of car A to m/s units:

$$72\left(\frac{\text{km}}{\text{h}}\right) = 72\left(\frac{1000 \text{ m}}{3600 \text{ s}}\right) = 20 \text{ m/s}$$

so the speed of car B is $20 + 4 = 24$ m/s
    Now turn over to the next frame.

12

We could describe the situation shown in the diagram of Frame 10 by means of an equation

$$v_B = v_A + v_{B/A}$$

in which

v_B is the speed of car B,

v_A is the speed of car A,

$v_{B/A}$ is the speed of car B relative to car A, and

we take all speeds as positive to the right.

This equation applies to the situation of Frame 10 quite generally, whatever the actual values of the speeds v_B, v_A and $v_{B/A}$. But when we substitute numerical values into the equation, the same units must, of course, be used throughout.

Here is a further exercise: if the speed of car A is $v_A = 45$ mile/h and that of car B is $v_B = 59$ mile/h, what is the relative speed $v_{B/A}$ expressed in m/s (1 mile = 1609 m)?

13

$$\boxed{6.26 \text{ m/s}}$$

Since v_B and v_A are both expressed in the same units, mile/h, we can substitute straight away in the equation $v_B = v_A + v_{B/A}$ and obtain the result $v_{B/A} = 14$ mile/h. This then has to be converted into m/s units:

$$14\left(\frac{\text{mile}}{\text{h}}\right) = 14\left(\frac{1609 \text{ m}}{3600 \text{ s}}\right) = 6.26 \text{ m/s}$$

Try another example before we move on: car B is moving at speed $v_B = 70$ km/h. Car A is moving 9 m/s slower than car B. Find the speed of car A in mile/h units.

$$\boxed{23.4 \text{ mile/h}}$$

Converting both speeds to mile/h:

$$v_B = 70\left(\frac{\text{km}}{\text{h}}\right) = 70\left(\frac{(1000/1609)\ \text{mile}}{\text{h}}\right)$$

$$= 43.5 \text{ mile/h}$$

$$v_{B/A} = 9\left(\frac{\text{m}}{\text{s}}\right) = 9\left(\frac{1/1609\ \text{mile}}{1/3600\ \text{h}}\right) = 20.1 \text{ mile/h}$$

so

$$v_A = v_B - v_{B/A} = 43.5 - 20.1 = 23.4 \text{ mile/h}$$

In the equation $v_B = v_A + v_{B/A}$ each term is the same kind of quantity, namely a velocity; so if we use the same *system* of units throughout, such as metres and seconds, it is automatic that all the terms in the equation will have the same units.

However, in many cases where we have an equation describing a physical situation, some of the terms of the equation are made up of several quantities, and it may not be immediately obvious that all terms *can* be measured using the same units. Take for example the equation

$$v = u + at$$

which relates the final velocity v, after a time t, to the initial velocity u of an object moving in a straight line with constant acceleration a.

v and u are both velocities, and will be measured with units of velocity.

What about the last term, at? If the equation is correct this must also be expressible in velocity units – but can it?

One way to find out is to substitute some notional values into the expression: if $a = 2 \text{ m/s}^2$ and $t = 5 \text{ s}$, what is the product at? (Be sure to state the units as well as the numerical value.)

15

$$\boxed{at = 10 \text{ m/s}}$$

The product $at = (2 \text{ m/s}^2) \times (5 \text{ s})$
$$= 10\left(\frac{\text{m}}{\text{s}^2}\right) \times \text{s}$$
$$= 10 \text{ m/s}$$

The units m/s of this product are, of course, units of velocity, so the term at *is* expressible in velocity units, and the equation is consistent. Provided v and u are also measured in m/s, the units will be the same for all terms in the equation, as required.

Now the values we chose for acceleration a and elapsed time t in Frame 14 were completely arbitrary. We could have checked that the equation is consistent, that is, that all terms can be measured with the same units, without using any numbers at all: it would have been quite sufficient to substitute the units alone into the equation, without any numerical values.

Consider another equation which applies to a body with constant acceleration,

$$v^2 = u^2 + 2as$$

in which s is the distance travelled by the object, and the other symbols have the same meanings as in Frame 14.

If the velocities v and u are measured in cm/s and the distance s in cm, find the units that must be used for the variable a to make the units of all terms in the equation the same. Are these units of acceleration?

16

$$\boxed{\text{cm/s}^2 (\text{which } \textit{are} \text{ units of acceleration})}$$

Working: with the velocities measured in cm/s units, the units of both v^2 and u^2 are cm²/s². We know that all terms in the equation must have the same units, so the units of the term $2as$ must be cm²/s², too.

The numerical coefficient 2 has no units, and the unit of the distance s is cm, so the unit of a must be cm/s². This *is* a unit of acceleration, so in the equation $v^2 = u^2 + 2as$ all terms can be measured in the same units.

17

So far our equations have related only distances and times, but many physical situations also involve forces and masses. The acceleration a of an object of mass m in a certain direction is related to the resultant force F acting on the object in that direction by Newton's Second Law $F = ma$.

As always when physical quantities are equated, or added or subtracted, all the quantities must be measured in the same units.

For example, we may choose to measure mass m in kg units and acceleration a in m/s^2 units. Then the force must be given in kg m/s^2 units, so that the units of the two sides of the equation will be the same, as required.

However, force is such a commonly occurring quantity in mechanics (fluid or solid) that we give a special name, the newton, to this kg m/s^2 unit. The newton is a *derived* unit, being dependent on the units of mass, distance and time which are themselves set by international standards.

This group of units – newton, metre, kilogram and second – forms a set of so-called *consistent units*, because in equations such as $F = ma$ they satisfy the requirement that the two sides of the equation must have the same units.

Consider a simple example. The equation $Ft = (mv - mu)$ states that, over a time interval t, the change of momentum $(mv - mu)$ of a mass m moving in a straight line is equal to the impulse Ft of the resultant force F acting on it. The diagram below illustrates the situation.

By substituting units into each term we can check whether it is possible for all terms in the equation to be measured with the same units.

Left-hand side: Ft units N s

Right-hand side: mv, mu units kg m/s

At first sight these are not the same; but remember that 'newton' is just a convenient name for a unit of force which is derived from the fundamental SI units of mass, length and time.

If we substitute for 'newton' the expression in terms of metre, kilogram and second units which is equivalent to it, what do we get for the units of the left-hand side of the equation?

18

$$\boxed{\text{kg m/s}}$$

Newtons are equivalent to kg m/s². The units of the left-hand side of the equation are N s, so replacing newtons by the equivalent kg m/s² we get

$$N\,s = \frac{kg\,m}{s^2} \times s = \frac{kg\,m}{s}$$

This is the same as the units of the right-hand side, so both sides of the equation can be measured with the same units, as of course they must be.

Now try another example: if the resultant force on a particle is F and the distance moved in the direction of this force is x, then

work done by force F = change of kinetic energy
$$F\,x = \tfrac{1}{2}mv^2 - \tfrac{1}{2}mu^2$$

Can you show that the same units can be used to measure all the terms in this equation, in other words that the equation is consistent?

19

$$\boxed{\text{Yes, the equation } \textit{is} \text{ consistent}}$$

As before, we can choose the newton, metre, kilogram, second group of units. Then the left hand side of the equation, $F\,x$, has units

$$N\,m, \text{ or } \frac{kg\,m}{s^2}\,m, \text{ or } \frac{kg\,m^2}{s^2}$$

On the right-hand side there are two similar terms, $\tfrac{1}{2}mv^2$ and $\tfrac{1}{2}mu^2$, and both of these have the same units. The numerical coefficient $\tfrac{1}{2}$ has no units, so the units are

$$(kg)\left(\frac{m}{s}\right)^2, \text{ or } \frac{kg\,m^2}{s^2}$$

so all three terms can be measured with the same units, and the equation is consistent.

The next frame is a short revision exercise, which you should work through before going on.

Revision exercise

Note that	$1 \text{ kg} = 2.20 \text{ lb}$	$1 \text{ dyne} = 10^{-5} \text{ N}$
	$1 \text{ ft} = 0.3048 \text{ m}$	$1 \text{ inch} = 25.4 \text{ mm}$

1 The viscosity of air at 15°C is quoted in an old set of tables as 1.79×10^{-2} dyne s/cm^2. Convert this to our more usual units, N s/m^2.

2 The density of benzene is 880 kg/m^3, while the density of octane is 43.9 lb/ft^3. Find the difference between the densities of the two liquids, quoting your answer in kg/m^3.

3 A gas whose density is 0.074 lb/ft^3 is flowing through a venturi, whose upstream diameter is 4.0 in and throat diameter is 2.5 in (see the diagram below).

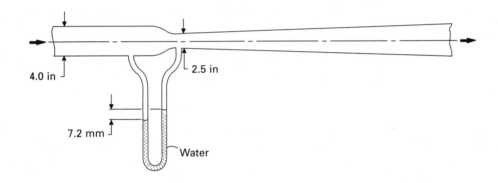

The manometer indicates a pressure difference of 7.2 mm of water, and the density of water is 1000 kg/m^3, of course.

Recalling that, in ideal conditions, the fluid velocity u at the throat is given by

$$u = \sqrt{\frac{2(p_1 - p_2)}{\rho(1 - (A_2/A_1)^2)}}$$

find the value of u, in m/s.

Answers: 1: 1.79×10^{-5} N s/m^2; 2: 175 kg/m^3; 3: 11.8 m/s

21

Dimensions and dimensional consistency

Suppose we do a physical experiment, for example by applying a force to a mass and observing the acceleration. The relationship between these variables is given by $F = ma$, and of course this equation applies whatever set of consistent units we may use to measure the variables with.

With any physical experiment, the actual physical quantities and the relationship between them are not affected by our choice of units.

So it ought to be possible to check that an equation is consistent, i.e. that the same units can be used to measure every term in the equation, without needing to use any particular set of units to carry out the check.

Let us denote our unit of length by [L], where [L] could be a metre, or a foot, or a kilometre etc. This general unit of length is often called a *dimension*; the square brackets are included to distinguish it from an ordinary variable.

Likewise, our unit, or dimension, of time is written [T], which could be a second, or a minute, or an hour etc.

Then the unit of velocity is derived from these and will be [L]/[T], distance travelled per unit time. For shortness this is usually written

$$\left[\frac{L}{T}\right]$$

So the unit of acceleration will be . . .?

22

$$\boxed{\left[\frac{L}{T^2}\right]}$$

Acceleration is increase of velocity per unit time, and its units are the units of velocity divided by time, that is

$$\left[\frac{L}{T}\right] \div [T], \text{ or } \left[\frac{L}{T^2}\right]$$

What will be the unit, or dimension, of volume?

23

$$\boxed{[L^3]}$$

A volume is of course the product of three lengths, so its unit must be the cube of the length unit, [L]. Remember to include the square brackets, to indicate that $[L^3]$ is a unit of measurement, not the cube of a variable.

In just the same way, our general unit of mass will be written [M], which could be a kilogram, or a tonne, or a gram etc.

These three units, or dimensions, of mass, length and time, are sufficient to form all the other units we need in mechanics. (Another unit, usually of temperature, has to be introduced for problems of thermodynamics, and yet another, usually of electric charge, for electrical problems, but these are outside the scope of this book.)

What are the dimensions, or units, in terms of [M], [L] and [T] of

(i) Mass flow rate (i.e. mass flowing per unit time)
(ii) Density?

24

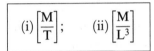

Here is the working:

(i) Mass flow rate, or mass per unit time, has units of mass/time. The unit of mass is [M] and the unit of time is [T], so the unit of mass flow rate is [M/T].
(ii) Density is mass/volume. The unit of volume is $[L^3]$, so the unit of density is $[M/L^3]$.

Each expression in square brackets, representing the units in terms of [M], [L] and [T] of mass flow rate, density etc., is often called the *dimensional formula*, or simply the *dimensions*, of the quantity.

Thus we say that the dimensions of density are $[M/L^3]$, the dimensions of acceleration are $[L/T^2]$ etc.

What are the dimensions of linear momentum?

25

$$\left[\frac{ML}{T}\right]$$

Linear momentum is mass × velocity, so in terms of [M], [L] and [T] its dimensions are

$$[M] \times \left[\frac{L}{T}\right], \text{ or } \left[\frac{ML}{T}\right]$$

So far we have *derived* the dimensions of velocity, acceleration, volume, mass flow rate, density and linear momentum from the three fundamental dimensions [M], [L] and [T] of mass, length and time. In Frame 17 we saw how we could derive the unit, or dimensions, of force from the units of mass and acceleration.

In terms of [M], [L] and [T], the dimensions of force are ...?

26

$$\left[\frac{ML}{T^2}\right]$$

Working: the relationship between force, mass and acceleration is given by the equation $F = ma$, in which, as with any equation that represents physical reality, the same units must be used to measure the quantities on both sides of the equation.

The dimension, or unit, of mass is [M], and the dimensions of acceleration are $[L/T^2]$, so the unit of force is the product of these:

$$[M] \times \left[\frac{L}{T^2}\right], \text{ or } \left[\frac{ML}{T^2}\right]$$

Now that we know the dimensions of force, we can find the dimensions of other quantities involving force.

What are the dimensions, in terms of [M], [L] and [T], of

(i) Pressure
(ii) Work (i.e. force × distance)?

$$(i) \left[\frac{M}{LT^2}\right]; \ (ii) \left[\frac{ML^2}{T^2}\right]$$

Working: (i) Pressure is force per unit area. The dimensions of force and area are $[ML/T^2]$ and $[L^2]$ respectively, so the dimensions of pressure are

$$\left[\frac{ML}{T^2}\right] \div [L^2] = \left[\frac{M}{LT^2}\right]$$

(ii) Work = force × distance, so its dimensions are

$$\left[\frac{ML}{T^2}\right] \times [L] = \left[\frac{ML^2}{T^2}\right]$$

We have come across instances where equations include numerical coefficients, such as the $\frac{1}{2}$ in the expression $\frac{1}{2}mv^2$ for kinetic energy, or the 2 in the equation $v^2 = u^2 + 2as$. These numbers are always the same, whatever consistent system of units we decide to use, so clearly they cannot have any units themselves. They are *dimensionless*.

Not all constants are dimensionless, however. For example, the gravitational acceleration, g, has a value which depends on the units used: 9.81 m/s^2, 981 cm/s^2, 32.2 ft/s^2 etc. Being an acceleration, it has dimensions $[L/T^2]$.

The gravitational potential energy of a body of mass m, height h above a datum, is given by mgh. What are the dimensions of gravitational potential energy?

$$\left[\frac{ML^2}{T^2}\right]$$

The dimensions of mgh are

$$[M]\left[\frac{L}{T^2}\right][L] = \left[\frac{ML^2}{T^2}\right]$$

You can compare this result with the one we obtained for the dimensions of work in Frames 26 and 27. The dimensions are of course the same – as they should be, since work is often equal to an increase or decrease of energy.

Carry on now to Frame 29.

29

There are some quantities that have no dimensions at all.

You are probably familiar with stress and strain, in steel specimens for example. Tensile strain, you may remember, is defined as the increase in length of a specimen divided by its original length.

The dimensions of strain are therefore [L] ÷ [L] , which is sometimes written as [1]: strain is a dimensionless quantity. The same units must of course be used to measure both the extension and the original length, but provided this is done the ratio will be the same, whatever units are being used. Strain itself has no units, and its value is a pure number.

The angle α shown below, when measured in radians, is given by $\alpha = \ell/r$, ℓ being the length of the arc subtended to radius r.

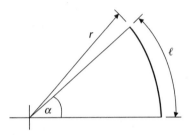

What are the dimensions of angle α?

30

[1]: angles are dimensionless

An angle is given by the ratio of two lengths, so it has no dimensions.

Radians are not the only units we can use to measure angles; degrees are more commonly used. Degrees can also be thought of as ratios of two lengths, and so are dimensionless, but when dividing the arc by the radius to obtain the angle in degrees we in effect use different units for the arc and the radius, so degrees incorporate an additional (dimensionless) multiplier.

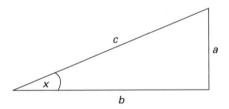

Trigonometrical ratios, such as $\sin x$ and $\tan x$, are all ratios of two lengths. Referring to the diagram above, $\sin x = a/c$, $\tan x = a/b$; so the dimensions of $\sin x$ and $\tan x$ are ...?

31

> They are dimensionless

Just as in the case of angles, the trigonometrical ratios are all ratios of two lengths and so are dimensionless. They have no units.

These trigonometrical ratios can all be expressed in the form of power series, (see for example K.A. Stroud, *Engineering Mathematics*), such as

$$\sin x = x - \frac{x^3}{6} + \frac{x^5}{120} - \cdots$$

$$\tan x = x + \frac{x^3}{3} + \frac{2x^5}{15} + \cdots$$

We call the quantity x the *argument* of $\sin x$, $\tan x$ etc. Now let's suppose for a moment that x could have dimensions, such as [L], for example.
  What would be the dimensions of successive terms of the power series expression for $\sin x$? Is it possible for the argument of $\sin x$ to have dimensions?

32

> No: x must be dimensionless

If x had dimensions, such as [L], then successive terms in the series for $\sin x$ would have dimensions [L], $[L^3]$, $[L^5]$ etc. They would all be dimensionally different, would need different units of measurement, and could not meaningfully be added together or subtracted.
  The only possibility is that the argument x must be dimensionless, so that all the terms in the power series are dimensionless. And the left-hand sides of the equations, that is $\sin x$, $\tan x$ etc., are all dimensionless too (as you already knew from Frames 30 and 31).

We sometimes come across expressions like $\sin \omega t$, $\cos kx$, $\sin(\omega t - kx)$, denoting various kinds of wave motion.
  Referring to the expression $\sin(\omega t - kx)$, in which t denotes time and x denotes distance, what must be the dimensions of ω and k?

33

$$\left[\frac{1}{T}\right]; \left[\frac{1}{L}\right]$$

The argument, $(\omega t - kx)$, has to be dimensionless, so both of the terms within it must be dimensionless. The dimensions of t are [T] and those of x are [L]; so the dimensions of ω and x must be the reciprocals of these.

Another well-known power series is the one for e^x:

$$e^x = 1 + x + \frac{x^2}{2} + \frac{x^3}{6} + \dots$$

What can you say about the dimensions of x, the exponent?

34

x must be dimensionless

As before, all the terms in the power series must have the same dimensions, or else they cannot be added together. The only way this can be achieved is for them all to be dimensionless; so the left-hand side of the equation, e^x, must also be dimensionless.

We are now able to find the dimensions of any quantity we are likely to meet in fluid or solid mechanics, and so to investigate whether all the terms in any physical equation are dimensionally consistent, that is, that they all have the same dimensions. Unless this is so, the equation cannot be correct.

Here is a simple example: in the constant acceleration equation $v = u + at$, find the dimensions of each of the three terms, and check that the equation is dimensionally consistent.

All three terms have dimensions [L/T], so the equation is consistent

Working: the term v on the left-hand side is the final velocity, so it has the dimensions of velocity, [L/T].

The first term on the right-hand side, u, is the initial velocity: also [L/T].

The final term at is the product of the acceleration a (dimensions [L/T^2]) and the elapsed time t (dimensions [T]), so its dimensions are $\left[L/T^2\right] \times [T] = [L/T]$. So the equation *is* dimensionally consistent, i.e. all terms in the equation have the same dimensions. Remember that the dimensions of each term only tell us what kind of units should be used to measure the variable; they do not tell us anything about the value of the variable.

Now here is Bernoulli's equation in one of its possible forms:

$$p + \tfrac{1}{2}\rho u^2 + \rho g z = \text{constant}$$

The first term is a pressure; we found in Frame 27 that the dimensions of pressure are [M/LT^2]. Remembering that ρ denotes density and z the height above a datum, work out the dimensions of the second and third terms; and what must be the dimensions of the constant on the right-hand side?

The dimensions of both terms are $\left[M/LT^2\right]$
The dimensions of the constant must also be $\left[M/LT^2\right]$

Working: the dimensions of $\tfrac{1}{2}\rho u^2$ are

$$\left[\frac{M}{L^3}\right]\left[\frac{L}{T}\right]^2 = \left[\frac{M}{LT^2}\right]$$

(the coefficient $\tfrac{1}{2}$ is dimensionless) and the dimensions of $\rho g h$ are

$$\left[\frac{M}{L^3}\right]\left[\frac{L}{T^2}\right][L] = \left[\frac{M}{LT^2}\right]$$

so both terms have the dimensions of pressure, as they must.

The constant on the right-hand side must have the same dimensions as all other terms in the equation, i.e. $\left[M/LT^2\right]$ also.

37

The fact that all the terms of an equation must have the same dimensions provides us with a very useful check on our theoretical work. We cannot be certain that an equation that is dimensionally consistent is right; but we *can* be absolutely sure that a dimensionally inconsistent equation must be wrong.

The equation below, which looks as if it is intended to relate the kinetic and potential energies of a particle in free fall, has an error in it.

$$\tfrac{1}{2}mv^2 = \tfrac{1}{2}mu^2 + mh$$

By finding the dimensions of each of the three terms in the equation, can you say what is wrong with it?

38

> The dimensions are $[ML^2/T^2]$, $[ML^2/T^2]$ and $[ML]$. These are not all the same, so there must be an error in the equation. The third term can be brought to the same dimensions as the other two by multiplying by a factor with dimensions $[L/T^2]$.

You have probably realised that $[L/T^2]$ are the dimensions of acceleration. This may suggest to us, if we didn't know already, that g, the gravitational acceleration, is the factor missing from the third term.

This example shows how a dimensional check on an equation not only may show when the equation is incorrect, but also often suggests what the error is.

Here is another example: if a windmill of swept area A operates in a wind of speed u, then the maximum power available from the wind might be (incorrectly) calculated to be $\tfrac{1}{4}\rho A u^2$, ρ being the density of the air. Find the dimensions of this expression, and compare them with the dimensions of power (remember that power is rate of doing work, i.e. work per unit time). Can you suggest the correct form of the expression?

> The dimensions of $\frac{1}{4}\rho A u^2$ are
>
> $$\left[\frac{M}{L^3}\right][L^2]\left[\frac{L^2}{T^2}\right] = \left[\frac{ML}{T^2}\right],$$
>
> which you may recognise as the dimensions of force, while the dimensions of power are those of work per unit time, or
>
> $$\left[\frac{ML^2}{T^3}\right]$$

This suggests that the expression should be not $\rho A u^2$ times some constant, but $(\rho A u^2 \times u)$ multiplied by a constant: i.e. a constant $\times \rho A u^3$.

This is indeed true. The correct expression for the power in the wind passing through a circle of area A is actually $\frac{1}{2}\rho A u^3$. This illustrates that dimensional reasoning can help us to detect errors in the form of expressions, and can often suggest what the correct form should be. It cannot, however, tell us the value of the constant numerical coefficient, because the coefficient is dimensionless. Thus the coefficient $\frac{1}{2}$ in the expression $\frac{1}{2}\rho A u^3$ could not be predicted by dimensional reasoning. To find its value, we have either to do some careful analysis, or carry out some experiments.

As a matter of interest, even an ideal windmill could not extract more than 59% of the power in the wind, i.e. not more than 59% of $\frac{1}{2}\rho A u^3$. The best practical windmills extract only 35% or less.

40

Here is an equation which describes laminar flow of a fluid between two parallel plates, where one plate is moving with speed U, and there is a pressure gradient in the x direction, $\mathrm{d}p/\mathrm{d}x$:

$$u = \frac{U}{h}y - \frac{y}{2\mu}\left(\frac{\mathrm{d}p}{\mathrm{d}x}\right)(h-y)$$

The equation gives an expression for the velocity u of the fluid at a particular distance y from the fixed plate.

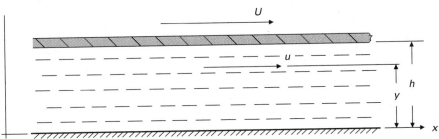

We wish to check that this equation is dimensionally consistent. There is nothing particularly difficult about this, but first of all we need to look at the dimensions of a derivative, like $\mathrm{d}p/\mathrm{d}x$. We will do this in the next frame.

41

A derivative, such as dp/dx, comes from the limit as δx tends to zero of $(\delta p/\delta x)$; so its dimensions are just those of p divided by those of x.

Likewise, the second derivative $d^2p/dx^2 = (d/dx)(dp/dx)$ comes from the limit as δx tends to zero of

$$\left(\frac{\text{the change in the value of } dp/dx}{\delta x} \right)$$

and its dimensions are those of p divided by those of x^2; and similarly for higher derivatives.

If you are in any doubt, think of how we read out a derivative like d^2p/dx^2: 'D-two-p by D-x-squared'. The bottom line of the fraction has the dimensions of x-squared, while the top has the dimensions of just the pressure p.

If x is a length, what are the dimensions of d^3x/dt^3, in terms of [L] and [T]?

42

$$\boxed{[L/T^3]}$$

The dimensions of d^3x/dt^3 are those of x divided by those of t^3, that is

$$[L] \div [T^3] = [L/T^3]$$

Now, going back to the equation we had before

$$u = \frac{U}{h}y - \frac{y}{2\mu}\left(\frac{dp}{dx}\right)(h - y)$$

the dimensions of the left-hand side of the equation are simply [L/T], the dimensions of a velocity.

The first term on the right-hand side, $(U/h)y$, is a velocity multiplied by the ratio of two lengths, so its dimensions are those of velocity also.

What about the remaining term? Find out what its dimensions are, using what you know about the dimensions of derivatives, and check that the equation is dimensionally consistent. (The viscosity, μ, has cropped up already, e.g. in Frame 20 of this programme, so you should be able to work out its dimensions.)

43

> The dimensions are $[L/T]$, so the equation is consistent.

The dimensions of the derivative dp/dx are those of pressure divided by those of distance, i.e.

$$\left[\frac{M}{LT^2}\right] \div [L] = \left[\frac{M}{L^2T^2}\right]$$

As you could work out from its definition, the dimensions of dynamic viscosity μ are $[M/LT]$, so the dimensions of the whole expression

$$\frac{y}{2\mu}\left(\frac{dp}{dx}\right)(h-y)$$

are

$$\frac{[L]}{[M/LT]}\left[\frac{M}{L^2T^2}\right][L] = \left[\frac{L}{T}\right]$$

so all three terms of the equation have the dimensions of velocity $[L/T]$, and the equation is dimensionally consistent.

44

This brings us to the end of this programme, except for the test exercise.

Before you tackle that, read the revision summary that follows on the next page. If there are any points of which you are not completely sure, turn back to that point in the programme and revise them before continuing.

45

Revision summary

1 *Consistency of units*

Quantities which are to be added, subtracted or equated must be measured in the same units.

2 *Conversion of units*

To convert a quantity to different units, a straightforward method is to replace the existing units by their exact equivalent quantities, as for example

$$90\left(\frac{km}{h}\right) = 90\left(\frac{1000 \text{ m}}{3600 \text{ s}}\right) = 25\left(\frac{m}{s}\right)$$

3 *SI units of force*

In the SI system forces are measured in newtons. The newton is a derived unit: it is a special name given to the unit $kg \text{ m/s}^2$, which arises directly from the equation $F = ma$. (We could just as well write '$kg \text{ m/s}^2$' each time. It is more convenient to write 'newtons', or simply 'N', but remember that '$kg \text{ m/s}^2$' is what this really means.)

4 *Dimensional formulae*

The units of a given quantity always have the same form, whichever system of units we use. Thus, the units of velocity may be ft/s, m/s, mile/h etc.: in every case the unit is a distance divided by a time.

This can be expressed in terms of dimensions [M], [L] and [T]. The result we call the *dimensions* or *dimensional formula* of the quantity. Thus the dimensions of velocity are [L/T], of density are $[M/L^3]$, etc.

5 *Dimensions of arguments in trigonometric functions etc.*

The argument x in functions like $\sin x$, $\tan x$ and e^x must be dimensionless. All of these functions can be expressed as power series in the argument x, and the terms of such series can only have the same dimensions if x, and therefore all the terms, are dimensionless.

6 *Dimensional consistency*

Quantities which are to be added, subtracted or equated must have the same dimensions – or else they cannot be measured in the same units. It is good practice to carry out regular dimensional checks during theoretical work.

Now work through the test exercise in Frame 46.

Test exercise

1 (i) Find the dimensions of modulus of elasticity ($=$ stress/strain).
  (ii) The kinematic viscosity ν of a fluid is defined as the dynamic viscosity μ
       divided by the density ρ. What are the dimensions of kinematic viscosity?

2 Check whether each of the following equations is dimensionally consistent:

  (i)

$$a = r\frac{\mathrm{d}^2\theta}{\mathrm{d}t^2} + 2\left(\frac{\mathrm{d}r}{\mathrm{d}t}\right)\left(\frac{\mathrm{d}\theta}{\mathrm{d}t}\right)$$

a : acceleration	r : length
θ : angle	t : time

  (ii)

$$F = B\rho u^2 \ell^2 + C\mu u \ell^2$$

F : force	u : velocity
B, C : dimensionless constants	ρ : density
ℓ : length	μ : viscosity

Programme 8

SIMILARITY AND
THE TESTING OF MODELS

1

An economical way to present numerical data

In the previous programme we saw how to find the dimensions of physical quantities, and that quantities which are added, subtracted or equated must have the same dimensions.

There are many instances where numerical information – the results of experiments, say, or the solutions of complex equations – is presented in the form of graphs, or tables of values. For example, the results of experiments to determine the pressure drop in fluid flowing through pipes are usually given as curves on a graph, and data on thermodynamic properties of steam and water are presented in tables. These graphs and tables can occupy many pages, and it usually takes some time to consult them. Using our knowledge of dimensions, we can often condense the information into a much more compact form.

To illustrate this we will consider a simple equation which we mentioned in the previous programme, the constant acceleration equation $v = u + at$.

Given values of the initial velocity u and the acceleration a, we can draw a graph showing how the velocity v varies with time t. For the values $u = 1.5$ m/s and $a = 1$ m/s^2, try sketching a graph of v against t. (Use a ruler to draw the two axes, of v vertically and t horizontally.)

2

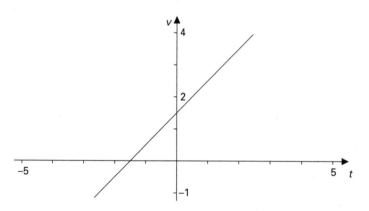

The equation $v = u + at$ is a first-degree equation in v and t, so the graph of v against t must be a straight line. Setting $t = 0$ in the equation, we get $v = u$, which gives the intercept on the v axis (1.5 m/s in this case); the gradient is $dv/dt = a$, of course, and in this case a is equal to 1 m/s^2. (If this is unfamiliar, you can follow it up in a suitable textbook such as K. A. Stroud, *Engineering Mathematics* – the section on curves and curve fitting.)

Using the same method, plot on the same axes the line for the values $u = -0.5$ m/s and $a = 2$ m/s^2.

3

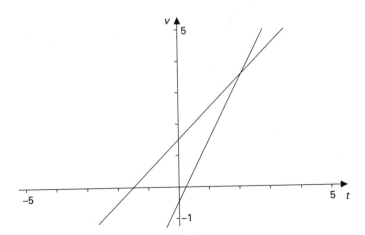

In this case the intercept on the v axis is at $u = -0.5$ m/s, and the gradient is $a = 2$ m/s^2; the line can be drawn straight away.

We could draw many more lines, for different pairs of values of u and a.

These lines can be used to find values of the velocity v at any given time t. For the case where the initial velocity is $u = 1.5$ m/s and the acceleration is $a = 1$ m/s^2, use your graph to find the velocity at time $t = 3$ s.

4

$$\boxed{4.5 \text{ m/s}}$$

This is easy enough, being just a matter of reading from one of the lines on our graph, though in this case we could find the velocity just as well, if not better, by solving the equation. Remember, though, that we are only using the equation $v = u + at$ as an illustration: in a real case the equation would not be one we could solve easily, if indeed we were able to write it down at all.

But we can only use the graphs to solve a problem if a line has already been drawn for the right pair of values of u and a, or at least for some nearby values. To make our graph widely applicable, a very large number of lines would have to be drawn, and this seems very cumbersome.

In the equation $v = u + at$, all terms have the dimensions of velocity, [L/T]. If we divide all the terms by a velocity – say, the initial velocity u – we get

$$\left(\frac{v}{u}\right) = 1 + \left(\frac{at}{u}\right)$$

What are the dimensions of each term in this equation?

5

[1] : all the terms are dimensionless

We are now going to treat the quantities in brackets, (v/u) and (at/u), as our variables, and plot a new graph. It looks like this:

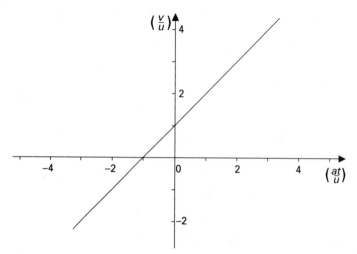

... just a single straight line. You may like to check that this line satisfies the equation $v/u = 1 + at/u$.

Returning to our earlier problem, where we wished to find v at time $t = 3$ s when $u = 1.5$ m/s and $a = 1$ m/s^2, with these values we have

$$\frac{at}{u} = \frac{1 \times 3}{1.5} = 2$$

From the graph above, we find that, when $at/u = 2$, $v/u = \dots$?

6

$$v/u = 3$$

So, with $u = 1.5$ m/s, we get $v = 3 \times 1.5 = 4.5$ m/s, just as before.

The attraction of using this form of presentation – in terms of dimensionless ratios – is that the *single* line shown contains all the information that previously we needed *many* lines to portray. We can pick *any* pair of values of the initial velocity u and the acceleration a, and find the velocity at any time t.

Try it for the following case:

initial velocity $u = 1.0$ m/s

acceleration $a = -0.5$ m/s^2

Using the graph shown in Frame 5, find the velocity v at time $t = 4$ s.

$$\boxed{v = -1 \text{ m/s}}$$

Here is the working:

$$\frac{at}{u} = \frac{(-0.5)(4)}{1.0} = -2$$

From the graph, when

$$\frac{at}{u} = -2, \frac{v}{u} = -1$$

so

$$v = -1 \times u = -1 \times 1 = -1 \text{ m/s}$$

Try using the graph again to solve this slightly different problem: if the initial velocity is $u = 2$ m/s, what acceleration is necessary to achieve a final velocity $v = 6$ m/s after 2.5 s have elapsed?

$$\boxed{1.6 \text{ m/s}^2}$$

In this problem we know the values of both v and u, so we can find the ratio (v/u) immediately:

$$v/u = 6/2 = 3$$

From the graph we find that, when $v/u = 3$, $at/u = 2$, and therefore

$$a = \frac{2u}{t} = \frac{2 \times 2}{2.5} = 1.6 \text{ m/s}^2$$

We could of course answer these questions more directly by using the equation $v = u + at$. But if we were dealing with a situation where we wished to present the data graphically as concisely as possible, the graph of one dimensionless ratio (v/u) against the other (at/u) would be much the best way of doing it.

This is exactly the situation we find when we are doing experiments to find the relationship between variables in a certain physical situation: we wish to present the results as concisely as possible, so that the relationship is quickly found. The best way to do this is usually to find dimensionless ratios of the variables, and then from the experimental results to calculate values of these ratios and plot them as points on a graph.

9

Let us suppose we wished to do some experiments to find the relationship between the distance s travelled in a straight line by an object, its initial velocity u, the elapsed time t and the constant acceleration a. (For the moment we will imagine we don't know the equation $s = ut + \frac{1}{2}at^2$.)

The first thought might be to plot graphs of s against t, for various pairs of values of u and a. We would get a set of graphs like these:

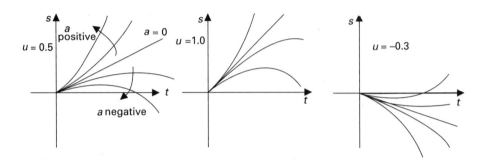

These graphs represent a great deal of experimental effort, each of the many lines requiring perhaps five or more measurements, and the form of the relationship between s, u, a and t is not very obvious from the graphs.

Now let's look at the situation if we plot a graph of dimensionless ratios. First we need to find some suitable ratios among the variables s, u, a and t: for the moment we can cheat a little and look at the equation $s = ut + \frac{1}{2}at^2$.

All the terms in this equation have dimensions . . . .?

10

$$\boxed{[L]}$$

s is a distance, so its dimensions are [L], and it is easy to check that the other two terms also have dimensions [L], as of course they must.

If we divide through by one of the terms, say ut, we get a dimensionless version of the equation

$$\left(\frac{s}{ut}\right) = 1 + \tfrac{1}{2}\left(\frac{at}{u}\right)$$

relating two dimensionless ratios (s/ut) and (at/u).

We will now run our imaginary experiment again, and plot a graph of one dimensionless ratio (s/ut) against the other (at/u).

11

So that you can plot the graph yourself as we go along, sketch out a grid like the one below on your own sheet of paper. You don't need to be very precise: it would be easiest to use squared paper if you have some handy, but plain or lined paper and a sketched grid will do just as well.

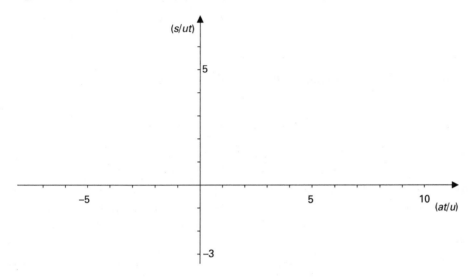

When you have prepared the grid, go on to the next frame.

12

For our first test, we must choose values for the initial speed u and the acceleration a: we could choose

$$u = 0.2 \text{ m/s and } a = 0.5 \text{ m/s}^2$$

We then carry out our test, noting the distance covered, s, at intervals of time. Here are the results:

t (s)	0	1	2	3	4
s (m)	0	0.46	1.38	2.84	4.78

(s/ut)	—	
(at/u)	0	

Bearing in mind that $u = 0.2$ m/s and $a = 0.5$ m/s^2, can you now fill in the spaces in the table? (Two places of decimals are sufficient.)

13

t (s)	0	1	2	3	4
s (m)	0	0.46	1.38	2.84	4.78

(s/ut)	—	2.30	3.45	4.73	5.98
(at/u)	0	2.5	5.0	7.5	10.0

Working: in the first column, $s = 0.46$ m and $t = 1$ s, so

$$\left(\frac{s}{ut}\right) = \frac{(0.46 \text{ m})}{(0.2 \text{ m/s}) \times (1 \text{ s})} = 2.30$$

$$\left(\frac{at}{u}\right) = \frac{(0.5 \text{ m/s}^2) \times (1 \text{ s})}{(0.2 \text{ m/s})} = 2.5$$

Both of these are dimensionless: they are simply numbers, with no units.

The values in the other columns of the table are calculated in the same way.

Now plot the four points corresponding to each pair of values for (s/ut) and (at/u) on your grid.

14

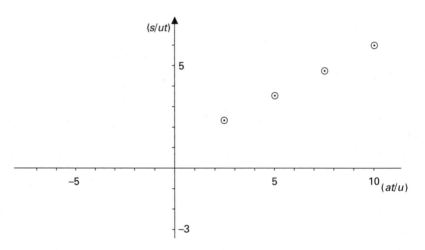

The four points lie roughly in a straight line. This is encouraging, but we have only done one test, with fixed values for u and a. With different values, we may get a different line, or even a curve.

Move on now to the next frame, where...

15

... we will select some new values for *u* and *a* and do another test. We will try $u = 0.4$ m/s and $a = 0.6$ m/s^2.

This time the results are:

t (s)	0	2	4	6
s (m)	0	2.03	6.42	13.14

(*s/ut*)	—			
(*at/u*)	0			

Again, fill in the spaces in the table and plot the three points on your graph.

16

Here is the completed table:

t (s)	0	2	4	6
s (m)	0	2.03	6.42	13.14

(*s/ut*)	—	2.54	4.01	5.48
(*at/u*)	0	3.0	6.0	9.0

The three new points fall close to the straight line through the four earlier points. This is beginning to look less like a fluke.

We will do one more test, this time with a negative initial velocity, to see if this produces a contradictory result: try $u = -0.5$ m/s, $a = 1.0$ m/s^2.

This time the results are:

t (s)	0	2	4
s (m)	0	1.03	5.95

(*s/ut*)	—		
(*at/u*)	0		

Fill in this (last!) table, and put in the last two points on the graph.

17

t (s)	0	2	4
s (m)	0	1.03	5.95
(s/ut)	—	−1.03	−2.98
(at/u)	0	−4.0	−8.0

Although they lie on the other side of the vertical axis, these two points also lie on the same straight line. Your final graph will look something like this:

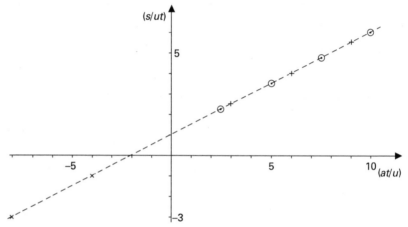

It is now clear that, for the three pairs of values of u and a that we chose, a single relationship exists between the dimensionless ratios (s/ut) and (at/u). Since we chose the values at random, this relationship is very likely a universal one that will apply *whatever* values of u and a we may choose.

You probably know that the equation of a straight line on x–y axes can be written as $y = mx + c$, where m is the gradient of the line and c is the value of y where the line cuts the y axis (if not, see, for example, K. A. Stroud, *Engineering Mathematics*). Have a look at our graph above, and see what the values are of the gradient and the intercept on the y axis. Can you now write down the equation relating the two dimensionless ratios?

18

> Gradient : 0.5; intercept on y axis : 1
> The equation is $(s/ut) = 0.5(at/u) + 1$

This is just $y = mx + c$, but with (s/ut) instead of y, and (at/u) instead of x.

19

The equation we have found, $(s/ut) = 0.5(at/u) + 1$, is easily rearranged to the more familiar form

$$s = ut + \tfrac{1}{2}at^2$$

By presenting our results in terms of dimensionless ratios we have been able to find the relationship between the variables by taking only *nine* readings. This is a very great improvement on the large number of readings we should have to take if we plotted directly graphs of s against t. Even if we did plot a number of these graphs, the relationship between the variables would still not be at all obvious.

The example we have used here, being based on an equation we already knew, is of course a rather artificial one. Usually the graphs that result from experiments will not turn out to be simple straight lines, but working in terms of dimensionless ratios still offers a tremendous saving of effort.

20

Summary

1 Numerical information can usually be condensed into a much more compact form by forming dimensionless ratios of the variables, and recording the values of these dimensionless ratios rather than the values of the variables themselves. This saves a great deal of space when making up tables of values, graphs etc.
2 These tables or graphs of dimensionless ratios contain exactly the same information as all the recorded values of the variables. Although we have to record far fewer values if we use dimensionless ratios, none of the important information is lost.
3 In experiments, it is especially useful to present the results in the form of dimensionless ratios among the variables. The resulting presentation is far more concise, and it is likely to be much easier to make useful deductions from data presented in this way.

Turn on now to the next frame.

21

So we shall often wish to find dimensionless ratios among the variables that are involved in a problem; but there are usually several possible ratios we could choose. In the case we have just considered, where we began by looking at the equation

$$s = ut + \tfrac{1}{2}at^2$$

in which all the terms have dimensions [L], we could have divided through by any of the terms, and obtained these ratios:

(dividing by s) $\dfrac{ut}{s}$ and $\dfrac{at^2}{s}$, or (dividing by at^2) $\dfrac{s}{at^2}$ and $\dfrac{u}{at}$

All of these are dimensionless. We could even raise them to a power, as for example

$$\left(\frac{ut}{s}\right)^2 \text{ or } \left(\frac{at^2}{s}\right)^{1/2}$$

A dimensionless ratio raised to any power remains dimensionless, of course. Now, how do we find suitable dimensionless ratios to use in a real situation? One method is covered in the next few frames.

22

We shall take an example from fluid mechanics, that of the drag force experienced by a smooth spherical body past which a fluid is flowing.

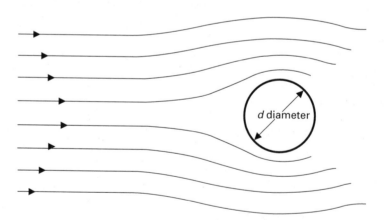

This drag force will be influenced by several factors. The diameter of the sphere will obviously be one such factor: the larger the body is, the greater the drag force it will suffer.

Can you think of some other factors that will affect the drag force on the body?

23

This is rather a hard question for you to answer at this stage, because you really need some experience in fluid mechanics to answer it fully; but perhaps you were able to think of one or two factors that will affect the drag force.

The *speed of the flow* is certainly going to have an effect on the drag force. We all know that a high wind is more likely to blow a fence down than a gentle breeze, and that pedalling a bicycle gets harder the faster you go.

We must also consider the characteristics of the fluid. It may be thick and treacly, or thin and runny: we would expect the drag force to be influenced by the *viscosity* of the fluid.

The *density* of the fluid will also be important, for if the fluid is very dense it is likely to require much more force to make it divert around the body than if it is rarified.

You may have suggested some other candidates – perhaps you thought of the roughness of the surface of the sphere, and certainly this could make a difference, but we did specify that the surface should be smooth. In fact the four quantities mentioned above are all we need.

24

So these four variables are likely to influence the drag force: the size of the body (we will choose its diameter d to indicate this), the speed u of the fluid (this should be measured a long way upstream, where it is unaffected by the presence of the body), the viscosity μ of the fluid, and its density ρ. If the force is F, we can write this as

$$F = \phi(d, u, \mu, \rho)$$

where ϕ represents some function whose form is unknown.

This is just a shorthand way of writing 'F depends on d, u, μ and ρ', and of course it does not give any indication of exactly *how* F will alter as the other quantities d, u, μ and ρ vary. All the equation says is that F depends in some way on the values of the four variables d, u, μ and ρ. We shall call these four variables the *independent variables*, and the drag force F we shall call the *dependent variable*.

If we were going to carry out some experiments to investigate the influence of the four independent variables on the dependent variable F, then it would be sensible to set out the results in the form of dimensionless ratios, so as to yield the most concise form of presentation possible. We need to know how to decide on suitable dimensionless ratios.

There are several ways of tackling this. We will look first of all at a method which is quite straightforward, even if it can sometimes be a bit laborious.

25

We will begin by supposing the function ϕ can be represented as just a product of powers of the independent variables, as follows:

$$F = \phi(d,\ u,\ \mu,\ \rho) = C \times d^\ell u^m \mu^n \rho^r$$

where C is a constant, and the diameter d is raised to the power ℓ, the speed u to the power m, and so forth.

The dimensions of the two sides of this equation must be the same, of course. Recalling that the dimensions of viscosity μ are [M/LT], we have

Left-hand side: $\left[\dfrac{ML}{T^2}\right]$ Right-hand side: $[L]^\ell \left[\dfrac{L}{T}\right]^m \left[\dfrac{M}{LT}\right]^n \left[\dfrac{M}{L^3}\right]^r$

In order for the dimensions of the two sides to be the same, we must have the same powers of M, L and T on each side. Considering the powers of L first, on the left-hand side it appears to the first power, while on the right-hand side the power of L is

$$\ell + m - n - 3r$$

Equating these:

$$1 = \ell + m - n - 3r$$

Now, see if you can produce similar equations for the powers of M and T.

26

for M :	$1 = n + r$
for T :	$-2 = -m - n$

There are four unknown quantities, ℓ, m, n and r, but as there are only three equations their values are not uniquely defined. We can eliminate some of them, though:

from the equation for M: $r = 1 - n$

from the equation for T: $m = 2 - n$

Using these to eliminate r and m from the equation for L we get

$$1 = \ell + (2 - n) - n - 3(1 - n)$$

so

$$1 = -1 + \ell + n$$

giving

$$\ell = 2 - n$$

Now we have found expressions for ℓ, m and r in terms of n. In the next frame we shall see what effect this has on our earlier equation for F.

27

Substituting for ℓ, m and r we get

$$F = C \times d^{(2-n)}u^{(2-n)}\mu^n\rho^{(1-n)}$$

Now

$$d^{(2-n)} = d^2 \times d^{-n} = d^2/d^n$$

Similarly

$$u^{(2-n)} = u^2/u^n$$

and

$$\rho^{(1-n)} = \rho/\rho^n$$

Putting all these into the first equation above and tidying up, we get

$$F = C \times \rho u^2 d^2 \left(\frac{\mu}{\rho u d}\right)^n$$

In this equation, the quantity $(\mu/\rho u d)$ is raised to the power n, in which the value of n is not defined by what we have done so far. The equation is, of course, dimensionally consistent, because that is how we have derived it; it remains dimensionally consistent *whatever* value the exponent n takes.

What does this tell you about the dimensions of the quantity $(\mu/\rho u d)$?

28

> It must be dimensionless

If the equation remains dimensionally consistent irrespective of the value we choose for the exponent n, then the quantity $(\mu/\rho u d)$ cannot have any dimensions at all.

We looked at some other dimensionless quantities in Programme 7, Frames 29–34; you might want to refer back if your memory is at all hazy.

Remembering that the dimensions of dynamic viscosity μ are [M/LT], work out what the dimensions of $(\mu/\rho u d)$ are, and convince yourself that it *is* dimensionless.

29

> The dimensions of $(\mu/\rho ud)$ are
>
> $$\left[\frac{M}{LT}\right]\left[\frac{M}{L^3}\right]^{-1}\left[\frac{L}{T}\right]^{-1}[L]^{-1}$$
>
> and this reduces to [1], confirming that $(\mu/\rho ud)$ is dimensionless.

This dimensionless ratio crops up very frequently in fluid mechanics. We generally use the reciprocal of it, $(\rho ud/\mu)$, which is known as the *Reynolds number*, after the eminent engineer Osborne Reynolds, to whom we shall be referring again later on. We shall denote the Reynolds number by *Re*.

With this notation, we have $F = C \times \rho u^2 d^2 \times (Re)^n$.

30

This is a good moment to think over what we have done: we began in Frame 25 by assuming that the drag force F could be represented by the expression

$$F = C \times d^\ell u^m \mu^n \rho^r$$

We then adjusted the exponents ℓ, m, n and r to make this equation dimensionally consistent, and ended up with the result

$$F = C \times \rho u^2 d^2 \times (Re)^n$$

But we have nowhere justified the original assumption that the drag force really can be expressed as a single product of powers of the variables d, u, μ and ρ, and indeed it seems rather unlikely that something so simple would be able to represent the phenomenon.

However, even a complicated function is usually expressible as a power series, in which (as we saw in Programme 7) the quantity occurring in the series has to be dimensionless. A much more general solution, then, is

$$F = \rho u^2 d^2 [C_0 + C_1(Re) + C_2(Re)^2 + \ldots]$$

The series enclosed in the brackets on the right-hand side of this equation is just a function of the Reynolds number *Re* written out in series form, so we can write more briefly

$$F/\rho u^2 d^2 = f(Re)$$

where f is an unknown function.

Carry on now to the next frame.

This is as far as dimensional reasoning alone will take us. Obviously the equation

$$\frac{F}{\rho u^2 d^2} = f(Re)$$

is not sufficient on its own to tell us how big the drag force on the sphere is, because the function f is unknown.

But by our dimensional analysis of the problem we have reduced the number of variables from *five* (the force F, size d, speed u, viscosity μ and density ρ) to only *two*, the dimensionless ratios $\rho u d / \mu$ (Reynolds number) and $F/\rho u^2 d^2$. This is a very useful achievement, which markedly reduces the amount of work we have to do if we wish to carry out experiments to investigate the drag force on spherical bodies. The equation above is also very helpful in guiding us if we carry out tests on models.

Now we will look at another example, that of medium-sized waves on the surface of the sea. The speed u at which these waves travel varies according to the wavelength λ, and it will also depend on the gravitational acceleration g.

What are the dimensions of the three quantities u, λ and g?

$$\boxed{u: \; [L/T]; \; \lambda: \; [L]; \; g: \; [L/T^2]}$$

Finding the dimensions of quantities like these should be straightforward now.

The speed u depends on the two variables λ and g, so we can write this

$$u = \phi(\lambda, g)$$

The (unknown) function ϕ could be expanded as a series in which each term has the form $C\lambda^\ell g^m$, so the equation can be written

$$u = \Sigma C\lambda^\ell g^m$$

In a general case the values of C, ℓ and m could differ from term to term of the series, but all of the terms of the series must have the same dimensions as each other, and as the left-hand side of the equation.

Taking the typical term $C\lambda^\ell g^m$ on the right-hand side, what are the dimensions of each side of this last equation?

33

The dimensions are : left-hand side [L/T]; right-hand side $[L]^\ell\,[L/T^2]^m$

You should now be able to write down two equations relating the exponents ℓ and m, to state the condition that the dimensions of the two sides of the equation must be the same.

34

$$1 = \ell + m; \quad -1 = -2m$$

The first equation is the condition that the powers of [L] should be the same on the two sides of the equation, and the second is the condition for powers of [T]. (You will notice that the dimension [M] is not involved in these equations. We have two equations, and only two unknowns, ℓ and m, so we are able to solve completely.)

Now, solve these two equations, to find the values of ℓ and m.

35

$$\ell = 1/2; \quad m = 1/2$$

You can easily check, by substituting these values into the equations, that they do satisfy them. If your solution is different, you must have made a mistake somewhere; check over your working before you continue.

The solution for the speed u is thus

$$u = \Sigma C \lambda^{1/2} g^{1/2} = C_1\sqrt{\lambda g} + C_2\sqrt{\lambda g} + \ldots$$
$$u = (C_1 + C_2 + \ldots)\sqrt{\lambda g}$$
$$= C\sqrt{\lambda g}$$

where C is a constant.

We can make use of this result straight away.

Waves on the surface of the sea having a wavelength 5 m are observed to travel at a speed of approximately 2.8 m/s. Applying the equation we have just derived, at what speed will waves whose wavelength is 10 m travel?

$$\boxed{3.96 \text{ m/s}}$$

Here is one method: if we call the speed and wavelength of the 5 m waves u_1, λ_1 and the speed and wavelength of the 10 m waves u_2, λ_2 then

$$\frac{u_2}{u_1} = \frac{(C\sqrt{\lambda g})_2}{(C\sqrt{\lambda g})_1}$$

and, since both C and g are the same whatever kind of sea-waves are occurring,

$$\frac{u_2}{u_1} = \sqrt{\frac{\lambda_2}{\lambda_1}}$$

Putting in the values, we get the speed of the 10 m waves to be

$$u_2 = u_1 \sqrt{\frac{10}{5}} = 2.8 \sqrt{2} = 3.96 \text{ m/s}$$

In each of the two examples we have looked at so far, we have seen that the relationship between the variables can be condensed into an equation involving only dimensionless ratios of those variables. Thus, instead of $F = \phi(d, u, \mu, \rho)$, we ended up with $F/\rho u^2 d^2 = f(Re)$, and instead of $u = \phi(\lambda, g)$, we got $u/\sqrt{\lambda g} =$ constant.

Rather than going through the process of writing down and solving simultaneous equations for the powers to which the variables are to be raised, it would be much more direct to find the dimensionless ratios right at the outset.

Turn now to the next frame, where we shall look at an example of this.

37

We have just done an example on medium-sized waves on the sea's surface. With these waves the restoring force (the force trying to flatten the surface out) is provided almost entirely by gravity.

By contrast, the restoring force for small waves – ripples – comes principally from surface tension. Denoted by the symbol s, this is the effective force per unit width of surface which arises from molecular attraction within the mass of fluid (see Programme 1, Frames 74–84).

It has been found that the speed u with which ripples travel depends on the surface tension s, the density ρ and the wavelength λ. Now we shall see if we can find, simply by inspection, a dimensionless ratio among these variables. First we write down the variables involved, together with their dimensions:

Variables:	u	s	ρ	λ
Dimensions:	$\left[\dfrac{L}{T}\right]$	$\left[\dfrac{M}{T^2}\right]$	$\left[\dfrac{M}{L^3}\right]$	$[L]$

Notice that the fundamental dimension [M] occurs in two of the variables; [T] occurs in two; and [L] occurs in three. We note also that the dimensions of one of the variables, λ, are simply [L]. Now if s is divided by ρ, this eliminates the dimension [M]. The dimensions of the ratio (s/ρ) are

$$[M/T^2] \div [M/L^3] = [L^3/T^2]$$

Next we can use the variable u to eliminate the dimension [T] from the above expression: since u involves [T] raised only to the first power, we need to divide by u^2. The resulting ratio $(s/\rho u^2)$ has dimensions

$$[L^3/T^2] \div [L^2/T^2] = [L]$$

Finally, dividing by λ will yield a dimensionless ratio, which is ...?

38

$$\boxed{s/\rho u^2 \lambda}$$

This ratio was quite easy to find. What we do in these cases is first to write down all the variables, together with their dimensions. Then we can begin to build up ratios of variables, eliminating one fundamental dimension at each stage of building. In this example we left [L] to last, because it is the easiest to eliminate, using the variable λ whose dimensions are [L].

39

A large road sign can be subject to considerable wind forces, the force being at a maximum when the wind comes from exactly behind the sign. The moment necessary at the base of the posts to hold the sign in its upright position is denoted by *B*.

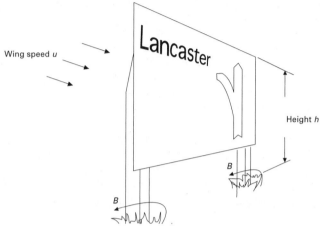

The moment *B* will depend on the height and width of the sign, the speed *u* of the wind, and the density ρ and viscosity μ of the air. We can only consider signs of a fixed shape, i.e. ones in which all lengths are in fixed ratios to one another, because these ratios are all dimensionless and if they could vary it would increase the number of variable dimensionless ratios beyond what we could cope with. This being so, just *one* length is enough to describe the size of the sign, including its width, area and thickness, because all these lengths are in a fixed ratio to each other. We shall use the height, *h*.

We wish to find dimensionless ratios among the variables *B*, *u*, ρ, μ and *h*.

First of all, what are the dimensions of the moment of a force?

$$\left[\frac{ML^2}{T^2}\right]$$

The moment of a force is the force multiplied by the distance of its line of action from the point about which the moment is taken, so its dimensions are those of force times distance, i.e. $[ML/T^2] \times [L]$.

We can now list the relevant variables and their dimensions:

Variables:	*B*	*h*	*u*	ρ	μ
Dimensions:	$\left[\dfrac{ML^2}{T^2}\right]$	$[L]$	$\left[\dfrac{L}{T}\right]$	$\left[\dfrac{M}{L^3}\right]$	$\left[\dfrac{M}{LT}\right]$

Can you form a dimensionless ratio from the first four of these variables?

41

> A possible form is $(B/\rho u^2 h^3)$

Here is the working: two of these variables involve the fundamental dimension [M], two involve [T], and all four involve [L]. Also, the dimensions of one variable, h, are simply [L]. This variable can be used to eliminate [L], which we will do last.

We can eliminate dimension [M] by dividing B by ρ. The dimensions of the result are

$$\left[\frac{ML^2}{T^2}\right] \div \left[\frac{M}{L^3}\right] = \left[\frac{L^5}{T^2}\right]$$

Next, [T] can be eliminated; we must divide by u^2. The dimensions are then

$$\left[\frac{L^5}{T^2}\right] \div \left[\frac{L}{T}\right]^2 = [L^3]$$

Finally, dividing by h^3 gives us a dimensionless ratio, $(B/\rho u^2 h^3)$. Any power of this ratio is also dimensionless, of course, but the form given is probably the most helpful one, because it has the dependent variable B conveniently raised to the first power.

The variable μ has not so far been included. We have already come across a well-known dimensionless ratio involving a density, a velocity, a size and a viscosity. It is commonly known as ...?

42

> The Reynolds number

So we have two dimensionless ratios: $(B/\rho u^2 h^3)$, and the Reynolds number $(\rho uh/\mu)$. The question is, are there any more?

We could also form a dimensionless ratio from the variables B, h, u and μ: $(B/\mu uh^2)$. However, this is simply the product of the two we have already found. There is no point in including it in our equation, because its value can be calculated immediately from the values of the other two ratios. It looks as if two dimensionless ratios are sufficient, in which case the relationship between the variables can be written

$$(B/\rho u^2 h^3) = \phi(\rho uh/\mu)$$

where ϕ represents an unknown function.

We will now address the question: how many dimensionless ratios can be found?

Buckingham's theorem

43

In the road sign example, there were five variables involved (including the dependent variable B), and we found two distinct dimensionless ratios. The reduction from *five* variables to *two* dimensionless ratios is equal to the number of fundamental dimensions involved in the problem, *three* in this case: [M], [L] and [T].

This is an example of the application of Buckingham's theorem, which states that

> if a situation involves n variables and r fundamental dimensions, the relationship between the variables can be written as an equation among p distinct dimensionless ratios, where (in most cases) $p = n - r$.

The problem we did on the speed of ripples on the surface of a liquid involved *four* variables and *three* fundamental dimensions, [M], [L] and [T], and so we were able to find *one* independent dimensionless ratio, $(s/\rho u^2 \lambda)$.

The very first example we did in this programme, where we used the equation $s = ut + \frac{1}{2}at^2$, had *four* variables (s, u, a and t) and just *two* fundamental dimensions, [L] and [T], so we were able to find *two* independent dimensionless ratios.

So all of these cases obey Buckingham's theorem. Here is another example.

44

A v-notch weir is a device for measuring the rate of flow of a liquid in an open channel. Such weirs are used on pump test rigs, effluent treatment plants, drainage systems and so forth. Exact analysis of these weirs is virtually impossible, but dimensional reasoning can be very helpful in reducing the number of measurements necessary to calibrate the weir.

The volume flow rate Q over the weir will depend on the height h of the liquid surface above the bottom of the notch, the density ρ and viscosity μ of the liquid, the gravitational acceleration g, and the angle θ of the notch. (We assume surface tension forces are negligible.)

Now, make up a table of these variables and their dimensions.

45

Variables:	Q	h	ρ	μ	g	θ
Dimensions:	$\left[\dfrac{L^3}{T}\right]$	$[L]$	$\left[\dfrac{M}{L^3}\right]$	$\left[\dfrac{M}{LT}\right]$	$\left[\dfrac{L}{T^2}\right]$	$[1]$

This should all be quite familiar. Now we wish to form dimensionless ratios from these variables, and before we start it will be useful to work out how many ratios we ought to be looking for.

In this problem there are *six* variables, and *three* fundamental dimensions. So how many distinct dimensionless ratios do we expect?

46

Three

The number of distinct dimensionless ratios is equal to the number of variables in the problem (six), less the number of fundamental dimensions (three), and the result of that is $6 - 3 = 3$ dimensionless ratios.

It is convenient to arrange to have the dependent variable appearing in only one dimensionless ratio, if at all possible. The dependent variable here is the volume flow rate, Q.

Can you make up a dimensionless ratio that includes Q?

47

A possible ratio is $(Q/g^{1/2}h^{5/2})$

You may have produced a ratio that looks quite different, such as $(Q\rho/\mu h)$, or indeed some power of either of these. All of these would be perfectly correct. Here is the working to produce the ratio given above.

Starting off with Q, whose dimensions are $[L^3/T]$, we can use the variable g to eliminate $[T]$. The dimensions of g are $[L/T^2]$, so we need to divide by the square root of g.

The dimensions of $(Q/g^{1/2})$ are $[L^3/T] \div [L/T^2]^{1/2} = [L]^{5/2}$.

To achieve our dimensionless ratio, we divide by $h^{5/2}$, giving $(Q/g^{1/2}h^{5/2})$.

Can you find two more dimensionless ratios, neither of them involving Q?

$$\boxed{(\rho g^{1/2} h^{3/2}/\mu) \text{ and } \theta}$$

First of all, we have already seen that angles are dimensionless, so the angle θ is itself one dimensionless ratio.

That leaves the variables h, ρ, μ and g. Dividing ρ by μ gets rid of the dimension [M]: the ratio ρ/μ has dimensions $[T/L^2]$.

Variable g can be used to eliminate [T]: again we need to use $g^{1/2}$, this time multiplying by it. The dimensions of $(\rho g^{1/2}/\mu)$ are $[L^{3/2}]$.

Finally we multiply by $h^{3/2}$, and we have a dimensionless ratio.

Of course, the ratios given are not the only ones possible. You may have produced ratios that are different but still dimensionless, and they will be equally correct. For example, your ratios might be the squares of the ones given here, which at least removes those rather awkward half powers.

49

We have found our three dimensionless ratios, so we can now write the relationship between them as

$$\frac{Q}{g^{1/2}h^{5/2}} = \phi\left(\frac{\rho g^{1/2}h^{3/2}}{\mu}, \theta\right)$$

The ratio on the left-hand side includes the dependent variable, Q, so we call it a *dependent* dimensionless ratio.

The two ratios on the right-hand side, in which the dependent variable does not appear, we call *independent* dimensionless ratios.

Turn over now to the next frame.

50

Testing of models

We have seen (Frames 22–30) that the drag force F on a spherical body of diameter d past which a fluid is flowing at speed u is given by

$$\left(\frac{F}{\rho u^2 d^2}\right) = \phi\left(\frac{\rho u d}{\mu}\right) = \phi(Re)$$

The form of the function ϕ is unknown, but if we made some experimental measurements, we should be able to plot a graph of $(F/\rho u^2 d^2)$ against Re. To cover a wide range of values of the Reynolds number, Re, we may need to use several spheres of different diameters, tested in several fluids with different densities and viscosities, moving at different speeds. The resulting graph would be like this:

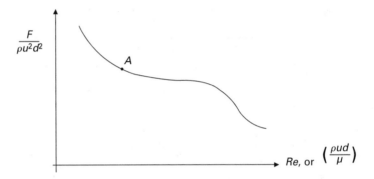

The fact that we get a single curve tells us that no other variables are involved in the problem. (If we left a relevant variable out of our dimensional analysis, we would get a scatter of points, not a unique curve.)

A single point on the curve, say point A, could represent two or more different measurements: one might be made using a small sphere with a dense fluid moving at a high speed, and another with a large sphere and a rarefied fluid moving at a low speed, but with the same value of the Reynolds number in both cases. $(F/\rho u^2 d^2)$ depends only on the Reynolds number, so if the Reynolds number is the same in the two cases, the value of $(F/\rho u^2 d^2)$ will also be the same, and we will get the same point on the graph for both.

> *The fact that one point on the graph can represent two or more different situations is the key to the testing of models.*

Provided the value of the independent dimensionless ratio(s) is the same in both the prototype (i.e. the full-scale version) and the model, the value of the dependent dimensionless ratio will be the same also.

For this example of the drag force on a spherical body, which do you think is the independent dimensionless ratio?

The Reynolds number

The dimensionless equation for this example is $(F/\rho u^2 d^2) = \phi(\rho u d/\mu)$.

The Reynolds number, $(\rho u d/\mu)$, is the relevant independent dimensionless ratio, because it involves only independent variables, while the ratio on the left-hand side of the equation, $(F/\rho u^2 d^2)$, is the dependent dimensionless ratio, because it contains the dependent variable F.

Here is an example: a communications station is to be built on a hilltop , and the reflector is to be protected by a radome, which is approximately a sphere 4 m in diameter. The designer of the radome, wishing to investigate the forces likely to be exerted by winds, decides to test a one-fifth scale model in a wind tunnel. For this model to be a true representation of the full-scale situation, we must make the value of the independent dimensionless ratios for the model the same as for the full-size version.

In this example there is only one independent dimensionless ratio: the Reynolds number. At the top of the hill the density of the air is 1.1 kg/m^3 and its viscosity is 1.8×10^{-5} N s/m^2. If the wind speed is 35 m/s, what is the value of the Reynolds number?

8.56×10^6

With these values, the Reynolds number is

$$\frac{\rho u d}{\mu} = \frac{1.1 \times 35 \times 4}{1.8 \times 10^{-5}} = 8.56 \times 10^6$$

As you can see from this, the Reynolds number can take very large values.

So for the model to be a true representation, its Reynolds number must also have the value 8.56×10^6.

When the value of the independent dimensionless ratios is the same for both the model and the prototype, and the model is an exact scale replica of the prototype, we say that the two situations are *dynamically similar*.

Being at one-fifth scale, the model radome is 0.8 m diameter. If the density and viscosity of the air in the wind tunnel are 1.22 kg/m^3 and 1.8×10^{-5} N s/m^2 respectively, what should the speed of the air in the wind tunnel be?

53

$$\boxed{157 \text{ m/s}}$$

The Reynolds number for the model in the wind tunnel is

$$\frac{\rho u d}{\mu} = \frac{1.22 \times u \times 0.8}{1.8 \times 10^{-5}}$$

and this must be equal to 8.56×10^6, the value for the full-scale radome. Solving this equation, we get $u = 157$ m/s.

You may have realised that it is not really necessary to calculate the actual value of the independent dimensionless ratio to obtain this result. All we need is to write an equation to state that the Reynolds number should be the same in both situations, and solve it directly for the speed u. For this case we get

$$\frac{\rho u d}{\mu} = \text{(full-scale)} \ \frac{1.1 \times 35 \times 4}{1.8 \times 10^{-5}} = \text{(model)} \ \frac{1.22 \times u \times 0.8}{1.8 \times 10^{-5}}$$

For example, the value of the viscosity is the same on both sides of the equation and so can be cancelled out.

54

We have found that the air speed in the wind tunnel has to be several times faster than the speed for the full-scale situation. This may pose a real difficulty, because even 157 m/s is beginning to approach the speed of sound at the wind tunnel (approximately 340 m/s), and when this happens the pressure, and so the density, of the air will vary appreciably around the model. This makes the model situation quite different from the case of the prototype, where the speed is lower and the pressure is virtually the same everywhere.

One way round this is to use a closed-circuit wind tunnel, in which the air can be compressed to several atmospheres, so that its density is increased. If our test on the model radome were to be conducted in such a wind tunnel, in which the density of the air is 11.0 kg/m^3 and the viscosity is the same as before, 1.8×10^{-5} N s/m^2, what would the air speed need to be in the wind tunnel?

$$\boxed{17.5 \text{ m/s}}$$

Again, for dynamic similarity the independent dimensionless ratio must be the same in both situations, and the Reynolds number is the relevant ratio.

$$\frac{\rho u d}{\mu} = \text{(full-scale)} \; \frac{1.1 \times 35 \times 4}{1.8 \times 10^{-5}} = \text{(model)} \; \frac{11.0 \times u \times 0.8}{1.8 \times 10^{-5}}$$

Solving for u, we get $u = 17.5$ m/s.

This is much more satisfactory, because this speed is nowhere near the speed of sound. There are still severe practical drawbacks, though, most notably the cost and complication of the compressed-air wind tunnel.

Another possibility we could consider is to use another fluid entirely, and one fluid that is cheap, non-toxic and readily available is water. Of course, liquids are different from gases, in that they form free surfaces (but our model will be tested in a closed pipe, so this will not be a problem), and also in being virtually incompressible. The air speeds ruling at the hill-top do not give rise to any of the phenomena associated with compressibility, so there is no reason why water should not be used. All we need to do, remember, is to make sure the relevant independent dimensionless ratio has the same value for the model as the prototype. Taking the following values:

	Air at hill-top	Water at model
Density	1.1 kg/m^3	1000 kg/m^3
Viscosity	1.8×10^{-5} N s/m^2	1.14×10^{-3} N s/m^2

find the required speed of the water in the model situation.

$$\boxed{12.2 \text{ m/s}}$$

We choose the speed to make the independent dimensionless ratio the same in the model and the prototype. So

$$\frac{\rho u d}{\mu} = \text{(full-scale)} \; \frac{1.1 \times 35 \times 4}{1.8 \times 10^{-5}} = \text{(model)} \; \frac{1.22 \times u \times 0.8}{1.14 \times 10^{-3}}$$

and solving for u we get $u = 12.2$ m/s.

57

The water tube is provided with a balance to measure the drag force on objects placed within it. In the conditions given, the drag force on the model radome is measured to be 35 kN – a very substantial force – and we now wish to predict the corresponding force on the full-scale radome.

Having arranged that the value of the independent dimensionless ratio, the Reynolds number, is the same for both the model and the prototype, we know that the value of the dependent dimensionless ratio $(F/\rho u^2 d^2)$ will also be the same for both cases.

What is the value of this dependent dimensionless ratio for the model?

58

$$\boxed{0.367}$$

Here is the working:

$$\frac{F}{\rho u^2 d^2} = \frac{35\,000}{1000 \times 12.2^2 \times 0.8^2} = 0.367$$

This ratio has the same value for the prototype (full-scale) version; so now what is the value of the drag force on the full-scale radome?

59

$$\boxed{7.9 \text{ kN}}$$

Working: $(F/\rho u^2 d^2) = 0.367$ for the full-scale radome, so

$$F = 0.367\,\rho u^2 d^2 = 0.367 \times 1.1 \times 35^2 \times 4^2 = 7913 \text{ N} = 7.9 \text{ kN}$$

It is interesting that the drag force on the actual spherical radome is a good deal less than the force on the model. This is because the model is tested in water, which is about 900 times as dense as the air which surrounds the actual radome, and at high values of the Reynolds number (such as we have here) it is the inertia of the fluid that gives rise to the greatest part of the drag.

Turn to the next frame, and we will do another example.

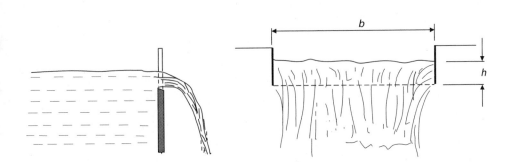

Water flows over a rectangular sharp-edged weir of breadth b, the upstream level of the water being height h above the crest of the weir. Assuming the breadth b is large enough for edge effects to be negligible, the discharge (i.e. the volume flow rate) is proportional to the breadth, so we shall use the flow rate per unit breadth (Q/b) as our dependent variable. This depends on the height h, the density ρ and viscosity μ of the water, and the gravitational acceleration g.

We have five variables here: (Q/b), h, ρ, μ and g. Make a table of these variables and their dimensions, as we have done before. How many independent dimensionless ratios can we form from these variables?

61

We can form *two* independent dimensionless ratios

Here is our table of variables and their dimensions:

Variables:	Q/b	h	ρ	μ	g
Dimensions:	$\left[\dfrac{L^2}{T}\right]$	$[L]$	$\left[\dfrac{M}{L^3}\right]$	$\left[\dfrac{M}{LT}\right]$	$\left[\dfrac{L}{T^2}\right]$

There are five variables, and the three fundamental dimensions $[M]$, $[L]$ and $[T]$ appear, so we expect $5 - 3 = 2$ independent dimensionless ratios.

Now we need to find two dimensionless ratios of these variables, only one of them including the dependent variable (Q/b). You should be able to do this without too much difficulty.

62

$$\boxed{\frac{(Q/b)}{g^{1/2}\,h^{3/2}}, \quad \frac{\rho g^{1/2}\,h^{3/2}}{\mu}}$$

The answers given are of course not the only possibilities. You may have obtained the squares of these, or the reciprocal, or products: for example, $(Q\rho/b\mu)$, $(\rho^2 gh^3/\mu^2)$ would be equally correct.

Using the two dimensionless ratios first given above, the relationship between the variables can be written as

$$\frac{(Q/b)}{g^{1/2}\,h^{3/2}} = \phi\left(\frac{\rho g^{1/2}\,h^{3/2}}{\mu}\right)$$

and this equation applies to *any* rectangular weir for which the breadth is large (so that the atypical flow at the edges forms only a small part of the total) and the equation applies for *any* liquid flowing over the weir.

Suppose a weir like this is to be used to monitor the flow of a liquid whose viscosity is 0.4 times that of water and whose specific gravity is 0.96. Rather than carry out tests on the prototype weir, it is decided to test a scale model using water as the fluid.

What is the appropriate scale for the model?

63

$$\boxed{1.79 \text{ times } \textit{larger} \text{ than the prototype}}$$

For the model to be a true representation of the prototype, the value of the independent dimensionless ratio $(\rho g^{1/2}\,h^{3/2}/\mu)$ must be the same for both. We only have ratios rather than actual values, so writing the values for the model as unity we have

$$(\text{prototype}) \ \frac{0.96 \times g^{1/2} \times (h_p)^{3/2}}{0.4} = (\text{model}) \ \frac{1 \times g^{1/2} \times (h_m)^{3/2}}{1}$$

so the scale is $(h_m/h_p) = (0.96/0.4)^{2/3} = 1.79$.

There is no hard and fast rule that a scale model must be smaller than the prototype. Where the prototype is a very small item, or where only large measuring equipment is available, a large-scale model is often appropriate.

Continuing with this example, if the model is 1.79 times as large as the prototype, what will be the ratio of the volume flow rate for the model weir to that for the prototype?

64

4.29

The dependent dimensionless ratio $[(Q/b)/g^{1/2}h^{3/2}]$ will have the same value in the model and the prototype, so the ratio of the volume flow rates will be

$$\frac{Q_{\text{model}}}{Q_{\text{prototype}}} = \frac{(bh^{3/2})_{\text{model}}}{(bh^{3/2})_{\text{prototype}}} = (1.79)^{5/2} = 4.29$$

The gravitational acceleration g can be omitted from the ratio because it is of course the same for the model and the prototype.

65

Testing of models – summary

1 In any model test the model must be an exact geometric replica of the prototype – even down to the roughnesses of the two surfaces being to scale. We then say that the model and the prototype are *geometrically similar*.
2 A model is a true representation of a full-size prototype when all the relevant independent dimensionless ratios have the same value in both the model and the prototype.
3 When these conditions are satisfied we say that the situations are *dynamically similar*.
4 The dependent dimensionless ratio will then also have the same value in both the model and the prototype.

66

Lift and drag coefficients

We return now to the question of the drag force on a body immersed in a stream of moving fluid. Taking road vehicles as an example, at all but the lowest speeds the drag force exerted by the air is much the largest force that opposes their level motion, so there are strong incentives to reduce the drag and hence both fuel consumption and atmospheric pollution.

To indicate the magnitude of the drag force experienced by different-shaped bodies (such as vehicles) we often use a *drag coefficient* C_D defined by

$$\text{Drag force } F = C_D \, \tfrac{1}{2}\rho u^2 A$$

where ρ is the density of the fluid, u is its velocity relative to the body, and A is an area of the body (usually the projected area viewed along the direction of flow of the fluid: the main exception to this is in the case of aerofoils, where the plan area of the aerofoil is used). You will recognise the term $\tfrac{1}{2}\rho u^2$ from Bernoulli's equation written in pressure terms: it represents the pressure increase that occurs if the flow is brought to a standstill. A drag coefficient of unity is equivalent to this value of pressure difference being exerted over the whole frontal area.

Rearranging this equation, we have $C_D = (F/\tfrac{1}{2}\rho u^2 A)$, which may be compared with our earlier dimensionless ratio $(F/\rho u^2 d^2)$.

What are the dimensions of the drag coefficient, C_D?

67

$$\boxed{\text{It is dimensionless}}$$

The dimensions of the area A are $[L^2]$, the same as those of d^2, so by comparison with the ratio $(F/\rho u^2 d^2)$ we see that C_D is dimensionless.

We have already seen that the dimensionless ratio $(F/\rho u^2 d^2)$ is not a constant, but varies in some manner as the Reynolds number varies. The same must apply to the drag coefficient C_D. (It is an over-simplification to quote a single figure for the drag coefficient of a body such as a vehicle, although for many road vehicles, which are rather bluff, i.e. not very near-perfect aerodynamic shapes, C_D is virtually constant at normal road speeds.)

Let's see how this works in a practical example: turn over now.

68

Example

A road-haulage truck has an approximately rectangular frontal area 2.1 m wide × 4.3 m high. To investigate the drag on the truck, a one-sixth scale model is to be tested in a wind tunnel.

   We can assume that the density and viscosity of the air are the same for the model as for the full-size truck. If the truck travels at 100 km/h, what is the appropriate air speed for the model in the wind tunnel?

$$\boxed{167 \text{ m/s}}$$

The drag coefficient for a truck of given shape depends only on the Reynolds number, so conditions in the wind tunnel will be similar to those for the full-size truck when the Reynolds number has the same value:

$$\left(\frac{\rho u \ell}{\mu}\right)_{\text{model}} = \left(\frac{\rho u \ell}{\mu}\right)_{\text{full-size}}$$

where ℓ denotes a length such as the height of the prototype or model: thus $\ell_{\text{model}}/\ell_{\text{full-size}}$ is one sixth.

   Now $u_{\text{full-size}} = 100$ km/h $= 100 \ (1000 \text{ m}/3600 \text{ s}) = 27.8$ m/s, and the density and viscosity of the air are the same for both, so

$$(u\ell)_{\text{model}} = (u\ell)_{\text{full-size}}$$
$$u_{\text{model}} = 27.8 \times 6 = 167 \text{ m/s}$$

This is a rather high speed for a wind tunnel. Suppose the wind tunnel we have is only capable of 75 m/s, less than half the speed at which conditions would be similar.

   Fortunately, as we have already said, the drag coefficient for bluff bodies such as road-haulage trucks varies only a little with Reynolds number, so we can obtain a quite good estimate of the drag coefficient by testing the model at 75 m/s.

   For our one-sixth scale model tested at 75 m/s, the drag force is 670 N. In these conditions, what is the drag coefficient?

70

$$C_D = 0.79$$

For the full-size truck the frontal area is $2.1 \times 4.3 = 9.03$ m^2, so for the model the area is $(9.03/6^2) = 0.251$ m^2.

$$C_D = F/\tfrac{1}{2}\rho u^2 A$$

so for our model

$$C_D = 670/(\tfrac{1}{2} \times 1.2 \times 75^2 \times 0.251)$$
$$= 0.79$$

So if we assume that the drag coefficient for the full-size truck has approximately the same value, what drag force will it experience when travelling at 100 km/h?

71

$$3.31 \text{ kN}$$

The drag force is

$$F = C_D \times \tfrac{1}{2}\rho u^2 A$$
$$= 0.79 \times \tfrac{1}{2} \times 1.2 \times 27.8^2 \times 9.03 \text{ N}$$
$$= 3.31 \text{ kN}$$

Just as a matter of interest, you may like to calculate the power required to overcome this drag force. (Remember that power is the rate of doing work, which in this case is the drag force multiplied by the speed.)

72

$$92 \text{ kW}$$

Working:

$$\text{Power} = 3.31 \times 27.8 \text{ kW}$$
$$= 92 \text{ kW}$$

Some further power will be consumed in overcoming rolling resistance, but at normal cruising speeds the drag force exerted by the air is much the larger component of the total drag.

Turn now to the next frame.

Aerofoil shapes, such as the wings of aircraft and the blades of turbines and windmills, experience substantial forces perpendicular to the direction of relative motion of the surrounding fluid. This force is called the *lift*.

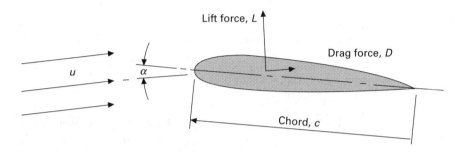

The lift force L on aerofoils of given shape at a given angle of incidence α depends on the density ρ and viscosity μ of the fluid, the velocity u of relative motion of the fluid, and the size of the aerofoil (we can use the chord length c – see the diagram above – as a measure of the size).

An exactly similar argument to that for drag forces leads to the relationship

$$\left(\frac{L}{\rho u^2 c^2}\right) = \phi\left(\frac{\rho u c}{\mu}\right) = \phi(Re)$$

The dimensionless ratio $(L/\rho u^2 c^2)$ could be used as a measure of the lift performance of the aerofoil. The lift coefficient in common use is defined slightly differently, by

$$\text{Lift force } L = C_L \tfrac{1}{2}\rho u^2 S$$

where S is the plan area of the aerofoil (the area of the aerofoil viewed perpendicular to the chord line). Rearranging this, we have

$$C_L = (L/\tfrac{1}{2}\rho u^2 S)$$

The drag coefficient for an aerofoil is defined using the same plan area S, as

$$C_D = (D/\tfrac{1}{2}\rho u^2 S)$$

where we have used the symbol D for the drag force.

Now here is an example: a certain aerofoil is rectangular in plan, with chord 2.2 m and span 15 m. If the lift coefficient is $C_L = 0.38$, find the lift force on the aerofoil when it is moving with speed 140 m/s through still air of density 0.85 kg/m^3.

74

$$\boxed{105 \text{ kN}}$$

The lift is

$$L = C_L \tfrac{1}{2}\rho v^2 S$$

The plan area S is equal to $2.2 \times 15 = 33 \text{ m}^2$.
  Therefore

$$L = 0.38 \times 171 \times 0.85 \times 140^2 \times 33 \text{ N}$$
$$= 105 \text{ kN}$$

As you might expect, both the lift coefficient C_L and the drag coefficient C_D vary with the incidence angle α. The graph below shows the variation of C_L for one particular shape of aerofoil. Graphs for other aerofoil shapes are similar, with the lift coefficient increasing with the angle of incidence, rising to a maximum value at around $15°$.

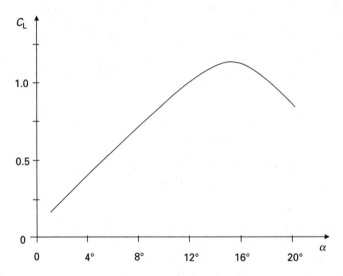

Ignoring the contribution of the aircraft's tail (which is usually small, but negative – pushing downwards rather than upwards) the lift provided by the wing is, in level flight, equal to the aircraft's weight. For an aircraft coming in to land, the air is denser (at lower altitude), but the aircraft will be travelling relatively slowly.
  If our aerofoil already mentioned forms the wing of an aircraft weighing 105 kN which on its landing approach is travelling at 58 m/s in still air of density 1.20 kg/m³, what lift coefficient is required from the aerofoil?

$$\boxed{C_L = 1.58}$$

The lift force required is $L = 105$ kN (although the aircraft is descending rather than flying level, its acceleration will be small and so it will be almost exactly in equilibrium), and the plan area of the wing is 33 m^2.

Then

$$C_L = 105 \times 10^3 / (\tfrac{1}{2} \times 1.2 \times 58^2 \times 33)$$
$$= 1.58$$

As you can see from the graph on the previous page, the best this shape of aerofoil can manage is a lift coefficient of about $C_L = 1.2$. How can we achieve sufficient lift to be able to land?

One way is to go faster – the lift force is proportional to u^2, so this is very effective – but landing at high speeds places heavy demands on undercarriage and tyres, and requires long and costly landing strips. Much the most common solution is to use flaps which alter the shape of the aerofoil to give greater lift, and also often increase its plan area.

This brings us to the end of this programme, apart from the revision summary and the test exercise. Read the revision summary carefully and make sure you have fully understood the content of the programme, then try the test exercise.

76

Revision summary

1 *Dimensionless ratios offer a more compact way of presenting numerical information*
Numerical information, such as the results of experiments or solutions of complex equations, is most compactly stored by forming the variables into dimensionless ratios and recording *their* values, rather than the values of the variables themselves.

2 *Buckingham's theorem*
If a physical situation involves n variables and r fundamental dimensions, we can form $(n - r)$ distinct dimensionless ratios.

3 *Expression of a relationship in dimensionless form*
Any relationship between physical variables can be expressed as an equation among a set of distinct dimensionless ratios of the variables. There will be fewer of these ratios than there were variables, so the dimensionless equation is more compact.

4 *Presenting experimental results in terms of dimensionless ratios*
As with other numerical information, experimental results are most concisely presented in the form of dimensionless ratios. In this form the relationship between the variables is most directly and economically found.

5 *Similarity*
Two situations are *dynamically similar* if all the relevant independent dimensionless ratios have the same value in the two cases. This is the condition that is normally required to be satisfied in tests on models. When this is so, the dependent dimensionless ratio also has the same value in the two cases.

6 *Lift and drag coefficients*
A body immersed in flowing fluid experiences a force parallel to the flow direction, called the *drag force*, D. Often it will also experience a force perpendicular to this direction, which is called the *lift force*, L. We can form dimensionless ratios $(D/\frac{1}{2}\rho u^2 A)$ and $(L/\frac{1}{2}\rho u^2 A)$, which are known as the *drag coefficient* and the *lift coefficient* and denoted by C_D and C_L respectively. A is a reference area, such as the frontal area or plan area. For a given body shape and orientation, C_D and C_L depend on the Reynolds number only.

Test exercise

1 Form a dimensionless ratio involving the following variables: pressure difference Δp, density ρ, length ℓ and volume flow rate Q.

2 A pendulum and its environment are defined by the values of a mass m, a length ℓ, the acceleration of gravity g and the angle of swing θ. Find a ratio of these variables that has the dimensions of time, and so deduce that the period T of the pendulum is given by

$$T\sqrt{g/\ell} = \text{function of } \theta$$

3 (a) In a certain situation a force F is found to depend on the density ρ of the fluid, the diameter d of the pipe in which it is flowing, the velocity u of the flow and the gauge pressure p. Form two suitable dimensionless ratios of these variables.

(b) To investigate the relationship between the variables the following readings are taken, using two different fluids:

Density ρ (kg/m³)	d (m)	u (m/s)	p (bar)	F (N)
1000	0.05	5.9	4.0	1183
1000	0.05	4.7	1.12	364
1000	0.05	8.0	1.95	704
850	0.02	8.5	6.1	297
850	0.02	5.5	1.8	94
850	0.02	12.4	1.2	115

Calculate the values of your two dimensionless ratios for each of these six cases. By plotting a graph, find the relationship between the dimensionless ratios, and hence find the relationship among the five variables.

4 (a) If the resistance force R to motion of a sphere through a fluid depends only on the density ρ and viscosity μ of the fluid, and the diameter d and the velocity u of the sphere, show that R is given by

$$R = (u^2/\rho) \, \phi(\rho u d/\mu)$$

Hence show that at very low velocities, when R is directly proportional to u,

$$R = k\mu u d$$

where k is a dimensionless constant.

(b) A fine granular material of specific gravity 2.5 is in uniform suspension in still water of depth 3 m. Considering the granules as spheres of 0.02 mm diameter, estimate how long it will take for the water to clear. Take $k = 3\pi$.

Programme 9

LAMINAR AND TURBULENT FLOW;

FLOW IN PIPES

1

Laminar flow and turbulent flow

The sketch shows a long tube along which water flows from left to right. A thin stream of coloured dye is introduced into the water on the centre-line of the tube.

Would you expect the stream of dye to be straight, as shown below, or

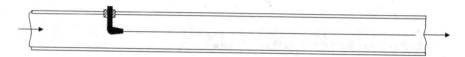

confused, as shown below?

2

> Either is possible

When the water is flowing slowly, the motion is orderly, and all particles move in straight lines parallel to the axis of the tube. The stream of dye will then be straight. This kind of flow is called *laminar flow*.

By contrast, in a fast-moving flow of water the particles move in a random way, in addition to the general left-to-right flow. The dye rapidly gets thoroughly mixed, and after only a short distance the water becomes a uniform pale colour. This is called *turbulent flow*.

But what do we mean here by 'fast' and 'slow'? In particular, at what speed does the flow change from orderly to random – from laminar to turbulent?

This question was investigated by the British engineer Osborne Reynolds at Manchester during the early 1880s, in one of the classic experiments of fluid mechanics. (We have already come across Osborne Reynolds in Frame 29 of Programme 8).

He used a thin filament of coloured dye in water flowing along a glass tube, so that the pattern traced by the dye could be observed. The water was stored in a tank in which it was allowed to settle for some time before each experiment, so that there would be no eddies remaining in the tank that might affect the behaviour of the water in the pipe.

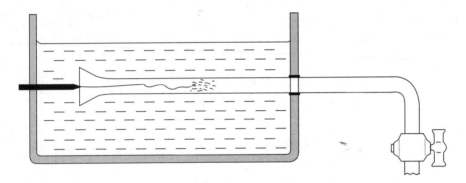

Reynolds observed what we have already discussed: that there are two kinds of flow. Furthermore, he showed that, when the value of the dimensionless ratio

$$\frac{\rho u d}{\mu}$$

is less than about 2000, the flow is always laminar. (Here u represents the *mean* velocity of the fluid, ρ and μ are the density and viscosity, and d is the inside diameter of the tube.) When the value of this ratio is greater than 2000, the flow is usually turbulent, unless special precautions are taken.

We have already met the ratio $(\rho u d/\mu)$ in the previous programme: it is now universally known as the Reynolds number. We denote it by Re.

Here is an example: water at 50 °C flows at a mean speed of 0.5 m/s along a tube of 5 mm diameter. The density of the water is 988 kg/m^3 and the viscosity is 0.548×10^{-3} N s/m^2. Is the flow likely to be laminar or turbulent? Remember, all you need to do is calculate the value of the Reynolds number.

4

$$\boxed{\text{Turbulent}}$$

Working: to determine the character of the flow, we need to calculate the value of the Reynolds number:

$$\frac{\rho u d}{\mu} = \frac{988 \times 0.5 \times (5 \times 10^{-3})}{0.548 \times 10^{-3}}$$
$$= 3830$$

and this is greater than 2000, so the flow is likely to be turbulent.

Whilst Reynolds' experiments were done using water, it has been found that his results apply equally to other fluids. Here is an example: glycerine at 25 °C is flowing down a pipe of inner diameter 20 mm at a mean speed of 0.5 m/s. The density of the glycerine is 1250 kg/m³, and the viscosity μ is 0.942 N s/m². Is the flow likely to be laminar or turbulent?

5

$$\boxed{\text{Laminar}}$$

Once again, we need to calculate the Reynolds number, and this time we find

$$\frac{\rho u d}{\mu} = 13.3$$

and this is less than 2000, so the flow will be laminar.

So far, we have been talking about liquids, but the flow of gases can also be either laminar or turbulent. The Reynolds number criterion applies in just the same way as with liquids.

The density and viscosity of carbon dioxide at 15 °C are 44 kg/m³ and 14.4×10^{-5} N s/m² respectively. If carbon dioxide flows along a tube of diameter 15 mm, what is the greatest velocity at which the flow will definitely be laminar?

6

$$\boxed{0.44 \text{ m/s}}$$

Working: for the flow to be definitely laminar, $\rho u d / \mu < 2000$. Rearranging:

$$u < 2000 \frac{\mu}{\rho d}$$

$$u < \frac{2000 \times 14.4 \times 10^{-5}}{44 \times 0.015}$$

$$u < 0.44 \text{ m/s}$$

Flow of fluids along pipes is obviously a very common occurrence, but, provided the fluid emerges at the other end, you may be wondering why we should worry whether the flow is laminar or turbulent. The answer is that there is a friction loss when fluid flows along a pipe, and this loss is greater when the flow is turbulent. Engineers often need to know how much extra pressure is needed to push the fluid along the pipe because of this friction. Before looking at this in detail, we shall investigate how the pressure drop is related to the shear stress between the fluid and the wall of the pipe.

7

Relationship between pressure drop in a pipe and shear stress at the wall

The diagram below shows a pipe of diameter d, in which a fluid is flowing steadily from left to right. At the point A the pressure is p, and at point B, a distance ℓ further downstream, the pressure has fallen to $(p - \Delta p)$.

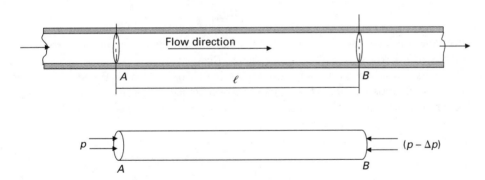

The fluid between A and B is subject to pressure forces, as shown in the lower part of the diagram. What is the resultant force to the right acting on the fluid between points A and B due to the pressure?

8

$$\Delta p \times \pi d^2/4$$

This is just the pressure difference multiplied by the area of cross-section of the pipe.

The fluid is flowing steadily, at constant speed, so the forces acting on it must be in equilibrium. The only axial (horizontal) forces on the fluid are the resultant pressure force, acting to the right, and the viscous shearing force exerted to the left on the fluid by the wall of the pipe.

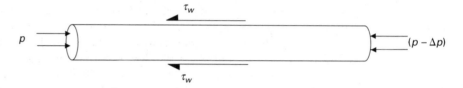

Denoting the shear stress at the wall by τ_w, the viscous shearing force acting on the fluid between points A and B is equal to τ_w multiplied by the area of the pipe wall, i.e.

$$\text{Viscous shearing force on the fluid} = \tau_w \times \pi d \ell$$

Now, by equating this to the axial force due to the pressure, find an expression for the pressure drop Δp over the length ℓ, in terms of τ_w and d.

9

$$\Delta p = (4\ell/d)\,\tau_w$$

This equation looks as if it should tell us the pressure drop Δp, but the trouble is that we do not know the value of the shear stress τ_w.

Fortunately, when the flow is laminar, we can work out how the velocity must vary over the cross-section of the pipe, and so calculate the shear stress.

Carry on now to the next frame.

10

Pressure drop in pipes when the flow is laminar

When a pipe is carrying a laminar flow of fluid, we know that, because the fluid has viscosity, the particles of fluid close to the wall of the pipe must be virtually stationary. (We looked at viscosity and the consequent shear stresses in fluids back in Programme 1, Frames 5–20. Turn back and review this section if your memory is hazy about it.)

At what point of the cross-section do you think the velocity of the fluid is likely to be the greatest?

11

> At the centre

The maximum velocity is at the centre of the pipe.

Now let us consider a cylindrical element of fluid of radius r and length ℓ, as shown. There is a viscous shear stress τ acting along the wall of the cylindrical element; this is not the same as the shear stress τ_w at the pipe wall.

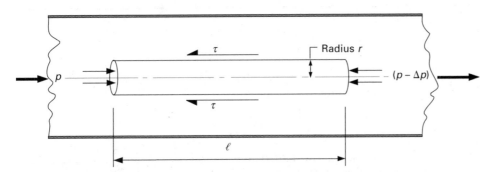

In the same way as before, the resultant pressure force (acting to the right on the element) is $\Delta p \times \pi r^2$, and the viscous shearing force (acting to the left) is $\tau \times 2\pi r\ell$ (τ is the viscous shear stress at radius r). Every particle of the fluid is moving with constant speed, so these two forces must be in equilibrium. Now, by equating the two forces, find π in terms of r, ℓ and Δp.

12

$$\tau = \frac{r}{2\ell}\Delta p$$

This should be quite straightforward.

You should recall from our earlier work on viscosity (Programme 1, Frames 5 to 20 again) that the shear stress is equal to the velocity gradient multiplied by a constant, μ. (If not, turn back and refresh your memory.)

Here we can write this in mathematical terms as

$$\tau = \mu \times \left(-\frac{du}{dr}\right)$$

The minus sign is included because du/dr is itself negative, and we want the result for τ to be positive. (du/dr is negative because the maximum velocity u is at the centre of the pipe, where $r = 0$, so u decreases as r increases.)

Now, combine this result with the equation at the top of the page to obtain a result for du/dr that does not involve τ.

13

$$\frac{du}{dr} = -\left(\frac{\Delta p}{2\mu\ell}\right)r$$

It is not difficult to integrate this equation:

$$u = -\left(\frac{\Delta p}{2\mu\ell}\right)\frac{r^2}{2} + C$$

not forgetting to include a constant of integration, C. To find the value of this constant, we can use the fact that, at the wall, where r is equal to the pipe radius R, the velocity u is zero. So, go ahead and calculate C (in terms of Δp, R, μ and ℓ).

14

$$C = \left(\frac{\Delta p}{4\mu\ell}\right) R^2$$

Now the equation for u can be written as

$$u = \frac{\Delta p}{4\mu\ell}(R^2 - r^2)$$

We see that u varies with r^2. In fact, the shape of the graph of u against r is like that of the curve $y = ax^2$. Do you know the name of this kind of curve?

A parabola

The diagram shows how the velocity u varies across the pipe. The curve is a parabola, and it represents the equation

$$u = \frac{\Delta p}{4\mu\ell}(R^2 - r^2)$$

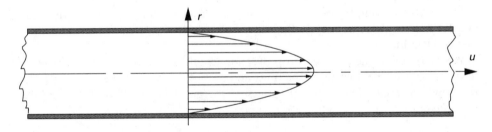

Evidently, the maximum velocity is at the centre of the pipe. What is this maximum velocity (in terms of Δp, μ, ℓ and R)?

16

$$u_{\max} = \frac{\Delta p}{4\mu\ell} R^2$$

The maximum velocity is on the centre-line of the pipe, where $r = 0$. All we need is to set $r = 0$ in the equation

$$u = \frac{\Delta p}{4\mu\ell}(R^2 - r^2)$$

to get the result shown at the top of the page.

If you are keen on integration, you can derive the total volume flow rate from the equation for u above by summing the flows through elements of radius r and width dr. We will content ourselves with just quoting the result:

$$\text{Volume flow rate } Q = \frac{\Delta p}{8\mu\ell} \pi R^4$$

This is known as the *Poiseuille equation*, or sometimes as the *Hagen–Poiseuille equation*. These two, Hagen (a German working in the USA) and Poiseuille (who was French), worked independently on laminar flow in pipes in the years around 1840. The equation has been very thoroughly confirmed by experiments.

Now try this example: water at 10 °C flows through a thin tube 3 mm diameter and 1.4 m long. The viscosity of the water is 1.30×10^{-3} N s/m². The volume flow rate is 0.085 l/min.

We wish to find the pressure drop over the length of this tube; but first find the mean velocity of the flow along the tube, and so find the value of *Re* and check that the flow is laminar. (Note that the units of the given volume flow rate are litres per *minute*.)

17

$$\boxed{\text{Mean velocity } u = 0.20 \text{ m/s}; \ Re = 462}$$

Working:

$$\text{mean velocity } u = \frac{Q}{A} = \frac{(0.085 \times 10^{-3})/60}{\pi \times (3 \times 10^{-3})^2/4}$$

$$= 0.20 \text{ m/s}$$

$$Re = \frac{1000 \times 0.20 \times 3 \times 10^{-3}}{1.30 \times 10^{-3}} = 462$$

Since the value of Re is less than 2000, the flow will certainly be laminar.

Now, using the Poiseuille equation, find the pressure drop Δp between one end of the thin tube and the other.

18

$$\boxed{1.30 \text{ kN/m}^2}$$

Working:

$$p = \frac{8Q\mu\ell}{\pi R^4}$$

$$= \frac{8 \times (0.085 \times 10^{-3}/60) \times (1.3 \times 10^{-3}) \times 1.4}{\pi \times (1.5 \times 10^{-3})^4}$$

$$= 1.30 \times 10^3 \text{ N/m}^2$$

A simple way to find the viscosity of a liquid is to allow it to flow from a container through a tube, and measure the rate of flow. Instruments used to do this are called *viscometers*.

In one common kind of viscometer, the liquid under test is placed in a container which has a small outlet tube of standard diameter in its base. The flow of a standard volume of liquid is timed.

A diagram of a viscometer of this kind is shown at the top of the next page.

19

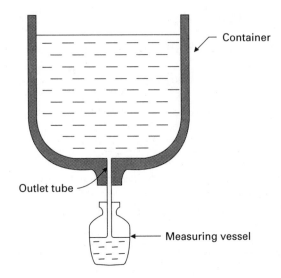

Container

Outlet tube

Measuring vessel

In a test of viscosity using one of these viscometers the initial depth of liquid is 120 mm, its density is 870 kg/m³, the diameter of the outlet tube is 2.4 mm and its length is 13 mm. The time for 50 cm³ to flow is 145 s.

First, we need to calculate the gauge pressure at the entrance to the tube, that is, at the bottom of the container. This is …?

20

$$\boxed{1024 \text{ N/m}^2}$$

The pressure is just hydrostatic, so all we need to do is to find ρgh. The volume flow rate is given by

$$Q = (50 \times 10^{-6})/145$$
$$= 3.45 \times 10^{-7} \text{ m}^3/\text{s}$$

Of course, the level of the liquid will fall during the test, the pressure will decrease, and so will the flow rate. The value for Q calculated above is the mean value. However, if the vessel is large compared with the 50 cm³ whose flow is timed, these changes should not cause a very large error.

Rearranging the Hagen–Poiseuille equation, the viscosity of the liquid is given by

$$\mu = \frac{\Delta p \pi R^4}{8Q\ell} = \frac{\Delta p \pi d^4}{128Q\ell}$$

Using this result, estimate the viscosity μ of the liquid.

$$\boxed{\mu = 0.186 \text{ N s/m}^2}$$

This is just a matter of substituting the known values into the equation.

Partly for the reasons already stated, the estimate of viscosity we have calculated is not likely to be quite accurate. Viscometers of the kind described are usually calibrated using liquids whose viscosity is already accurately known. Users are supplied with tables, so that the times of flow can readily be converted into viscosity values.

Another important reason why the estimate is not a very good one is that the outlet tube is so short that true laminar flow does not have an opportunity to develop. In the next frame we look at what happens to the pattern of flow at the entrance to a pipe.

22

Entrance to a pipe: the development of the flow pattern

When fluid enters a pipe from a large tank or reservoir, the velocity of the fluid is at first almost uniform across the pipe, except close to the wall, where there is a very steep velocity gradient.

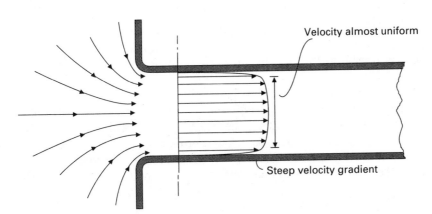

The severe shearing in the layer close to the wall has an immediate effect on adjacent layers, slowing down their motion. But the volume flow rate must remain the same at all points along the pipe, in accordance with the principle of continuity.

As the outer layers of fluid slow down, what must happen to the speed of flow near to the middle of the pipe?

23

The speed of the middle layers must increase

...because the overall mass flow rate must remain the same.

Not surprisingly, this process of slowing down the outer layers and speeding up the inner ones takes place over a considerable distance. Indeed, the fluid will theoretically never quite reach a steady situation where the velocities are no longer changing. In practice, we say that the flow is *fully developed* when the velocities at all points on the cross-section are within 1% of their ultimate values.

We shall look first at the situation when the eventual pattern of flow in the pipe is laminar. We have already quoted the Hagen–Poiseuille equation (Frame 16)

$$Q = \frac{\Delta p}{8\mu\ell}\,\pi R^4$$

which gives the volume flow rate Q in terms of pressure drop per unit length $\Delta p/\ell$, fluid viscosity μ and pipe radius R.

The mean velocity u of fluid flow along the pipe is equal to the volume flow rate divided by the area of cross-section of the pipe. Find an expression for this mean velocity.

24

Mean velocity $u = (\Delta p/8\mu\ell)R^2$

The mean velocity is just the volume flow rate Q divided by the cross-sectional area of the pipe, πR^2.

Since the velocity close to the entry is almost uniform across the whole pipe, the velocity there is virtually equal to the mean velocity. Once the flow is fully developed, the maximum velocity is at the centre of the pipe cross-section, so the fluid on the centre-line has the greatest amount of accelerating to do.

What is the ratio of the maximum velocity (see Frame 16) to the mean velocity?

25

> The ratio is 2: max velocity = 2(mean velocity)

The fluid at the centre of the pipe cross-section has to accelerate from the mean velocity, at the entry to the pipe, to twice that velocity. When the Reynolds number is close to 2000, the distance needed from the entry may be as much as 114 times the diameter of the pipe before the flow is fully developed.

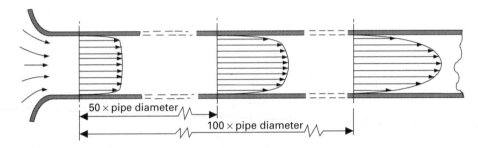

The development of laminar flow in a pipe is shown in the diagram above.

26

All this refers to the laminar flow situation; what about when *Re* is greater than 2000, so that the flow is turbulent? In that case, the velocity of any individual particle keeps varying: it will have a varying axial component, along the pipe, and it also varies in the transverse plane.

It is still useful to draw a velocity profile across the pipe, but when the flow is turbulent we have to recognise that the profile refers only to the *axial* component of velocity, and also that at each point of the cross-section this has to be averaged over time because the velocity keeps varying.

The velocity profile cannot be calculated, and it has to be found by careful experimental investigation. A typical velocity profile is shown on the next page.

27

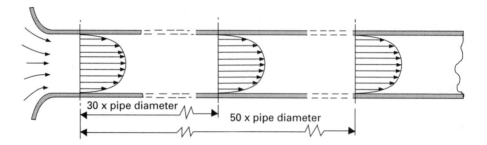

30 x pipe diameter

50 x pipe diameter

The velocity profile is much flatter than in the case of laminar flow. This is not so very surprising, in view of the fact that the fluid particles are continually jostling about and changing position: they cannot be expected to change their axial velocity very much as they move about from one point of the cross-section to another.

Full development is reached more rapidly when the flow is turbulent: a distance from the entry of about 50 times the pipe diameter is usually sufficient.

Because the motion of particles in turbulent flow is virtually impossible to predict, we cannot calculate the velocity distribution and hence the pressure drop as we did for laminar flow, but we do still have the result we derived in Frames 6–8 that the pressure drop over a length ℓ of pipe is given by

$$\Delta p = (4\ell/d)\tau_w$$

This is true regardless of whether the flow is laminar or turbulent.

We noted in the previous programme that recording experimental results in terms of dimensionless ratios of the variables makes things a lot easier, and this is what is always done in this case. (We shall be using ideas from Programme 8 fairly heavily in the next few frames, so it would be worth re-reading it if you don't remember it too well, before carrying on with this programme.)

First of all, we need to list the variables that are involved in the problem. The dependent variable is τ_w. The character of the flow is governed by the value of the Reynolds number, so the variables involved in Re must all have an influence on the shear stress τ_w. Write down as many variables as you can think of on which τ_w must depend.

$$\boxed{\rho, \ u, \ d, \ \mu}$$

All of these variables are involved in the Reynolds number, so it seems very likely they will all have an influence on the shear stress τ_w too.

Physically, we would certainly expect the viscosity μ to have an effect on τ_w. Because they are involved in the velocity gradient, the velocity u and diameter d will also influence τ_w.

You may, very reasonably, be wondering what the density ρ can have to do with the shear stress. The answer is that, in turbulent flow, there is a continuous process of momentum exchange as particles move from the fast-moving centre of the pipe to the relatively sluggish outer regions, and vice versa. The more dense the fluid is, the more momentum has to be gained or lost in this process – so clearly the density *does* have an effect on τ_w.

Thus τ_w depends on ρ, u, d and μ. This makes a total of five variables. We can list them, with their dimensions:

Variables:	τ_w	ρ	u	d	μ
Dimensions:	$\left[\dfrac{M}{LT^2}\right]$	$\left[\dfrac{M}{L^3}\right]$	$\left[\dfrac{L}{T}\right]$	$[L]$	$\left[\dfrac{M}{LT}\right]$

Can you now form a dimensionless ratio of the first three of these variables? (If you are in any doubt about this, turn back to Programme 8 and reread Frames 37 onwards.)

29

$$\tau_w / \rho u^2$$

This is the form you are most likely to have found, but $\rho u^2 / \tau_w$ is also dimensionless; so is the square root of either form, or indeed any other power of them. All of these answers would be equally correct.

Now, how many distinct and independent dimensionless ratios do we expect to find? The answer to this question is provided by Buckingham's theorem (Programme 8, Frame 42) which says that in this situation, where we have *five* variables and *three* fundamental dimensions (M, L and T), the relationship between the variables can be written as an equation between $(5-3) = 2$ distinct dimensionless ratios.

Having found one dimensionless ratio already, we need just one more. The Reynolds number involves all four independent variables, and is the obvious ratio to choose.

So now we have the two dimensionless ratios:

$$\tau_w / \rho u^2 \text{ and } \rho u d / \mu$$

You may well recognise the quantity ρu^2, or something like it, from Bernoulli's equation. Can you write down Bernoulli's equation, in the form where all the terms have dimensions of pressure?

30

$$p + \tfrac{1}{2} u^2 + \rho g h = \text{constant along a streamline}$$

The middle term, $\tfrac{1}{2}\rho u^2$, can be thought of as representing the increase in pressure that occurs when fluid is brought to rest from its velocity u – as in the case of a pitot tube, for example.

Because $\tfrac{1}{2}\rho u^2$ has a direct physical meaning, we generally take $(\tau_w / \tfrac{1}{2}\rho u^2)$ as our first dimensionless ratio, instead of $(\tau_w / \rho u^2)$. $(\tau_w / \tfrac{1}{2}\rho u^2)$ can be thought of as the ratio of the shear stress at the wall to the pressure rise due to stopping the fluid completely. (A pressure is a force divided by an area, so it is just another kind of stress.)

31

Friction factor

Instead of our earlier statement, that

$$\tau_w \text{ depends on } \rho, \; u, \; d \text{ and } \mu$$

we can now write the version involving only the two dimensionless ratios:

$$(\tau_w / \tfrac{1}{2}\rho u^2) \text{ depends on } (\rho u d / \mu)$$

When the flow is turbulent, we know we cannot calculate the value of τ_w, so we have to look at the results of experiments to find out just how $(\tau_w / \tfrac{1}{2}\rho u^2)$ varies with Reynolds number. By using dimensionless ratios, we have been able to reduce the number of variables involved from five in the original statement to only two. This makes the presentation of the experimental results much more straightforward; it also much reduces the amount of experimental work that has to be done.

The most common way of presenting the data is in the form of a graph of $(\tau_w / \tfrac{1}{2}\rho u^2)$ against $(\rho u d / \mu)$.

We already know the ratio $(\rho u d / \mu)$ as the Reynolds number. The ratio $(\tau_w / \tfrac{1}{2}\rho u^2)$ is also given a name: it is called the *friction factor*, denoted by the symbol f:

$$f = \tau_w / \tfrac{1}{2}\rho u^2$$

In the next frame a graph of the friction factor against the Reynolds number is given for a smooth pipe, so turn over now (but if you are from the USA, read the next paragraph!).

[In the USA a friction factor four times larger is used:

$$f_{USA} = 4(\tau_w / \tfrac{1}{2}\rho u^2)$$

This is still dimensionless, of course, and either ratio is equally good. It is just a matter of what you are used to. When reading charts like the one in the next frame, it is vital to know whether the friction factor is the American one or the European one, or else your results may end up a factor of four in error. In this book we shall use f to denote $\tau_w / \tfrac{1}{2}\rho u^2$, without the additional factor.]

32

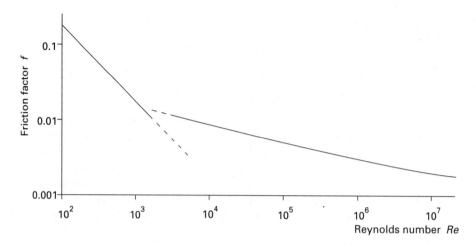

In the graph above, probably the first thing you will notice is that the line relating the friction factor f to the Reynolds number is in two sections, one for Reynolds number values up to 2000 or a little over, and the other for values of Re more than 3000 or so. What do we know about the character of the flow when the value of the Reynolds number is less than 2000?

33

> The flow is laminar

So the first line relates to laminar flow; the second refers to turbulent flow conditions.

Now, the friction factor is defined by $f = \tau_w / \frac{1}{2}\rho u^2$, and we know that the pressure drop along a length ℓ of pipe is related to the shear stress at the wall by

$$\Delta p = \frac{4\ell}{d} \tau_w$$

Combining these equations:

$$\Delta p = 4f \frac{\ell}{d} \left(\tfrac{1}{2}\rho u^2\right) \tag{a}$$

When the flow is laminar, we have already seen (Frame 24) that the mean velocity u of the fluid flow along a pipe is given by

$$u = (\Delta p/8\mu\ell)R^2 = (\Delta p/32\mu\ell)d^2 \tag{b}$$

Now, substitute the expression (a) for Δp into equation (b) and solve for the friction factor f. What do you get?

$$f = 16\mu/\rho du$$

There is something familiar-looking about the ratio $\mu/\rho du$. Rewriting the equation above:

$$f = \frac{16}{\rho du/\mu}$$

We now see – you may already have seen – that this can be written as

$$f = \frac{16}{Re}$$

Thus, *when the flow is laminar, the friction factor is inversely proportional to the Reynolds number.*

The graph in Frame 32 of f against Reynolds number is plotted on logarithmic scales, so this inverse relationship appears as a straight line with negative slope.

35

For the section of the graph of f against Re where the flow is turbulent, the slope of the line is also negative, but the gradient is much less than when the flow is laminar.

The curve for turbulent flow can be represented by an empirical formula, and several such formulae have been proposed. All of these formulae are a matter of fitting an equation to the experimental results, and for most purposes they do not offer any advantage over the chart.

This is especially true when you realise that the formulae that are straightforward enough to use apply only to smooth pipes. As you might expect, the value of the friction factor is usually greater when the inner surface of the pipe is rough. Our graph can be made much more useful if the friction factors for rough pipes are included.

The roughness is usually measured by the average height of the surface bumps, denoted by the symbol k. In line with our policy of presenting the information in the most economical way possible, we need a dimensionless ratio involving the roughness k – a distance – and one or more of the other five variables τ_w, ρ, u, d and μ.

What ratio would you suggest?

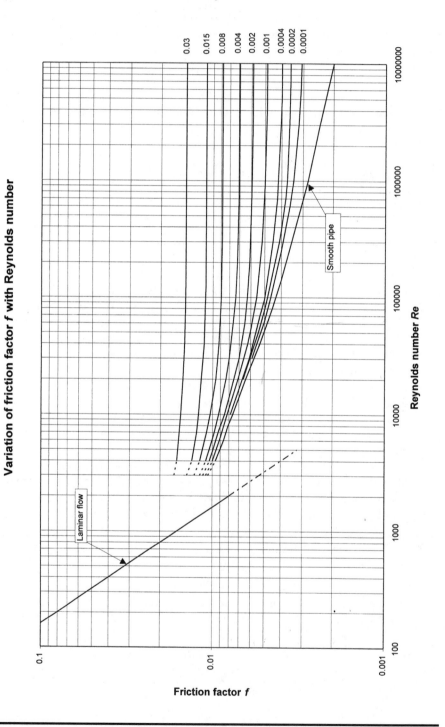

Variation of friction factor f with Reynolds number

$$\boxed{k/d}$$

This is not the only possible answer, but it does seem the most obvious one. It has the great advantage that two pipes of different diameter that have the same value of k/d are *geometrically* similar; in other words, one of the pipes is an exact scale model of the other.

The chart opposite is a graph of friction factor against Reynolds number, for various values of the roughness ratio k/d. It is based on the experimental work of several investigators, but it is usually called a Moody diagram, after the American engineer who drew it up.

To show how the diagram is used, consider a pipe whose roughness ratio is 0.004 with a fluid flow passing along it such that the Reynolds number is 2×10^5.

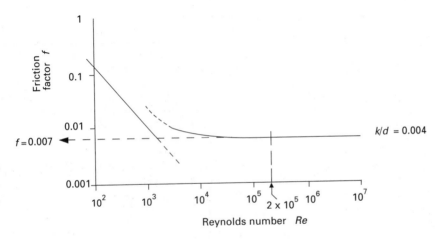

The sketch above shows how to read the value of the friction factor f from the chart: the value is approximately 0.007.

Now an example for you to try: a pipe of roughness $k/d = 0.002$ carries a flow at Reynolds number $Re = 5 \times 10^4$. Use the Moody chart to find the value of the friction factor.

$$\boxed{f = 0.0067}$$

This should have been straightforward. Here is another example: water at 15 °C flows along a pipe of diameter 6 mm at a mean speed of 0.25 m/s. The roughness ratio of the pipe is 0.003, and the viscosity of the water at 15 °C is 1.14×10^{-3} N s/m^2. What is the friction factor in this case?

38

$$\boxed{f = 0.012}$$

Working: first we must find the value of the Reynolds number.

$$Re = \frac{\rho u d}{\mu} = \frac{1000 \times 0.25 \times (6 \times 10^{-3})}{1.14 \times 10^{-3}}$$

$$= 1316$$

and then we can use the Moody chart to find the friction factor, $f = 0.012$.

Since Re is less than 2000, the flow is laminar, and we could equally well find the value of f by calculation, using

$$f = 16/Re$$

and you may like to check that this gives the same result.

39

Finding the pressure loss or head loss in a pipe due to friction

To estimate the pressure loss due to friction in a length of pipe, all we need is to substitute the values into the equation we labelled (a) in Frame 33:

$$\Delta p = 4f \frac{\ell}{d} \left(\tfrac{1}{2}\rho u^2\right)$$

Here is a worked example: water at 15 °C is flowing through a pipe of diameter 25 mm and roughness $k = 0.10$ mm at a mean speed of 2.4 m/s. We wish to find the pressure drop due to friction in a 50 m length of this pipe.

First we need to find the Reynolds number:

$$\frac{\rho u d}{\mu} = \frac{1000 \times 2.4 \times 0.025}{1.14 \times 10^{-3}}$$

$$= 5.26 \times 10^4$$

which is greater than 2000, so the flow is turbulent.

The roughness ratio is

$$k/d = 0.1/25$$

$$= 0.004$$

From the Moody chart, what is the value of the friction factor?

$$f = 0.0075$$

Since we have to read from the chart, you may have got a slightly different value, but it should be close to 0.0075.

Now, to find the pressure drop due to friction in the 50 m length of pipe we need to use the equation

$$\Delta p = 4f \frac{\ell}{d} \left(\tfrac{1}{2} \rho u^2 \right)$$

Substituting in the values:

$$\Delta p = 4 \times 0.0075 \times \frac{50}{0.025} \times \left(\tfrac{1}{2} \times 1000 \times 2.4^2 \right)$$
$$= 1.73 \times 10^5 \text{ N/m}^2$$

The calculation is quite straightforward. Friction causes a pressure drop of 1.73 bar – a quite substantial amount.

Now here is an example for you to try: a garden hose, 12 mm bore (i.e. 12 mm internal diameter) and 30 m long, carries 16 l/min of water at 15 °C. The roughness of the inner surface of the hose is $k = 0.002$ mm. We wish to find the pressure drop over this length of hose; but first of all we must find the value of the Reynolds number. What do you get?

$$2.48 \times 10^4$$

Working: the flow velocity is

$$u = \frac{16 \times 10^{-3}/60}{\pi \times 0.006^2}$$
$$= 2.36 \text{ m/s}$$

so the Reynolds number is

$$Re = \frac{1000 \times 2.36 \times 0.012}{1.14 \times 10^{-3}}$$
$$= 2.48 \times 10^4$$

Now find the value of the roughness ratio (k/d), and so evaluate the friction factor f.

42

$$(k/d) = 0.000\ 17;\ f = 0.0061$$

Working:

$$k/d = 0.002/12$$
$$= 0.000\ 17$$

Using the Moody chart with $Re = 2.48 \times 10^4$ and $(k/d) = 0.000\ 17$, we find that the friction factor is

$$f = 0.0061 \text{ approximately}$$

Finally, find the pressure drop over the 30 m length of hose.

43

$$1.70 \times 10^5 \text{ N/m}^2$$

All we have needed to do here is to substitute the values into the equation

$$\Delta p = 4f \frac{\ell}{d} \left(\tfrac{1}{2}\rho u^2\right)$$

The next frame gives you an opportunity to make sure you have fully understood what we have done so far in this programme. Try to complete the questions before turning to the solutions on the next page: they are all quite straightforward.

Revision exercise

44

1 A pipeline 700 mm in diameter carries a flow of methane gas at 15 °C and gauge pressure 3 bar. The density of the gas is 2.70 kg/m^3 and its viscosity is 1.15×10^{-5} N s/m^2. The mean velocity of flow of the gas is 0.95 m/s.

Is the flow laminar or turbulent?

2 Find the friction factor for the conditions given in Question 1, and estimate the pressure drop in a 100 m length of the pipeline. The roughness value of the inner surface of the pipeline is $k = 0.28$ mm.

3 Diesel fuel flows along a pipe 2.3 m long, whose bore (internal diameter) is 4 mm. The density and viscosity of the fuel are 850 kg/m^3 and 1.80×10^{-3} N s/m^2 respectively. If the pressure drop over the length of the pipe is 1.4 kN/m^2, estimate the volume flow rate of fuel along the pipe.

(Hint: since the bore is small, assume the flow is laminar and use Poiseuille's equation to find the flow rate. Then find the flow velocity, and hence the Reynolds number, to check that the flow is indeed laminar.)

45

Solutions

1 To find out whether the flow is laminar or turbulent, we must find the value of the Reynolds number.

$$Re = \frac{2.7 \times 0.95 \times 0.7}{1.15 \times 10^{-5}}$$
$$= 1.56 \times 10^5$$

Since this is much greater than 2000, the flow will be turbulent.

2 The roughness ratio of the pipe is

$$k/d = 0.28/700$$
$$= 0.0004$$

From the Moody chart, we find the friction factor:

$$f = 0.0048$$

Finally, we find the pressure drop:

$$\Delta p = 4f \frac{\ell}{d} \left(\tfrac{1}{2} \rho u^2\right)$$
$$= 4 \times 0.0048 \times \frac{100}{0.7} \times \tfrac{1}{2} \times 2.7 \times 0.95^2$$
$$= 3.34 \text{ N/m}^2$$

3 As suggested, we shall make use of the Poiseuille equation straightaway.

$$Q = \frac{\Delta p}{8\mu\ell} \pi R^4$$
$$= \frac{(1.4 \times 10^3) \times \pi \times (2 \times 10^{-3})^4}{8 \times (1.80 \times 10^{-3}) \times 2.3}$$
$$= 2.12 \times 10^{-6} \text{ m}^3/\text{s}$$
$$= 2.12 \text{ cm}^3/\text{s}$$

Finally we must check that the Reynolds number is indeed less than 2000: the mean velocity is $Q/A = 0.169$ m/s, and hence

$$Re = 850 \times 0.169 \times 0.004/(1.8 \times 10^{-3})$$
$$= 319$$

46

When dealing with flow in pipes we are continually needing to calculate the Reynolds number; this always includes both the viscosity and the density of the fluid.

To reduce the effort involved in this, and also the risk of making mistakes, the ratio of the viscosity to the density is often quoted in tables. This ratio is denoted by the Greek letter ν, pronounced 'nu', and is called the *kinematic viscosity* of the fluid.

To avoid confusion, the quantity that we have so far been calling the viscosity, that is, the ratio of the shear stress to the velocity gradient, is sometimes called the *dynamic viscosity*. This is denoted by the symbol μ, of course.

Thus

$$\text{kinematic viscosity } \nu = \frac{\text{dynamic viscosity } \mu}{\text{density } \rho}$$

The dimensions of dynamic viscosity are [M/LT], and the dimensions of density are [M/L^3], of course. What are the dimensions of kinematic viscosity?

47

$$\boxed{[L^2/T]}$$

This is just a matter of dividing [M/LT] by [M/L^3].

Typical units of kinematic viscosity are m^2/s. For most fluids the numerical value of the kinematic viscosity in these units is very small. For example, water at 15 °C has a kinematic viscosity $\nu = 1.14 \times 10^{-6}$ m^2/s, and for air at 15 °C the value is $\nu = 1.48 \times 10^{-5}$ m^2/s.

We see that the dimensions and units of ν involve only length and time; this is why it is given the name *kinematic* viscosity, kinematics being the study of motion without regard to forces or inertias.

The values of both μ and ν depend very much on the temperature. The viscosity of liquids generally *decreases* as the temperature rises, whereas the viscosity of gases *increases* as temperature rises.

Here is an example to do: hot water at 50 °C is flowing along a pipe 5 mm diameter at a mean speed of 0.42 m/s. At this temperature the kinematic viscosity of the water is $\nu = 5.55 \times 10^{-7}$ m^2/s. Will the flow be laminar or turbulent?

48

Turbulent

Working:

$$Re = \frac{\rho u d}{\mu} = \frac{u d}{\nu}$$
$$= 0.42 \times (5 \times 10^{-3})/(5.55 \times 10^{-7})$$
$$= 3784$$

and this is greater than 2000, so the flow will be turbulent.

In the revision questions in Frame 44, the third question asked us to find the flow rate, given the pressure drop over the pipe. This can be done directly from the Poiseuille equation if the flow is laminar, but when conditions are turbulent the flow rate cannot be found so directly.

To illustrate a possible method in these cases, we will work through an example: water at 12 °C is supplied to a 20 mm diameter steel pipe at 6 bar gauge pressure. The pipe is 65 m long, the roughness is $k = 0.02$ mm, and at the end of the pipe the water is discharged to the atmosphere. We wish to estimate the volume flow rate of the water.

It seems likely that the flow will be turbulent. The roughness ratio is given by

$$k/d = 0.02/20$$
$$= 0.001$$

Referring to the Moody chart opposite Frame 36 (it is worth putting a book mark in that page – we shall be referring back to it a few more times yet!), we see that the friction factor for this value of roughness at large Reynolds numbers levels out at $f = 0.0049$. We shall therefore start off with this value of f, and see what we get, using our by now familiar equation

$$\Delta p = 4f \frac{\ell}{d} \left(\tfrac{1}{2} \rho u^2 \right)$$
$$6 \times 10^5 = \frac{4 \times 0.0049 \times 65 \times \tfrac{1}{2} \times 1000 \times u^2}{20 \times 10^{-3}}$$

Solving for u, we get $u = 4.34$ m/s.

Given that the kinematic viscosity for the water is $\nu = 1.22 \times 10^{-6}$ m²/s, now calculate the value of the Reynolds number.

$$\boxed{71\ 150}$$

This value, being much greater than 2000, certainly confirms that the flow must be turbulent. However, our work so far has been based on a guessed value of the friction factor. We now have to check whether our value was right, and, if not, go through the calculations again with an improved value.

So, taking Re as 71 150, and recalling that the roughness ratio for the pipe is $k/d = 0.001$, use the Moody chart to find a new estimate of the friction factor.

$$\boxed{f = 0.0058}$$

This is a larger value of friction factor than our original estimate. Therefore the flow velocity must be less than we had previously calculated, the Reynolds number must actually be less than 71 150, the friction factor will be larger than 0.0058 ... and so on.

Fortunately, the friction factor varies only quite slowly with Reynolds number, and it seems reasonable to assume the true value will be only a little larger than 0.0058: we will try the value $f = 0.0059$.

Taking this value of f and the same pressure drop and other conditions as before, what will our estimate be now of the mean velocity u of the water flow along the pipe?

$$\boxed{3.96\ \text{m/s}}$$

Working: we use the equation relating Δp to u^2 that we used in Frame 48, except that the new value of f has to replace the old one. Solving for the mean velocity u, we get the figure of 3.96 m/s.

Before we finally find the volume flow rate, calculate the new value of Reynolds number, so that we can check that the friction factor value we have used is accurate enough.

52

$$\boxed{Re = 64\,920}$$

If you now look at the Moody chart again, you will see that, with the roughness ratio of 0.001, this value of Re does give a friction factor of about 0.0059, so our calculation is reasonably accurate.

Finally, we can find our estimate of the discharge, or volume flow rate.

53

$$\boxed{1.24 \text{ l/s}}$$

This is simply the mean velocity, $u = 3.96$ m/s, multiplied by the cross-sectional area of the pipe.

The solution is now complete, to an adequate level of accuracy. When the pressure drop is given, and flow is turbulent, a trial-and-error solution like the one we have just done is unavoidable. Luckily the friction factor f varies only slowly with Reynolds number, and velocity u is proportional to the square root of f, so the trial-and-error solution for u converges very quickly.

In all our efforts so far, we have assumed that we are dealing with continuous runs of horizontal pipe, but things are not usually as simple as this. In many practical situations the pipe will not be purely horizontal. Parts of it may be sloping, or even vertical.

The pipe may also include changes of diameter, and the continuity principle tells us that, when there are changes of diameter, the velocity of the flow must change too.

Before we embarked on this programme, we had often tackled the question of flows without losses, but where the elevation and/or the velocity were not constant. Besides continuity, what other important equation have we normally used to find how the pressure varies in a flow where both the height and the velocity are changing?

54

| Bernoulli's equation |

Written in the form where all of the terms have dimensions of energy per unit mass, Bernoulli's equation is

$$\frac{p}{\rho} + \frac{u^2}{2} + gz = \text{constant along a streamline}$$

and (as you should remember!), it applies only to incompressible, steady flow without losses.

The 'constant' on the right-hand side of the equation may be regarded as the total energy of the flow, per unit mass. When flow conditions are being compared over short distances, the total energy may indeed be virtually constant, but when we are dealing with a long pipe system the total energy at the downstream end may be much less than it was upstream. In that case, the sum of the three terms on the left-hand side of the equation will be less at the downstream end of the pipe than at the upstream end; it will certainly not be constant.

The work we have done so far in this programme has shown how to calculate the loss of pressure when the pipe is straight and horizontal, and the pressure drop is purely due to viscous friction losses: we can now use this knowledge to find out by how much the Bernoulli 'constant' declines in flow along a pipe, including cases where a pipe undergoes changes of height and diameter.

It is quite possible to work in terms of energy per unit mass here, but there are alternative forms of Bernoulli's equation that give results that seem more relevant to the situation of flow along a pipe. If we multiply the equation through by the density ρ, the equation is then in terms of pressure, which corresponds more closely with what we have done so far in this programme. Comparing conditions at points 1 (upstream) and 2 (downstream), the Bernoulli equation can be written

$$p_1 + \tfrac{1}{2}\rho u_1^2 + \rho g z_1 = p_2 + \tfrac{1}{2} u_2^2 + \rho g z_2$$

When there is a pressure loss due to friction, the two sides of this equation are no longer equal. To which side of the equation does a term representing the friction pressure loss have to be added to make the equation balance?

55

| To the right-hand side |

The sum of the three terms is less at the downstream point 2 than at the upstream point 1, so we have to add the pressure lost due to friction to the right-hand side of the equation to make up this deficit.

The equation is now

$$p_1 + \tfrac{1}{2}\rho u_1^2 + \rho g z_1 = p_2 + \tfrac{1}{2}u_2^2 + \rho g z_2 + \text{(friction pressure loss } \Delta p)$$

To see how this works, we will look in the next frame at an example: the case of a sloping pipe.

56

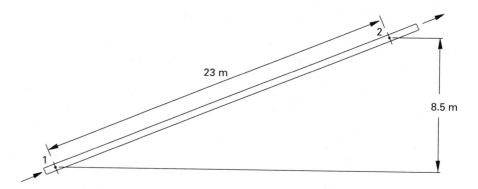

A fluid of density 1150 kg/m³ flows from point 1 to point 2 along the 12 mm tube at a velocity of 2.9 m/s. The friction factor is $f = 0.0068$.

The gauge pressure at point 2 is to be 2.0×10^5 N/m². We wish to find the gauge pressure needed at point 1.

First, we will estimate the pressure loss due to friction. We use our familiar equation:

$$\Delta p_{\text{friction}} = 4f \frac{\ell}{d} \left(\tfrac{1}{2}\rho u^2 \right)$$

Put in the values, and see what you get.

$$2.52 \times 10^5 \text{ N/m}^2$$

Now, to find the gauge pressure p_1, all we have to do is to substitute into Bernoulli's equation, as set out in Frame 55.
    What do you get for this?

$$5.48 \times 10^5 \text{ N/m}^2$$

Working: substituting into the equation exactly as it is in Frame 55, we have

$$p_1 + \tfrac{1}{2}\rho(2.9)^2 + 0 = 2.0 \times 10^5 + \tfrac{1}{2}\rho(2.9)^2 + (1150 \times 9.81 \times 8.5) + 2.52 \times 10^5$$

We have taken our datum to be level with point 1 on the pipe, so that the elevation z of this point is zero; the elevation of point 2 is 8.5 m. The velocity terms $\tfrac{1}{2}\rho(2.9)^2$ are the same on both sides of the equation, because the pipe diameter is constant; these terms therefore cancel.
    Solving for the gauge pressure p_1, we get the value 5.48×10^5 N/m².

When a pipeline is used to transport a fluid over a long distance, the pipe has to follow undulations in the terrain, and it is then convenient to work in terms of *head* rather than pressure. The idea of head was first introduced in Programme 4 (Frames 68–80), where we put Bernoulli's equation into the form

$$\frac{p}{\rho g} + \frac{u^2}{2g} + z = C \text{ (constant)}$$

in which each term of the equation has the dimensions of length.
    If it is a long time since you worked through Programme 4, you will find it helpful to re-read Frames 68–80 of that programme before going on, to refresh your memory.
    In the next few frames, assuming you have done that, we look at the situation where water flows from a reservoir along a long pipeline. First of all we shall consider the case where the pipe is of the same diameter over the whole length, so that the velocity u of the water is constant all the way along.

59

Just to remind you of what we did in Programme 4, if we take Bernoulli's equation in the form

$$\frac{p}{\rho g} + \frac{u^2}{2g} + z = C$$

the three terms on the left-hand side of the equation are called the *pressure head*, the *velocity head*, and the *elevation* respectively. All of them have units of length.

The elevation, which is simply the height of the pipe above a datum level, appears directly in the equation: this is why this form of Bernoulli's equation is very suitable for instances where the height of the pipe varies along its length.

The term C on the right-hand side is called the *total head*; it is equal to the sum of the pressure head, the velocity head and the elevation. If there were no losses the total head would be constant all the way along the pipe.

60

In all real cases, though, the total head is not constant, but declines gradually along the pipe because of friction losses. The diagram below is of a pipeline laid over an undulating landscape. At every point along the pipe, the height of the total head line above the datum is equal to the sum of the elevation, the pressure head and the velocity head.

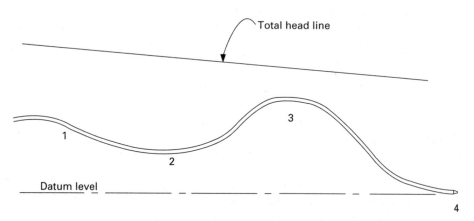

Remembering that in this case the velocity head is constant along the pipe, at which point of the pipe do you think the pressure head will be least?

61

At point 3

At every point along the pipe, the sum (pressure head + velocity head + elevation) is equal to the total head, that is, to the height of the total head line above the datum level. Therefore the sum (pressure head + velocity head) is at its smallest when the pipe comes closest to the total head line: this occurs at point 3.

The diagram below illustrates how the dimensions add up.

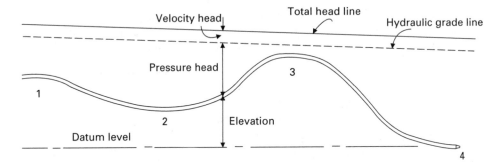

As you should recall from Programme 4, the dashed line, drawn below the total-head line by a distance equal to the velocity head, is called the *hydraulic grade line*. At each point along the pipe, the pressure head corresponds to the height that the liquid would rise in a vertical gauge glass, or piezometer; the hydraulic grade line is the line that follows the top of these imaginary liquid columns.

If the hydraulic grade line goes below the pipeline, the pressure head is then negative, and the pressure in the pipe is less than atmospheric. Can you remember the name given to a part of the pipe in which the pressure is less than atmospheric?

62

A siphon

All of this was covered in Programme 4, and should not be new to you: see Frames 77–80 of that programme if in doubt. It is by no means uncommon for pipelines to include sections at less than atmospheric pressure. The main problem with such siphon sections is that air or vapour may collect at the highest point and impede the flow; the lower the pressure, the more likely this is.

63

For several purposes – deciding how large a pump to install, for example, or working out where, if at all, the pressure will fall below atmospheric – engineers need to be able to work out the loss of total head due to friction along a pipeline.

Armed with the work we have done in this programme, we can work out the head loss due to friction in any section of pipe. Calculating this head loss due to friction is very similar to finding the pressure drop due to friction. We used the equation

$$\Delta p = 4f \frac{\ell}{d} \left(\tfrac{1}{2}\rho u^2\right)$$

to find the pressure drop. The pressure head is equal to the height of a column of the liquid needed to generate the corresponding pressure. Can you derive from this an expression (in terms of f, ℓ, d, u etc.) for the head loss due to friction?

64

$$\boxed{\text{Head loss due to friction} = 4f \frac{\ell}{d} \frac{u^2}{2g}}$$

Working: the pressure generated by a column of liquid is given by $p = \rho g h$.

Rearranging this, the height of the column is given by $h = p/\rho g$. Thus, to turn a pressure into a head, we need to divide by ρg, and this gives the equation above.

Here is an example: a pipe 15 cm diameter carries water at 15 °C, whose density is 1000 kg/m^3 and kinematic viscosity is 1.14×10^{-6} m^2/s. The mean speed of the water along the pipe is 2.3 m/s. The roughness of the pipe is $k = 0.25$ mm. We wish to find the slope of the decline in the total head line, that is, the head loss per unit length of the pipe.

First of all we need to find the value of the friction factor f, and this requires us to find the Reynolds number. What is the value of the Reynolds number in this case?

65

$$3 \times 10^5$$

The Reynolds number is given by $Re = ud/\nu$, and you should have found no trouble in calculating it.

Now, calculate the roughness ratio for the pipe, and use the Moody chart opposite Frame 36 to find the value of the friction factor f.

$$f = 0.0058$$

Working: the roughness ratio is

$$k/d = 0.25/150 = 0.00167$$

and using the Moody chart with $Re = 3 \times 10^5$ we find $f = 0.0058$ approximately. Finally, we can find the head loss per unit length of pipe. If we divide the equation through by ℓ, we have

$$\frac{\text{Head loss due to friction}}{\ell} = 4f\frac{1}{d}\frac{u^2}{2g}$$

and this gives the head loss per unit length of pipe directly. Now, substitute in the values, and see what you get.

67

Head loss is approx 4.2 cm per metre length

Working:

$$\frac{\text{Head loss}}{\ell} = 4 \times 0.0058 \times \frac{1}{0.15} \times \frac{2.3^2}{2 \times 9.81} = 0.042$$

This result, being a ratio of lengths, is dimensionless. Both of the lengths must have the same units, of course. One possibility is to use metres, in which case we have a slope of 0.042 m per m, or approximately 4.2 cm per m.

In this case the diameter and roughness of the pipe are constant all the way along its length. Often one or other of these quantities, or both, will change at points along the pipe, and then the head loss per unit length – the slope of the total head line – will alter. We look at an example where this happens in the next few frames.

68

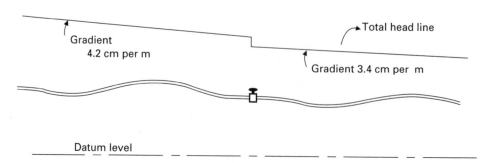

In this diagram the first part of the pipeline is the 15 cm pipe for which we have just done the calculation. With a flow velocity of 2.3 m/s, the head loss per unit length is 4.2 cm per metre length.

The second part has the same diameter but the inner surface is less rough, and the head loss in this section is only 3.4 cm per metre.

These gradients of the total head line are shown on the respective sections of the diagram.

There is a valve at the join between the two pipes. To complete our calculation of the total head all the way along the pipe, we need to be able to estimate the loss of energy, or the loss of head, at the valve. In fact, there will be a head loss at all valves, pipe bends, changes of diameter, and indeed all kinds of fittings.

Because valves and some fittings are rather complicated in shape, it is not usually possible to estimate the head loss from theory, but fortunately there is a wealth of experimental data to go on. This shows that, at all but very low values of Reynolds number, the head loss at a fitting is proportional to the square of the fluid velocity. This can be written as

$$\text{Head loss} = K\frac{u^2}{2g}$$

In other words, the head loss is equal to some constant K times the velocity head in the pipe $u^2/2g$. (The constant K is then dimensionless.)

For this example, the loss coefficient K for the valve is 0.45.

What is the head loss in the valve?

$$\boxed{12 \text{ cm}}$$

Working: the head loss in the valve is

$$K\frac{u^2}{2g} = 0.45 \times \frac{2.3^2}{2 \times 9.81}$$

$$= 0.12 \text{ m}$$

We can now draw a complete diagram, showing the total head line and the hydraulic gradient line:

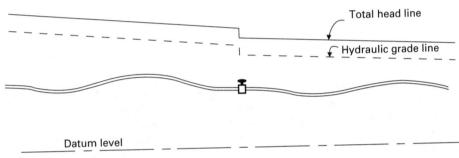

This diagram applies only for the one flow speed, 2.3 m/s. If the flow speed is altered, the friction losses in the pipes and the valve will also change. For example, if the flow speed is increased by 5%, the head loss due to friction in all parts of the system (being proportional to the square of the flow speed) will rise by a factor 1.05^2, i.e. by approximately 10%, so the slope of the decline of the total head line will be greater. The velocity head will also be increased by 10% (approximately), so the hydraulic gradient line, although still parallel to the total head line, will be 10% further below it.

Clearly, increasing the flow rate through the pipe will reduce the pressure head everywhere, and there will be a greater risk of the pressure falling below atmospheric and pockets of vapour forming.

We now come to our final topic for this programme: flow through pipes that are not circular.

70

Friction losses in non-circular pipes

Everything we have done so far in this programme refers to pipes of circular cross-section, which is much the most common shape, but other shapes are used in certain circumstances. Ducting for air flow, for example, is often rectangular. We can obtain estimates of the pressure drop in non-circular pipes and ducts by similar methods to those we used for circular pipes.

Take the case of the odd-shaped pipe shown below:

The area of the cross-section is A, and the perimeter is S. Then the resultant force on the fluid within the pipe to the right due to the pressure difference Δp is $A\Delta p$.

If we assume the shear stress at the wall τ_w is uniform all round the perimeter, then the viscous shearing force acting on the fluid in length ℓ of the pipe is $S\ell\tau_w$. Equating these:

$$\tau_w = \frac{A}{S}\frac{\Delta p}{\ell}$$

The ratio A/S has the dimensions of length, and is often called the *hydraulic mean depth*, denoted by the symbol m. Alternatively, it is sometimes called the hydraulic radius.

This result is quite general, and applies to any shape of pipe.

If the pipe is actually circular of diameter d, what is the value of the hydraulic mean depth m?

$$m = d/4$$

Working: the area of the cross-section is $\pi d^2/4$, and the perimeter is πd. The hydraulic mean depth for a circular pipe is the ratio of these, which is $d/4$. (This is equal to *half* the actual radius of the pipe, and for this reason the alternative name, hydraulic radius, can lead to confusion and is better avoided.)

Now, if we take our equation for the pressure drop in a circular pipe

$$\Delta p = 4f\,\frac{\ell}{d}\,(\tfrac{1}{2}\rho u^2)$$

we can rewrite this in terms of the hydraulic mean depth as

$$\Delta p = f\,\frac{\ell}{m}\,(\tfrac{1}{2}\,\rho u^2)$$

and the equation is then still exact for a pipe of circular cross-section.

It seems reasonable to expect that it will also give quite accurate results for pipes whose cross-section is not too wildly different from a circle.

Here is an example: we consider a rectangular duct 400 mm × 250 mm. First of all we must calculate the hydraulic mean depth m for the duct.

$$m = 77 \text{ mm}$$

Working:

$$m = \frac{400 \times 250}{2(400 + 250)}$$
$$= 77 \text{ mm}$$

and now, if we know the value of the friction factor f, we can calculate the pressure drop over any length of this duct. We usually get the value of f from the Moody chart; but for this we need the Reynolds number ud/ν, and also the roughness ratio k/d. We are faced with a problem here, because we have no diameter value to insert in these expressions. But in the previous frame we have a relationship between the diameter d of a circular pipe and the hydraulic mean depth m. Rewriting this with d as the subject, what do we get?

73

$$\boxed{d = 4m}$$

In the case of a circular pipe, the diameter is equal to four times the hydraulic mean depth.

For pipes that are not circular, but whose cross-section is not *too* different from a circle, we can use the same equation $d = 4m$ to provide an equivalent diameter.

What is the equivalent diameter for our 400 mm × 250 mm rectangular duct?

74

$$\boxed{308 \text{ mm}}$$

Working:

$$\text{Equivalent diameter} = 4 \times \text{hydraulic mean depth}$$
$$= 4 \times 77$$
$$= 308 \text{ mm}$$

Now we shall use this result to help provide an estimate of the pressure drop in the duct when conveying air at a mean speed $u = 6.9$ m/s. The roughness of the inner surface of the duct is taken as $k = 0.10$ mm.

First we must find the value of the Reynolds number, based on our equivalent diameter of 308 mm. The kinematic viscosity of the air is 1.50×10^{-5} m²/s.

What do you get?

75

$$\boxed{Re = 1.42 \times 10^5}$$

The roughness ratio, again based on the equivalent diameter, is equal to 0.10/308, which is equal to 0.0032.

Now use the Moody chart (opposite Frame 36) to find the value of the friction factor f.

$$\boxed{f = 0.0047}$$

Now we can find our estimate of the pressure drop per unit length in the duct.
We use the equation

$$\frac{\Delta p}{\ell} = f \, \frac{1}{m} \, (\tfrac{1}{2}\rho u^2)$$

and we shall take the density of air to be 1.20 kg/m^3.
What do you get for this?

$$\boxed{1.74 \text{ N/m}^2 \text{ per metre length}}$$

This is just a matter of substituting the values we have calculated into the equation.

This pressure drop is quite small, at least by comparison with typical pressure drops when liquids are conveyed by pipes, but because the volumes of air pumped are usually relatively large the power needed to blow air along the duct may be quite substantial, especially if the duct is long. Suppose the length of the duct is 85 m.
Then the power needed is given by

$$\begin{aligned}
\text{pumping power} &= \text{(force applied to fluid)} \times \text{velocity} \\
&= \text{(pressure} \times \text{area)} \times \text{velocity} \\
&= \text{pressure} \times \text{(volume flow rate)} \\
&= (1.74 \times 85) \times (6.9 \times 0.40 \times 0.25) \\
&= 102 \text{ W}
\end{aligned}$$

This concludes this programme, apart from the revision summary on the next page. When you have checked the summary, there is a short test exercise in the following frame – make sure you have understood and absorbed all the contents of the programme and the revision summary before you try the test exercise.

78

Revision summary

1 Flow in a pipe is always laminar when the Reynolds number is less than about 2000, and is turbulent when the Reynolds number is greater than 2000 (unless very special care has been taken to prevent it).

2 The pressure drop in a pipe of diameter d and length ℓ is given by the equation

$$\Delta p = 4f \, \frac{\ell}{d} \, (\tfrac{1}{2}\rho u^2)$$

in which u is the mean velocity of the flow and f is the friction factor.

3 The friction factor f depends only on the Reynolds number and the roughness ratio of the pipe. Its value can be read from a Moody chart (opposite Frame 36 of this programme).

4 The roughness ratio is the ratio of the average height k of the bumps on the inner surface of the pipe to the pipe diameter d.

5 The kinematic viscosity of a fluid, ν, is defined as the ratio of the dynamic viscosity μ to the density ρ.

6 The total head at a point in a fluid is the sum of the terms

$$\frac{p}{\rho g} + \frac{u^2}{2g} + z$$

When fluid flows along a pipe with negligible friction, the total head does not vary along the pipe. In real cases, the total head declines in the direction of flow. The gradient can be found from the equation in item 2 above.

7 The hydraulic mean depth m of a pipe is the ratio of the area of cross-section to the perimeter. For a circular pipe $m = d/4$. The value of m is readily calculated for non-circular pipes. Provided they are not too irregular in shape, the pressure drop in such pipes can be estimated from the equation

$$\Delta p = f \, \frac{\ell}{m} \, (\tfrac{1}{2}\rho u^2)$$

Test exercise

1 A pipe of internal diameter 55 mm and roughness $k = 0.07$ mm carries a liquid whose density ρ is 950 kg/m^3 and kinematic viscosity ν is 1.4×10^{-6} m^2/s. The flow rate is 4 l/s.
   (a) Find the value of the Reynolds number. Is the flow turbulent or laminar?
   (b) Using the Moody chart (opposite Frame 36) estimate the friction factor.
   (c) Estimate the pressure drop due to friction in a 100 m length of the pipe.
2 This pipe is installed in a factory with the downstream end 10 m higher than the upstream end, where the gauge pressure is 250 kN/m^2. With flow conditions as given in question 1, estimate the pressure at the downstream end of the pipe.
3 A horizontal pipe, 10 mm internal diameter and of roughness 0.01 mm, carries water of density 1000 kg/m^3 and kinematic viscosity 0.9×10^{-6} m^2/s. The length of the pipe is 220 m.
   The gauge pressure at the upstream end is 140 kN/m^2, and at outlet the water is discharged directly to atmosphere.
   Estimate the volume flow rate through the pipe. (You will need to use a trial-and-error method.)

80

Further problems

1 Water at 15 °C flows at 0.2 l/s along a pipe of diameter 0.5 m. Show that the flow will be laminar, and find the drop in pressure due to friction in a 100 m length of the pipe.

2 A liquid of dynamic viscosity 0.38×10^{-3} N s/m² and density 900 kg/m³ flows at 2.5 m/s through a pipe of internal diameter 10 mm. The roughness of the pipe is $k = 0.02$ mm. Estimate the pressure drop per metre due to friction.

3 Oil of kinematic viscosity $\nu = 5 \times 10^{-5}$ m²/s flows through an inclined tube of diameter 12 mm. The oil entering the tube is at atmospheric pressure, and the end of the tube where the oil emerges is also at atmospheric pressure. Find the inclination of the tube to the horizontal if the mean speed of flow of the oil is to be 0.2 m/s.

4

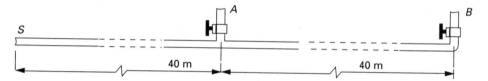

Water from a supply S at 15 °C is piped to two consumers A and B through a pipe of 30 mm diameter. The roughness of the pipe is $k = 0.12$ mm. Distances SA and AB are both 40 m. (a) When valve A is closed and B draws 15 l/min of water, find the head loss in the pipe from S to B. (b) When both A and B draw 15 l/min, find the head loss from S to B. (c) Valve B is now closed. If the head loss in the pipe from S to A is 3.5 m, find the flow rate in l/min.

5 Water from a mountain-top reservoir is carried down through a pipeline to a Pelton turbine 400 m below the level of the water in the reservoir. At the turbine the water emerges to atmospheric pressure through a nozzle of diameter 20 mm. Neglecting all friction losses, find the volume flow rate of water, and the ideal power available from this flow.

The pipe is 1300 m long and 80 mm internal diameter, and its internal roughness k/d is 0.002. If it is desired to operate at a flow rate of 15 l/s, find the head loss in the pipe, and find also the size of nozzle which should then be used at the Pelton turbine.

Programme 5

1	0.448 m/s	1	22.1 m/s
2	(a) 32.3 m/s;	2	0.70 m/s
	(b) 0.137 kg/s	3	869 l/min
3	(a) 18.7 kN/m^2	4	44 kN/m^2; 691 l/min
	(b) 218 W		

Programme 6

1 18.4 N, at 31° to the vertical

2 3.02 kN, at 30° to the horizontal

3 1032 N to the right

1 16.7 N, at 29° above horizontal

2 256 m/s

3 $A(p + \rho u^2)$

4 6.4 kN to the right

5 (a) 27 m/s
    (b) 28.1 N downwards;
        140 N to the right

Programme 7

1 (i) $\left[\dfrac{M}{LT^2}\right]$; (ii) $\left[\dfrac{L^2}{T}\right]$

2 (i) consistent

   (ii) not consistent (first and second terms [ML/T^2]; third term [ML^2/T^2])

Programme 8

1 $(\Delta p \ell / \rho Q^2)$; or some power of this ratio, or its reciprocal

3 (a) (F/$\rho u^2 d^2$) and (p/ρu^2), for example. Other forms, such as the product of these, are possible, and are equally correct.

Programme 9

1 (a) 66.1 × 10^3; turbulent
   (b) 0.0058 approx.
   (c) 57 kN/m^2

2 100 kN/m^2

3 86 l/min

1 0.0149 N/m^2

2 7.3 kN/m^2 per metre length

3 13.1°

4 (a) 0.61 m
   (b) 1.43 m
   (c) 54 l/min

5 27.8 l/s; 109 kW;
   177 m; 17 mm diameter

INDEX